THE PATHOLOGY OF THE U.S. ECONOMY

Also by Michael Perelman

CLASSICAL POLITICAL ECONOMY, PRIMITIVE ACCUMULATION AND THE SOCIAL DIVISION OF LABOR

FARMING FOR PROFIT IN A HUNGRY WORLD: CAPITAL AND CRISIS IN AGRICULTURE

INFORMATION, SOCIAL RELATIONS AND THE ECONOMICS OF HIGH TECHNOLOGY

KARL MARX'S CRISIS THEORY: LABOUR, SCARCITY AND FICTITIOUS CAPITAL

KEYNES, INVESTMENT THEORY AND THE ECONOMIC SLOWDOWN

The Pathology of the U.S. Economy

The Costs of a Low-Wage System

Michael Perelman
Professor of Economics
California State University

St. Martin's Press

First published in Great Britain 1993 by
MACMILLAN PRESS LTD
Houndmills, Basingstoke, Hampshire RG21 2XS
and London
Companies and representatives
throughout the world

ISBN 0–333–58909–2

A catalogue record for this book is available
from the British Library.

10   9   8   7   6   5   4   3   2
03   02   01   00   99   98   97   96   95

Printed in Great Britain by
Antony Rowe Ltd
Chippenham, Wiltshire

First published in the United States of America 1993 by
Scholarly and Reference Division,
ST. MARTIN'S PRESS, INC.,
175 Fifth Avenue,
New York, N.Y. 10010

ISBN 0–312–09528–7

Library of Congress Cataloging-in-Publication Data
Perelman, Michael.
The pathology of the U.S. economy / Michael Perelman.
p. cm.
Includes bibliographical references and index.
ISBN 0–312–09528–7
1. United States—Economic conditions. 2. Industrial relations–
–United States. 3. Monetary policy—United States. 4. Finance–
–United States. 5. Wages—United States. I. Title.
HC103.P417 1993   92–44985
330.973–dc20   CIP

To my mother
whose strength and courage has been an inspiration to me

Contents

List of Tables and Figures xii

Acknowledgements xiii

1 The Setting of the Decline **1**
A Preview of the Book 1
The Roots of Economic Mismanagement 3
The Failure of Economic Policy 4
The Role of Crises 6
The Challenge Ahead 8
The Golden Age of Capitalism 10
Post-War Decline 16
The Falling Rate of Profit 18
The Decline and Falling Profit Rates 19
Poverty and the Distribution of Income 22
The Oil Shock as a Consequence of the Economic
    Decline 23
The Decline as a Complex Economy-wide Process 25
Economics and Oversimplification 27
Summary 28

**2 The Attack on Labour Accelerates the Economic
    Decline** **30**
The Post-War Labour-Management Accord 30
The Breakdown of the Labour-Management Accord 31
Rebellion on the Shop Floor 32
The Social Dynamics of the Economic Decline 34
The Decline and Social Discord 36
How Business Attacked Labour 37
Unemployment and Labour Discipline 40
Scorched Earth Economics 41
A Catastrophe for Labour 44
Adding Insult to Injury 46
The Disastrous Expansion of Low-Wage Service
    Employment 48

Contents

How Businesses' Defeat of Labour Impairs the
Labour Force 51
Unplanned Fiscal Costs of Labour's Defeat 54
The Haitian Road to Economic Development 55

3 Government and the Decline 58
Keynes and the Credibility of Government 58
The Dark Side of Keynesian Theory: Military
Keynesianism 58
The Advantage of Waste 60
The Rise of a Garrison State 62
The End of the Excessive Faith in Government
Economic Management 63
The Abdication of Government from Economic
Responsibility 65
The Nirvana of Deregulation 67
The Contraction of the Government and the Economic
Decline 68
Education, Human Capital and the Economic Decline 70
The Decline in Public Education as a Cumulative Process 71
Test Scores and the Economic Decline 74
The Cost of Crippling Public Education 75
How the Economic Decline Reacts with the Education
System 77
The Deterioration of the Public Capital Stock 78
The Social Cost of Deteriorating Public Capital 79
Transportation and Public Capital 81
Inadequate Infrastructure and the State of the
U.S. Economy 83
Infrastructural Decline as Part of the General Decline 85
Future Infrastructural Needs 86
The Erosion of the Stock of Public Data for the U.S.
Economy 88
The Strategic Importance of Public Data 90

4 The Role of the Military in the Economic Decline 93
Military Spending as Class Warfare 93
The Benefits of Military Power 96
The Economic Failure of Military Keynesianism 98
The Changing Nature of Military Spending 100

The Question of Spillovers from Military Research and
  Development   101
The Pernicious Influence of Excessive Military Spending   104
How Military Spending Might Actually Harm the
  Military   105
The Class Nature of Military Keynesianism   107

**5   Keynesian Policy, Monetary Policy, and the
Weakening of Competition   109**
The Logic of Keynesian Policy and Cumulative
  Economic Processes   109
The Contradictory Nature of the Business Cycle   110
Keynes's Heresy   112
Keynesian Policies and Replacement Investment   114
Capital Widening versus Capital Deepening   116
Keynesian Policies and the Ageing of the Capital Stock   118
Monetary Policy and Capital Renewal   121
High Interest Rates and the Economics of a Short Time
  Horizon   122
The Economics of the Chinese Wall   124
The Costs of an Ageing Capital Stock   126
The Economics of Patching   128
Investing for Rapid Pay-back during the Depression   130
On the Ageing of the U.S. Capital Stock   131
The Short Pay-back Period and the Decline in U.S.
  Competitiveness   133
Crisis and Competition in the U.S. Economy   135
The Overhang of Phantom Capacity   137
The Elimination of Phantom Capacity   138
Creative Redeployment of Old Capital Goods   140
The Elimination of Productive Capacity   142
The Big Question   143

**6   Finance, the Falling Rate of Profit and
Economic Devastation   145**
Finance and the Momentum of the Decline   145
Falling Profits and Rising Interest Rates   146
The Falling Rate of Profit and Increasing Risk   147
What Banks Ideally Do   149
On the Regulation of the Financial System   150

The Circumvention of Bank Regulation   152
New Dimensions to Speculation   154
Finance and the Decline of U.S. Manufacturing   155
The Falling Rate of Profit and Capital Renewal   157
The Inefficiency of Corporate Takeovers and
    Leveraged Buyouts   158
Financial Capital versus Industrial Capital   160
The Unproductive Labour Dissipated in Corporate
    Takeovers   161
Unproductive Labour and the Hobbling of the
    Corporate Sector   163
Financial Services and Unproductive Labour   165
Tracking the Elusive Profit Rate   168
The Dual Nature of the Profit Rate   170

**7 De-industrialization and the Rise of the Service
    Economy**   **172**
Post-industrial Vision   172
The Hollow Economy and the Dangers of Post-industrial
    Utopianism   173
The Electronics Industry in the Age of Post-industrialism 175
Services and High Technology   178
The Demand for Services and the Proximity to
    Manufacturing   179
Does De-industrialization Exist?   182
Is De-industrialization the Rule in Market Economies? 185
Debates over De-industrialization   187
Investment and Taxes   188
Creativity Again   191

**8 High Wages, Enlightened Management, and
    Economic Productivity**   **192**
High Wages as a Defence against De-industrialization   192
The Two Faces of Management-Labour Relations   193
The Internal Politics of Management-Labour Relations   195
The Advantage of a Co-operative Policy toward Labour   198
The Economy of High Wages   199
Efficiency Wages   201
The Tradition of the United States as a High-Wage
    Economy   202

High Wages and Protectionism 204
A Test of the Theory of High Falling Wages during the
 Great Depression 205
Mitigating Factors 209
The Dissipation of the Residual Momentum of High
 Wages 210
High Wages in an International Context 211
Surprise! Unions Can Promote Productivity 212
How Good Management Can Prod Labour to Work
 Hard 215
Low Wages and the Structure of De-industrialization 216
Creativity and Economics 217
Creative Destruction and Destructive Creativity 220

9 Conclusion **221**

Bibliography 222

Index 247

List of Tables and Figures

Tables

1.1	The Deteriorating Performance of the U.S. Post-war Macroeconomy	18
1.2	Growth in Profit Rates for Non-Financial Corporations	19
1.3	Real Hourly Earnings in 1977 dollars	22
2.1	Caption??????/	56
5.1	Age Distribution of Machine Tools in the United States	132
5.2	International Distribution of Machine Tool Ages (percentages)	132

Figures

3.1	Cross-Country Comparison of Productivity Growth and Public Investment to GDP Ratio	84
7.1	Capital Intensity in Services and Manufacturing	180

xii

Acknowledgements

I wish to thank Gary Francis, Robert O'Brien and David Eldridge for their many excellent suggestions.

1 The Setting of the Decline

A Preview of the Book

This book tells the story of the deterioration of the U.S. economy. In this work, I contend that the difficulties that the U.S. economy faces today reflect long-term problems that have been festering for many decades. We cannot remedy these ills by short-term policy adjustments.

Many people prefer to locate the root of the current economic ills to be an excess of the selfishness that characterized the 1980s. I cannot accept that narrow interpretation of the decline. Instead, I will argue that what we see as a recent upsurge in signs of selfishness is more of a predictable reaction to the decline rather than a cause.

Of course, selfishness has contributed to the decline. We shall see that a number of groups have been so greedy that they became blinded to their own best interests. For example, business perceives that it will profit in the short-run by doing anything in its power to cut wages. Business leaders are intent on following what I call, 'The Haitian Road to Development.' When the majority of businesses attempt to cut wages, they reduce the income of their potential customers. More importantly, they cripple the labour force and thereby undermine its productivity. In the end, profits will suffer along with wages.

We see a similar degree of ineptitude on the part of the government. During the early post-war period, fearing a repeat of the Great Depression, both business and the public supported the government's attempt to stabilize the economy. Although stabilization policy initially helped to reduce the intensity of the business cycle, it also reduced competitive pressures. We will see that, as a result, stabilization policy impeded the economic modernization, preparing the way for an economic decline. Again, a policy backfired because those in control failed to understand how the economy works.

As the decline gained momentum, business, as well as the public at large, perceived that they would benefit by cutting taxes and limiting government activity. As a result, they helped to create a lax regulatory structure, which led to instability and chaos. The savings and loan bailout alone may eat up much of the expected savings from the tax cut. Again, we see a failure to recognize self-interest.

To cope with the drop in revenues, the government let the public infrastructure of roads and public works deteriorate enough to hobble the economy. Education suffered, further damaging productivity and profits – still another example of a policy failure.

Although business and the public oppose the government in general, they agreed that their interests are served by a huge military build-up. Here too they were mistaken. These military expenditures further sap the vitality of the economy, so much so that they ultimately threaten to weaken the military itself.

Each of these policies turned out to have disastrous results. Now we watch industry after industry wither, while real wages fall, and homelessness, hopelessness and a multitude of other social and economic ills multiply. We will trace these misperceptions of self-interest to economic forces that emerged from the process of economic decline.

We will see that these forces, as well as the decline itself, are part of the normal process of a market economy. In addition, I show that, even though many of our current economic problems are unavoidable, an inability to understand the decline has reinforced our economic problems.

Two influences in particular have been especially destructive. First, business and political leaders have failed to recognize that the decline is a long-term process. This misperception led them to think that a short-term solutions could be adequate. Given this mind-set, whatever improves the prospects for the next quarterly report or the next election remains uppermost in their minds. This approach is unfortunate because a technologically advanced economy depends on investment in durable plant and equipment. Such investment decisions require a long-term perspective. In addition, inappropriate economic decisions can scar the labour force for generations.

Second, economists have saddled us with a pervasive belief in a utopian vision of a market economy. In reality, the market is not the harmonious arrangement that abstract economic theory suggests. In particular, market economies require strong competitive pressures if they are to remain healthy.

Within the context of a market economy, the government should allow competitive forces to rid the economy of inefficient investments and management practices, while helping individuals to adjust to the dislocation which is part and parcel of a market economy. Instead, government policies protect business inefficiencies and leave workers more or less to fend for themselves when competitive forces uproot their jobs.

Although competitive pressures should be allowed to sweep away inefficiencies, we should understand that these pressures can take two forms. First, firms can engage in cut-throat competition, which can lead to depressions, which, in turn, create widespread hardship and suffering.

I recommend that we pursue a different form of competitive pressure; namely, high wages. Increasing wages can provide the pressure to coerce firms to adopt the best available technologies. Some individual firms will be unable to compete on the basis of higher wages, but other firms can emerge to take their place.

My suggestion runs counter to our current economic policies. The Haitian road that we presently follow leads to a demoralized labour force. The road I am suggesting leads to an improved labour force capable of lifting economic productivity. I do not pretend that this road will be smooth. Market economies are by nature contradictory beasts that impose frequent hardships, but the road that I am recommending certainly is superior to the Haitian road, which threatens to destroy our society unless it is reversed soon.

The Roots of Economic Mismanagement

Although the annihilation of the U.S. economy is not preordained, it is not beyond the realm of possibility. This book will explore some of the pressures that are currently threatening to push the U.S. economy to the point of destruction. I realize that the notion of economic self-destruction of the economy is not very popular.

Certainly, few trained economists in the United States today accept Marx's contention that capitalism is inevitably destined to self-destruct. Indeed, capitalism has proved to be far more resilient than Marx had ever imagined.

The U.S. economy, in particular, stands as a stark testimony to the resilience of capitalism. In the United States, capitalism has withstood an epidemic of political and economic mismanagement. In fact, everywhere you look you will see signs of mismanagement. You will see mismanagement of the labour force, of resources, of corporate assets, as well as general financial, political and economic mismanagement. The U.S. economy has surrendered its lead in sector after sector. Still, even though the economy may not work well, despite widespread mismanagement, it has avoided self-destruction.

Although capitalism has not self-destructed, it does give signs of losing its vitality. In addition, many of the signs of mismanagement, which seem to be responsible for the decline, are, in fact, an understandable response to more fundamental forces.

This book looks at these underlying forces that have sapped the strength of one particular capitalist economy – that of the United States – rather than capitalism as a whole. The progressive economic fragility of the United States economy is interesting in its own right, given the size of the economy.

I hope that this book will also cast some light on the nature of capitalism as a whole. Certainly, the fate of the largest capitalist economy will exercise a considerable influence on the system as a whole. Of course, just as a forest can thrive while individual trees expire, the course of the U.S. economy does not necessarily determine the future of capitalism. Nonetheless, the fate of the U.S. economy may foreshadow the future of those economies that are rising to challenge the U.S.

The Failure of Economic Policy

The training of professional economists teaches them that an economy is naturally healthy unless irrational policies interfere with the normal functioning of the market. Given this perspective, many economists see their calling as pursuing the search for ways to root out those policies that prevent the market from doing its job. One school of economic thought, popularly associated with the University of Chicago, dogmatically insists that any attempt whatsoever to improve the workings of the market constitutes mismanagement. According to this world-view, a market economy without any government interference would naturally perform smoothly and efficiently, benefitting all concerned. Unfortunately, such an ideal, efficient economy is no more possible than a frictionless machine.

The other main school of economic thought – let us call it the 'Economic Management School' – accepts that the unregulated market has some imperfections, but this school contends that a judicious dose of proper economic management can rid the economy of those imperfections.

I take issue with both schools of thought. Specifically, both schools of thought suffer from a faulty conception of mismanagement. The Chicago school is utopian to the extreme.

In a sense, the Economic Management School is no less utopian than the Chicago School. It interprets market imperfections as epiphenomena – isolated problems that are unrelated to each of the other symptoms rather than part of a systemic malaise. Accordingly, it assumes that proper management can treat these problems one-by-one and that a few simple policies will suffice to ensure the health of a market economy.

For the Economic Management School, a government that either fails to address existing market imperfections or addresses them in an improper fashion can be accused of mismanagement. The Economic Management

School accepts the need for some kind of piecemeal economic management, but would have us believe that a well-managed economy with the appropriate economic controls can function about as well as the Chicago School ideal of an unregulated market.

In contrast to the Economic Management School, the Chicago School of laissez faire economics understands the need to understand the economy holistically. It realizes that attempts to manage one part of the economy create pervasive effects throughout the economy. Hence piecemeal reforms cannot provide adequate solutions. Unfortunately, the Chicago school incorrectly draws the utopian conclusion from this realization that, left to its own devices, the market functions perfectly.

In fact, the market is far from a perfect mechanism. A careful study of the history of the U.S. economy bears out my contention. During the early post-war period, the Economic Management School was predominant. In part, we can trace this pervasive belief that piecemeal reforms could significantly improve our society to the unique history of the post-World War II economy.

We shall see that the sequence of a depression followed by a wartime boom, created a powerful economic momentum. Each time a new problem emerged, policy-makers confidently devised new programs to cope with the problem. Each policy came with grand promises of future benefits.

By 1970, the momentum of the post-war boom had dissipated, leaving the economy tottering on the brink of crisis. From that point on, most policies, whether they increased or decreased government involvement in the economy, proved to be dismal failures, or at best, patchwork solutions.

This crisis discredited the Economic Management School and prepared the way for the renewed ascendancy of the even more dangerous medicine prescribed by Chicago school. Yet, as deregulation and the market came to be the watchwords of the day, the economy moved even closer to the precipice. The public became more aware that neither school was capable of rectifying the economy. Economist jokes became rampant.

Still, we are loathe to recognize the hopelessness of our simplistic policy nostrums. Many people in the United States still carry the conviction that prosperity is the norm. They are still confident that some policy – maybe deregulation, maybe some fine tuning here and there, or even a routine overhaul – will get the economy running smoothly once again.

Ever hopeful, they await a new Moses to lead them, into the promised land of economic prosperity. More often than not the public becomes disenchanted with its leaders as quickly their policies prove inadequate to the task.

The widespread suspicion of our economic leaders is well deserved. The leaders to whom we turn generally behave with extraordinary irresponsibility. How many leaders of business or government have been willing to acknowledge the extent of the present impasse? The media have been no better. Instead, of a clear analysis of our predicament, we are treated to plethora of confident remedies to correct for previous mismanagement. We find innumerable proposals for political reform, tax reform, labour reform, but each of these reforms is as insufficient to the task as all the earlier reforms.

Why should these reforms be any more effective than post-reforms? Policy makers from both schools were equally confident about the efficacy of the reforms that they proposed in the past. They failed to anticipate the seemingly unavoidable, unwelcome consequences of their actions. We are quick to condemn them for their past errors, which we regard as mismanagement.

On closer inspection, we get a somewhat different picture of the policy-makers' records. Much of what appears as mismanagement, is really the inevitable failure of any attempt to correct the problems associated with a market economy with piecemeal reforms. Even policies that retrospectively appear to be based on pure stupidity make sense in the context of the political expediency in which these policies were framed.

In short, a market economy embodies powerful negative forces that can not be exorcised simply by adopting some intelligent economic policy. In the case of the United States, we will see that some policy measures – for example, higher wages – offer the possibility of somewhat better economic performance, but even these policies still entail serious difficulties.

Although a full-blown crisis has not yet arrived, more and more people are coming to doubt that prosperity is just around the corner. So Marx maybe was not so wrong after all. Capitalism may be in the process of self-destructing, even though the process has not been nearly as rapid as Marx and many of his followers believed. Even if the U.S. economy does not self-destruct, it is due for a long and painful period of adjustment. This book is intended to provide a framework for understanding the nature of this adjustment.

The Role of Crises

At this time, I will mention an underlying thesis of this book based on the central role of competition in a market society. Let me state it here once and let you judge for yourself based on the evidence that I will present in later chapters whether or not you accept it: Simply put, market economies require strong competition and strong competition breeds depressions and recessions.

I accept that market economies can survive for extended periods of time with a relatively weak level of competition. During such periods, economies can avoid depressions or even serious recessions. The first decades following the World War II are a case in point. At the time, most firms in the United States were in such a strong position that the level of competition did not represent much more than a minor inconvenience.

Such conditions cannot last forever. During periods when the level of competition is not very intense, competitive pressures are too weak to discipline business effectively. When economies lack discipline over an extended period of time, problems accumulate as careless and wasteful practices become more common.

Eventually, some external event – say an oil shock or a major bankruptcy – unleashes waves of competitive pressure, creating a recession or even a depression. The more time that has past since the economy has last experienced a depression, the more vulnerable the economy will be and the greater probability that the depression will be intense.

Depressions create terrible hardships, but the market has no other means of maintaining its vigour. Depressions and recessions are similar to auto-immune systems. If business is relatively strong, a moderate depression will mostly eliminate the least efficient firms and cause others to improve become stronger by improving their economic practices. As a result, the remaining population consists of a higher proportion of efficient firms than before. Once this sort of depression subsides, the economy will be stronger that it was on the eve of the depression.

If the weakness reaches a certain level, these economic crises can get out of hand and become virulent. When depressions turn into full-blown crises, they can cripple or even destroy the economy, indiscriminately sweeping away healthy firms along with relatively inefficient businesses. Instead of merely ridding the economic organism of sick and diseased elements, these crises eat away at the vital organs, threatening the very existence of the organism. Unlike biological systems, where such self-consuming outbreaks are rare, market economies are likely to experience these self-destructive attacks without some institutional protection.

I know from lectures and talks that I have given that this thesis makes most people uncomfortable, probably because it challenges their comfortable belief in the possibility of perpetual prosperity. Most people do not·want to think that depressions are an essential part of a market society, but our present policy precludes any other means of maintaining competitive pressures.

I will show that a policy of high wages offers an alternative to depressions as a means of creating market pressures. I do not pretend that high wages are a panacea, but this policy is far more attractive than a serious depression. After all, depressions – even modest depressions – are not tidy affairs. Many people will suffer. They are wasteful. A good number of efficient firms will fall by the wayside along with those least worthy of survival. Nonetheless, market economies require these depressions to free them of many of inefficiencies that made the depression occur in the first place.

Competition works like the natural fire cycle in a forest. Fires can destroy many trees, but they also clear the way for new growth alongside the healthy trees that survive the fire. Foresters attempt to prevent to preserve the forest, but without a fire for an extended period of time, litter builds up on the forest floor. When a fire does occur, it will have such a reservoir of fuel on the forest floor that the fire can wipe out the forest altogether.

In effect, fire prevention can both enhance and threaten forest ecology. In this sense, depressions serve a vital purpose within a market economy even though they can threaten the very survival of a market economy. Both too much and too little competition can threaten market economies. In any case, one cannot hope to eliminate market pressure without erecting an alternative to a market system.

Our policy-makers have behaved like foresters who have protected the trees from the destructive fires for too long. Now, a substantial economic correction is long overdue, so much so that when it arrives it may threaten the foundations of the U.S. economy.

The Challenge Ahead

Mainstream economists do not generally realize the close association between competition and depressions. Proponents of both the Chicago and the Economic Management schools mostly contend that economies can benefit from competition without enduring the inconvenience of depression. Indeed, both schools teach that depressions need not occur. In effect, they implicitly assume that competitive pressures are steady or do not fluctuate significantly. Consequently, they believe that competition can be effective without threatening to turn into a depression. As I just noted, raising wages might forestall a depression, but this policy entails serious risks and uncertainties.

This common misunderstanding of the nature of competition and crises within a market economy has induced policy-makers to pursue policies in a vain attempt to vanquish the business cycle. The effect of these policies has been to diminish the strength competitive forces, increasing the likelihood of a severe depression.

As a result of these policies, our economy no longer resembles a strapling, accustomed to the dangers and the rigors of a competitive jungle. Instead, our economy has become more like a tragic bubble-boy, who weakens daily in an atmosphere of loving care.

Today, many industries just seem to crumble in the face of increased competition. In other sectors of the economy, we see firms responding to increased competition with what, at first, seems to be vigor, but later turns out to nothing more than a convulsion. The financial sector seems to be a case in point. For example, many people greeted the junk bond movement as a progressive force that could benefit the industrial as well as the financial sectors of the economy. Instead, the junk bond movement merely helped to spread the contamination faster.

The image of a bubble in a discussion of the economy suggests a related metaphor – that of a fragile, easily punctured object. Indeed, the decade-long attempt to shield the bubble-boy economy has so distorted the situation, that we now find ourselves neglecting the human inhabitants within the bubble in order to protect the bubble itself.

This tragic reversal, in which we spend billions of dollars to shore up the financial structure by scrimping on what we spend for people, cannot continue indefinitely. Sooner or later the economic decline will deepen, causing even more widespread pain and suffering.

When Marx said that capitalism would self-destruct, he actually meant that, eventually we would consciously choose a form of society that is good for people rather than for markets. So far Marx has been wrong about the nature of this choice. Instead, in the post-war U.S. economy, which is the subject of this book, we have ended up with a market economy in which the state has protected business from market forces – leading to a feeble, bubble-boy economy.

Already, the U.S. economy seems to be falling behind in the world economy, even as the world economy as a whole seems to be slowing down. Maybe we should not be surprised at this turn of events. After all, world economic leadership has always been transitory. Portugal, Spain, Holland and England had been the world leaders in earlier ages. Why should we expect leadership to be permanent for the United States?

This book contains no simple solution for reversing the decline. Instead, my prime object is to issue a warning that, under the present regime consisting of piecemeal management often followed by thoughtless deregulation, neither the economy nor the people will prosper. With that said, let us turn to our analysis of the post-war U.S. economy so that you can judge for yourself.

The Golden Age of Capitalism

Background to the Golden Age

At the end of World War II, the United States held a seemingly unchallengeable economic position, in part due to the war. The war brought much new capital on line. It sparked innovations that gave the United States the lead in much modern technology. It left the economies of the traditional competitors of the United States in ruins.

This economic strength seemed at the time to be all the more dramatic, considering that the U.S. economy had only recently emerged from the ashes of the Great Depression. In fact, the striking dichotomy between the Depression and prosperity is somewhat misleading. Although the achievements of the post-war prosperity may seem to represent a transcendence of the failures of the Depression, in reality, the Depression also did much to pave the way for the post-war recovery.

To begin with, the Great Depression set off a wave of intense competition that forced many firms to scrap a good deal of outmoded plant and equipment. By 1939, U.S. firms had replaced one-half of all their manufacturing equipment that had existed in 1933 (Staehle 1955, p. 127). Although the total amount of investment during the Depression was relatively small, much of that investment was directed toward modernizing existing plant and equipment. Thereafter, U.S. business produced as much output as a decade before with 15 per cent less capital and 19 per cent less labour (Staehle 1955, p. 133). This investment, coupled with the increase in productive capacity during the war, made the capital stock of the post-war United States the envy of the world.

In addition, financial conditions at end of World War II were almost ideal. The Depression unleashed a wave of bankruptcies, which wiped out much of the U.S. corporate debt. It frightened financial institutions enough to make them concentrate on high quality investments whenever possible. By the end of World War II about 70 per cent of world's monetary gold stock resided in U.S. vaults (Magdoff and Sweezy 1983, p. 9).

The subsequent war-time prosperity provided unprecedented corporate liquidity. Banks held many of their assets in the form of highly liquid U.S. government securities. In short, the sequence of a depression followed by the war helped to prepare the way for prosperity by lowering expectations for the post-war economy.

The association between increased government spending and the recovery made a deep impression on the economics profession, especially in the United States. Many economists reasoned that, since the Depression was ended by the war, ending the war would inevitably throw the economy back into a depression once again.

An economic advisor to the Secretary of Commerce wrote, 'in the summer of 1946, unemployment may exceed 7 million, as rising civilian employment and reductions in working hours turn out to be insufficient to absorb the additions to the labor force consequent upon the rapid discharge of workers from the armed forces' (Bassie 1946, p. 126.)

This prognosis was widely shared. A Philadelphia journalist, Joseph Livingston, surveyed economists about their predictions for the near future. In June 1947, he found that economists were expecting prices to fall 6.64 per cent during the following year (Carlson 1977). Declines of this magnitude only occur during a severe economic downturn.

The public shared this pessimistic view of the future. In 1945, a Roper poll showed that less than 41 per cent of the population of the United States believed that a post-war recession could be avoided (Wolfe 1981, p. 14).

To the best of my knowledge, only one economist, James O'Leary, understood that something new was afoot (O'Leary 1945). In a remarkable article, based on a paper that he delivered at the 1944 annual meetings of the American Economic Association, O'Leary gave a number of reasons why the post-war economy should prosper. First of all, he reasoned that many families had deferred their purchase of expensive consumer goods for an extended period of time. For example, many consumers had been unable to afford cars during the depression. Later during the war, the government rationed production to free up the automobile plants to build tanks and trucks. As a result, the stock of automobiles was quite old.

O'Leary realized that the effect of this backlog of consumption would be all the more powerful because many families had first liquidated their consumer debt and then accumulated considerable savings during the war. Consequently, a broad group of people had both the wherewithal and the desire to purchase expensive consumer goods, setting the stage for a post-war boom.

Although O'Leary's interpretation of post-war conditions is commonplace today, it fell on deaf ears at the time he first made his views known. So while most economists predicted a dramatic decline in prices, O'Leary's contrarian predictions turned out to be correct. Prices did not fall at all. Instead, they rose at a rate of 8.09 per cent (Carlson 1977).

Robert J. Gordon concluded, 'Surely the greatest *economic* surprise of the first postwar decade was the failure of anything resembling a postwar depression to occur' (Gordon 1980, p. 115). Because the healthy economic conditions of the time were so unexpected, business responded even more enthusiastically than might have otherwise been the case.

The Great Depression helped to prepare the political, as well as the economic climate in which the post-war prosperity blossomed. Back in the 1920s, the dominant political mood was to trust the market to ensure continuing prosperity. The Coolidge administration faithfully represented the temper of the middle class of the time.

Once the Depression struck, much of the public lost confidence in laissez faire. Economists in the United States began to read with intense interest works of the eminent British economist, John Maynard Keynes, whom we shall now discuss.

The Political Economy of the Golden Age

During the early post-war period, the experience of the Depression was still fresh in the minds of the American people, who remembered that their ordeal lasted more than a decade. They were intent on avoiding a repetition of the Great Depression at all costs. In this spirit, they accepted the notion that a multitude of New Deal programs failed to get the economy rolling until the massive military build up began.

Economists shared the popular view that government involvement was essential to continued prosperity. The idea took hold that the government could prevent depressions by intervening in the economy to manage the level of economic activity. Although some business leaders remained hostile to government intervention (Collins 1981), others actively lobbied for a tame rendering of the new economic policy of the New Deal, recognizing its obvious benefits (Stein 1969; and Neal 1981, pp. 15–22).

During the early post-war period, many economists were becoming aware of the ideas of John Maynard Keynes (Stein 1969; Keynes 1936). Although Keynes' theory was both complicated and vague, in the United States the most common, albeit incorrect, interpretation of his work stressed that government spending was the most effective means of shoring up a weak economy (see Perelman 1989).

Although Keynes preferred productive investment, he facetiously suggested that the government could just as well bury old bottles filled with money to put people to work. One group could bury the bottles while another would dig for them (Keynes 1936, p. 129). In effect, anything that could stimulate enough spending could get the economy back on its feet.

Keynes's theory seemed reasonable enough in many respects. If the bottle buriers and bottle diggers received money for their superfluous services, they would spend it on goods and services. The companies that sell to them would buy from other companies, bringing life to all sectors of the economy. This notion that investment sets a cumulative process in motion lies at the heart of Keynesian policy.

Despite their fear of a depression, many business and political leaders resisted the popular proposition that the government had the responsibility to fight unemployment in general. The fate of the proposed Full Employment Act of 1946 was symptomatic of the business's ambivalence about the relative roles of the government and the market. Initially, the act promised that 'every American able to work and willing to work has the right to a useful and remunerative job.' Martin Neil Baily's observation that the Employment Act of 1946 'expressed the political will to avoid recession or depression' was only partially correct (Baily 1978, p. 15), since the political will extended only in so far as it left the free play of the market intact.

By 1946, the urgency of the Depression conditions had subsided. Conservative political forces whittled away at the bill. Congress removed the word, 'Full,' from the title of the Employment Act of 1946. Instead of promising full employment, Congress inserted the reminder that 'it is the policy of the United States to foster free competitive enterprise' to reassure business (Bailey 1950; see also Wolfe 1981, p. 53).

In the final version of the law, the forces of moderation in the Congress went even further, reducing the requirement of full employment to an intention (Santoni 1986, pp. 11–2). Robert Lekachman concluded: 'Congress had carefully removed the political sting from S. 380's tail. The law merely asked the president only to prepare one more report. Congress was asked to do no more than study it' (Lekachman 1966, p. 174).

Despite the absence of any legislative requirement, the government still seemed to behave as if this meek version of the Employment Act actually constituted a modest commitment to the principle of full employment. Yes, recessions periodically infected the economy, but they were relatively mild. Each time the economy threatened to go into another deep slump, a mix of fiscal and monetary policies managed to keep the economy afloat. As Milton Friedman noted, individuals and business became convinced that, 'unless the recession is *exceedingly* minor, explicit action will be taken' (Friedman 1968; and 1980, p. 79).

Indeed, during the first eight years after the passage of the Employment Act, the official unemployment rate averaged below 4 per cent (Editors of *Monthly Review* 1983, p. 3). In reality, this enviable record owed little to a strong commitment on the part of the government. Instead, the economy was so healthy that the modest efforts on the part of the government sufficed to keep the economy strong.

Nonetheless, as the memories of the Great Depression receded into the hazy past, leaders of business, government and the great universities deluded themselves into believing that they had somehow mastered the art of managing the economy. When the economy temporarily slackened off during the Eisenhower years, followers of John Maynard Keynes assured the world that a renewed regimen of their policies would ensure another burst of prosperity. At the time, Paul Samuelson insisted that with proper fiscal and monetary policy the economy could have full employment and whatever rate of capital formation and growth it wanted (Stein 1969, p. 363).

In the words of Joseph Garbarino: 'By 1955, the American economy had experienced ten years of fairly high level post-war prosperity and had weathered two minor recessions. The basis for concluding that a new economic era based on government's long-term commitment to stability and on industry's rationalized long range planning was at hand' (Garbarino 1962, p. 415).

Coming on the heels of the Great Depression, the surge in wartime demand vaulted the economy into what seemed to be an age of almost perpetual prosperity. Indeed, during the Golden Age, everything seemed to be in place for an economy without depressions or recessions. Depression year promises of a chicken in every pot gave way to an expectation of two cars in every garage.

Who would have guessed that, for many of the citizens of the United States, the fear of not even having a home, let alone a garage, would become a reality within a couple of decades? Who could have anticipated that we would soon add such hideous words as homelessness, rust-belt and de-industrialization to our vocabulary?

Overconfidence and the Return of the Business Cycle
For the most part, this dream of perpetual prosperity seemed to be within reach. Between 1947 and 1972, the average weekly earnings measured in 1977 dollars for total private non-agricultural work rose from $123 to $198 (President of the United States 1990, p. 344).

During the Kennedy Administration, the government expressed a commitment to maintaining this prosperity by applying the policy tools developed during the post-war period. In light of the strong economic performance at the time, the tentative spirit of the Employment Act of 1946 gave way to an overarching confidence in the government's ability to control the economy. Walter Heller expressed this spirit, writing: '[W]e now take for granted that the government must step in to provide the essential stability at high levels of employment and growth that the market mechanism, left alone, cannot deliver' (Heller 1966, p. 9).

Indeed, the economic successes of the Kennedy years redoubled the confidence in powers of macro-economic management. Confidence eventually gave way to overconfidence. Economists convinced themselves that their scientific training endowed them with the ability to fine tune the economy. For Arthur Okun: 'More vigorous and more consistent application of the tools of economic policy contributed to the obsolescence of the business cycle pattern and refutation of the stagnation myths' (Okun 1970, p. 37, and 1980, p. 163).

Even the Council of Economic Advisors, caught up in the economic utopianism of the time, reported in 1965 that: 'both our increased understanding of the effectiveness of fiscal policy and the continued improvement of our economic information, strengthen the conviction that recessions can be increasingly avoided and ultimately wiped out' (cited in Wolfe 1981, p. 69).

This faith in the possibility of continuous prosperity became so ingrained that, by 1967, an international conference of influential economists was convened in London to discuss whether the economists had actually vanquished the business cycle forever (Bronfenbrenner 1969a). Although most of the participants remained unconvinced of the ultimate demise of the business cycle, such skepticism was far from universal.

A few economists warned that those who believed in the myth of perpetual prosperity were extrapolating from a mere two decades of experience in using their economic techniques (R. A. Gordon 1969, p. 4). This word of caution left most economists unfazed. Circles close to the center of the Democratic Party policy-makers also remained under sway of the idea that depressions had been conquered, once and for all (R. A. Gordon 1969, p. 4).

Most importantly, the business community accepted the notion that threat of a depression was a thing of the past. Investors who bet on the continuation of prosperity were more often than not rewarded for their optimism at the time. Although the successful investors could content themselves with the thought that they were sensible business people who recognized sound economic propositions, they typically based their expectations on the delusion that the inevitable downturn was unlikely, if not impossible.

Optimistic expectations did seem to be capable of fueling the post-war economic boom by stimulating a vigorous investment program, which would ensure that markets would be strong enough to sustain a high level of economic activity for decades on end. In this vein, Paul Samuelson assured the readers of his 4 November 1968 column in *Newsweek* that the new Keynesian economics works: 'Wall Street knows it. Main Street, which has been enjoying 92 months of advancing sales knows it' (cited in DuBoff and Herman 1972).

Indeed, the performance of the economy during the first decades of the post-war period seemed to justify the confidence of the Keynesians. In terms of 'growth, price and distribution . . . the first two decades after World War II may well be a close approximation to the best that in practice can be obtained from a capitalist economy' (Minsky 1982, p. 376). Not surprisingly, promoters of the new economic policy became giddy with their early successes. They enthusiastically spread the gospel of perpetual prosperity, promising the faithful that they could manipulate the economy so exactly that capitalism could supposedly proceed from now on, untroubled by the periodic crises, which had plagued capitalism in the past.

Today, the salad days of the early post-war period are over. The economy slides deeper into decline. Economists still nostalgically long for the Golden Age. They ask themselves, what went wrong? Why does productivity not continue to grow the way it did in the early post-war period?

Only now are economists coming to pose the questions differently: What were the unusual features that made the Golden Age so much better than the norm (Griliches 1988, p. 19)? Even so, the mainstream of economic thought has not come to grips with the grim reality that such prosperity cannot continue indefinitely in a market economy.

Markets have an intrinsic rhythm of boom and bust. After an economy runs at full throttle for a period of time, strains and pressures build up in the form of excessive speculation and imbalances due to inappropriate investments by overly optimistic firms. Such is the nature of the capitalist economy. It requires periodic recessions or even depressions in order to steady itself.

In fact, the U.S. economy has spent the majority of time during the previous century enmeshed either in depressions, recessions or wars. Time and time again, the economy would emerge from one of these periods of turmoil, enjoy a period of prosperity, and then sink back again.

Post-War Decline

Economists generally have difficulty in anticipating the outbreak of an economic bust. Indeed, a few months after Samuelson published his naively optimistic 1968 *Newsweek* article, the economy entered a prolonged period of relative stagnation, although people did not realize what was happening at the time. With the benefit of hindsight, we now recognize that many of the symptoms of decline came to light just around this time.

Although economic optimism remained relatively strong, social and political optimism was eroding at the time. Two non-economic events were especially effective in shattering the hope and confidence of the post-war period. Neither was the stuff that we would expect to read in the business pages, but on a deeper level, both demonstrated the limits of the U.S. economy. First, the war in Vietnam made the citizens of the United States recognize the limits of the economic power of this nation. People in the United States were dumbfounded that a country as small and as poor as Vietnam could withstand against the military might of the United States, which seemed all-powerful only a couple of decades earlier.

The Vietnam War was not merely a symptom of economic weakness. It was also a major contributor to the economic decline, as we shall see later. As the damage from the Vietnam War spread though the economy, political cynicism became rampant. The public lost faith in the government. The Nixon Administration attempted to stem the tide of anti-government feelings by using illegal means to stop the flow of information from the government, leading to the Watergate Scandal. In this environment, with the economy in shambles and a sizeable portion of the executive branch of the government under indictment, faith in Keynesianism and the government's ability to control the economy evaporated. Conservative economic theory became ascendant.

Second, the racial turmoil of the 1960s reminded affluent, middle-class whites that not everybody was sharing in the great post-war prosperity. At first, the government was confident that it could extend the benefits of the Golden Age to less privileged groups of Americans. Later, as the economy slowed down, this optimism receded. Some white Americans regarded affirmative action program as a substantial threat that they would have to do with less in order that African-Americans could join the economic mainstream.

These two concerns – the Vietnam War and racial disharmony – were bound up with each other. During the war, non-white soldiers made up a disproportionate share of the combat troops. Many young white men, especially those from privileged families, found shelter in military deferments or service away from the front lines.

Parenthetically, a good many of the prominent figures who avoided military service in their youth have seen the error of their ways. Now that they have reached the critical age where military service is no longer a threat, they have become the most vocal proponents of a strong military

*Table 1.1   The Deteriorating Performance of the U.S.
Post-war Macroeconomy*

	1948–66	*1966–73*	*1973–79*	*1979–87*
Real GNP Growth Rate (%)	4.4	3.2	.6	2.2
Real Wage Growth Rate (%)	2.6	2.1	0.4	0.0
Unemployment Rate (Ave. %)	5.2	4.6	.8	7.7
Inflation Rate (Ave. %)	2.0	5.1	8.9	5.2
After Tax Profit Rate (%)	6.9	7.0	5.5	6.0
Rate of Capital Accumulation (%)	3.5	4.3	.5	2.8

Source: Bowles, Gordon and Weisskopf (1989).

presence. In fact, what optimism that remains in the contemporary United States seems to be grounded on a pride in military strength.

The Falling Rate of Profit

The decline has taken a severe toll on the working people of the United States. In 1972, the average weekly earnings in 1977 dollars for total private non-agricultural work stood at $198. Since then earnings have declined dramatically, reaching $168 in 1988 (President of the United States 1990, p. 344). Although inflation has slowed recently, unemployment continues high and investment remains weak.

In almost every respect, the United States is falling behind, while German-led continental Europe and Japan are moving ahead in economic power.

In order to understand the nature of this deterioration of the U.S. economic position, we must first take account of the decline in profits. In a market economy, capitalists or the managers in their employ make the key economic decisions. Although capitalists enjoy power, perks and other privileges, ultimately they must earn a profit to succeed. So as a first approximation, we can proceed with the assumption that capitalists' single objective is to make a profit, putting aside for the moment the need to understand the economy in all its complexity.

The before-tax rate of return on fixed capital and inventories declined by more than 30 percent between 1948 and 1987 (Michl 1991, p. 271). The magnitude of this decline is dramatic enough to merit our attention, despite the undeniable limitations of the data.

Because profits are high during booms and low during recessions, we normally compare average profit rates for an entire cycle to eliminate the problem of comparing a boom year with a bust year.

Table 1.2   Growth in Profit Rates for Non-Financial Corporations

Years	Profit Rate Growth (Per Cent per Annum)
1948–51	0.34
1951–55	–1.52
1955–59	–3.64
1959–65	4.01
1965–72	–5.36
1972–77	–1.40
1977–81	–5.67
1981–85	6.08

Source: Michl (1988a, p. 13).

Table 1.2 gives an estimate of the profit rate over the first eight post-war business cycles. Each period in Table 1.2 represents a complete cycle.

The first two post-war cycles suggest a period of relative stability. Profit rates fell on the whole, but not dramatically. Next, we see the profit rate falling substantially during the late Eisenhower years, followed by the initial Vietnam War boom. As the military build up overheated the economy, profits subsequently deteriorated. Profit rates continued to erode until after the Reagan recession. During the final cycle, covered in the table, the profit rate recovered somewhat, approximately to where it was in 1970, but nowhere near the peaks of the early 1960s.

This growth in the rate of profits during the last cycle does not seem to be a harbinger of the end of the decline. Profits rose in part because they had fallen so low during the previous cycle. In addition, profits rose because business was able to hire workers so cheaply; not because it was able to employ them particularly efficiently. I will return to this subject later.

The Decline and Falling Profit Rates

Although many influences can affect profit rates, Tom Weisskopf has proposed a useful way of decomposing the profit rate into the product of three major factors: first, the share of profits in the national income; second, the capital stock that would be required to produce the national income if the economy were operating at full capacity; and third, the current output as a fraction of the full capacity output (Weisskopf 1979). Although economists usually identify profitability with efficiency, Weisskopf's decomposition of the profit rate reveals how the profit rate can move independently of changes in business efficiency.

At best, Weisskopf's first factor is only loosely related to efficiency.

Theoretically, business could increase the share of profits in the national income as a reward for developing new and more efficient methods of producing the products that it sells; however, the profit share can change for other reasons that are unrelated to efficiency. For example, the share of wages, interest or rent can vary because of political factors, such as tax laws or rent controls.

Since the majority of people in the United States work for their living, the largest share of national income goes to labour. Because the shares that go to interest or rents are relatively small, the rise in these non-wage shares would have to be nothing short of spectacular to compensate for the fall in real wages. As a result, we should expect that the wage structure will be a crucial determinant of Weisskopf's first factor and that changes in the labour market would have a significant impact on the first factor.

These changes in the wage structure may have nothing to do with efficiency. A changing political climate can allow business or labour to push the wage level one way or another, regardless of changes in efficiency. Obviously, the political tide has been moving against labour in recent decades. For example, even though the real wage has been falling, the productivity of labour has actually been growing. We might be able to credit business efficiency with increasing the productivity of labour, except that the collapse of the wage structure is far more dramatic than any productivity advances.

This combination of an increase in productivity and a decline in wages is certain to augment Weisskopf's first factor: the profit share. With falling real wages, the share of profits will grow, unless one of two conditions are met: either the productivity of labour falls faster than the real wage (which did not happen) or some other groups, such as those who earn interest, are able to gain so much that their windfall wipes out the benefits from the fall in the real wage rate.

In short, unless a decline in the quality of labour would be responsible for the falling real wage – a notion that some economists do suggest, even though labour productivity has been growing – then the shrinking wage translates into an expansion of profits, irrespective of any efficiencies.

Tom Michl made an impressionistic calculation, which is very instructive in this regard. He estimated how much the share of wages would vary for each percentage change in the rate of labour productivity. He found that during the period 1948–70, roughly corresponding to what we had earlier called the Golden Age of capitalism, a one percentage point change in labour productivity tended to increase the wage share by 1.21 percent, meaning that labour was able to capture rewards over and above the increases in labour productivity at the time. In the later period, labour was much less fortunate. From 1970 to 1986, the estimate fell to 0.56 per cent, suggesting that labour earned only about one-half of its productivity increases (Michl 1988b).

Michl's estimates suggest that during the period in which the economic decline appeared, the share of wages in the national income began to fall due to causes that were unrelated to labour productivity. His calculations support the notion that we cannot uncritically attribute shifts in Weisskopf's first factor to efficiency during the period of the economic decline.

Weisskopf's third factor depends on the overall level of economic activity rather than business efficiency since individual business managers have little control over this factor. The policies of the federal government and the Federal Reserve Board are more important influences on the level of overall economic activity.

Only the second factor directly relates to efficiency. Weisskopf's statistical analysis indicated that the first and third factors could not explain much of the fall in the rate of profit. The second factor seemed more important.

Tom Michl made a similar diagnosis of the fall in the rate of profit. He found that, from 1948–70, the profit rare fell mainly as a result of a rise in the share of wages, mainly in the late 1960s. During the 1970s, although wages did not escalate, the rate of profit declined largely as a result of increases in the price of raw materials (Michl 1991, p. 271). During the 1980s, neither rising wages nor raw materials prices could explain why profits would remain low (Michl 1988a). Instead, a deeper structural problem seems to be at work. Something was blocking business from operating efficiently. In this book, I will attempt to identify the nature of this blockage.

We will see that, although profits are an important business incentive, the economic decline is more than a matter of dollars and cents. It works its way into the fabric of our society. For example, many recent observers of the U.S. business environment write as if the morality of business leaders has taken a recent turn for the worse. True, even firms that have cultivated good reputations in the past have seem to now behave in ways that the public would have considered shocking a few decades ago.

This trend owes more, however, to the decline in profits than to a sudden epidemic of immorality. A fall in profitability encourages firms to cut corners to protect their earnings. Under such conditions, many firms display a wanton disregard for their workers, the environment, and even their own customers.

Table 1.3　Real Hourly Earnings in 1977 dollars

1947	$3.06
1950	$3.36
1960	$4.27
1973	$5.38
1980	$4.89
1989	$4.80

Source: Economic Report of the President (1990, p. 344).

Poverty and the Distribution of Income

Lest the decline in the rate of profit cause us to become overly concerned with the fate of the well-to-do, we should note that during the 1980s, the upper 1 per cent of the families in the United States, who were already doing quite well, increased their average income by an astounding $233,322 per family, a gain of 74 per cent. Indeed, more and more people are enduring poverty and the differences between rich and poor are becoming more extreme. For example, during the 1980s, income gains for the bottom 95 per cent of the families were non-existent (Mishel and Frankel 1991, p. 25).

In short, the United States increasingly resembles a typical Third World economy. Each year more and more children drop below the poverty line. In 1973, 14.2 per cent of all people under 18 years of age were poor; by 1988, 19.6 per cent were poor (Mishel and Frankel 1991, p. 175).

As a result, in 1989, the share of the national income going to the upper 1 per cent exceeded that of the bottom 40 per cent (ibid., p. 27). This disparity in income is all but unknown in advanced economies. It is more typical of Latin American economies.

The state of labour in the United States is another clear indicator of the nature of economic decline. Table 1.3 below, shows that during the Golden Age, real hourly, non-agricultural wages steadily rose from $3.06 in 1947, reaching a high point in 1973 of $5.38 (all wages measured in 1977 dollars). Since then, real hourly wages have steadily declined, falling to $4.80 (in 1977 dollars) in 1989 (Economic Report of the President 1990, p. 344).

In short, the economic decline hurts people in most walks of life, except for those at the very peak of the economy. Of course, the poorest were hurt the most, but the hardship of the decline extended even to those who were relatively well off. By 1986, a average male with a college diploma was earning 2 per cent less in real terms than a similar person would have earned in 1973. Of course, a male with only a high school degree fared even worse, earning 16 per cent less than he would have in 1973 (Levy 1988, p. vii).

Some people rationalize the gross inequities in the United States with a conviction that the poor are just too lazy to get a job. In fact, a good number of the poor are physically unable to participate fully in the labour markets. For example, in 1979, the peak of the last business cycle for which we have information, the heads of two-thirds of all poor families were either a person who was elderly, disabled, a student, or a woman with a child under 6 years of age. In contrast, in 1939, only one-third of all poor households fell into these categories (Danziger and Gottschalk 1986, p. 405; Levitan and Shapiro 1987).

Others try to explain the growing inequality by unfavorable demographic changes in the United States. Such experts contend that educated white males receive more wages because they are 'naturally' the most productive workers. More and more workers are young, or women or from disadvantaged ethnic groups that earn less income.

In truth, demographic explanations are incapable of explaining such a major shift in the distribution of income. We will do better if we understand these shifts in terms of the economy-wide process of an economic decline rather than viewing it exclusively from the perspective of the very poor or of labour.

The Oil Shock as a Consequence of the Economic Decline

Many people prefer to look for single causes for the decline. For example, many still believe that we can trace the economic decline to the rise in oil prices during the 1970s. We can just as easily make the case that the pressuring arising during the early years of the economic decline was responsible for the oil shock. We have already noted that the inability of the U.S. economy to finance the Vietnam War without severe disruption was one of the early symptoms of the economic decline.

The events growing out of the Vietnam War helped to bring on the oil shock in several ways. First, the attempt to wage war in Vietnam set off a round of inflation. In addition, wheat, a raw material which many oil producing countries imported, soared in value. For example, Number 2, Hard Amber Durham, soared in price from $2.17 per bushel in 1972 to $6.60 in 1973 (U.S. Department of Agriculture 1980, p. 29). Although oil prices were quoted in dollars, they had been relatively stable.

In this environment, oil was a depreciating asset in a double sense. The petroleum exporters saw the depletion of their oil reserves as a long-term threat to their long-term economic health. The petroleum exporters were keeping a good deal of their proceeds in dollar denominated bank accounts. They saw the value of these accounts falling because of inflation (Sampson

1975, p. 251). They saw the value of their oil reserves falling as they became increasingly depleted. They had to pay more for the goods that they were importing, while the price of their principal export stagnated. Increasing oil prices seemed equitable in this light. That the price hikes coincided with the 1973 Embargo was largely coincidental (ibid., p. 252).

The Vietnam War helped to provoke the oil price increases in another way. Seeing the strains that the Vietnam War placed on the economy, Richard Nixon and his Secretary of State, Henry Kissinger, proposed the Nixon Doctrine, which held that the U.S. would support surrogates who would carry out our policies in the Third World. In this way, the U.S. could shift at least some of the burdens of defence onto other nations.

The job of the U.S. policeman for the Middle East fell to the Shah of Iran. Not satisfied with playing the simple cop on the beat, the Shah got swept up with illusions about his grandeur. He went on a shopping binge for sophisticated weaponry, well beyond the means of his treasury (see Hulbert 1982, Chapter 3).

The decline seemed to contribute to the shock in another way, which is harder to document, but was widely understood at the time. A number of sources report that Kissinger was acting to keep oil prices high in 1974 (Hulbert 1982, pp. 78–79).

Hulbert suggests that his motives were to help the Shah afford to purchase expensive weapons from the United States. I lean toward a different explanation. During the early 1970s, the U.S. was increasingly unable to compete in international merchandise trade. Encouraging the Shah to keep oil prices high seemed to give U.S. industry a leg up on its rivals.

Although the United States was dependent on imported oil, the U.S. dependence was much less than that of its two most important economic rivals: West Germany and Japan. Increased oil prices stood to do much more damage to industry in West Germany and Japan than in the United States (Castells 1980, p. 85). Certainly, the financial markets thought so. As soon as the oil prices rose in 1973, speculators began to dump their yen, marks and francs for dollars (Tanzer 1975, p. 91).

The U.S. hopes for an advantage from the oil shock came to naught. Rising oil prices actually hurt the United States more than most of its rivals.

The Japanese proved to be especially adept in adopting methods to cope with higher energy costs. Today, for example, the Japanese economy produces 2.24 times the real output for the same energy input as in 1973 (Chipello and Brauchli 1990). In contrast, U.S. firms were all to often inclined to make do with the equipment than they had on hand, until more intense international competition finally forced a series of devastating plant closings throughout the country. As a result, the United States uses about 2.5 times as much energy per person for commercial uses as Japan (ibid.). Again, a policy that was supposed to arrest the economic decline turned out to make it more severe.

The Decline as a Complex Economy-wide Process

Despite the abrupt materialization of the decline, it had been developing over decades. We can liken the process to the movement of a gigantic ship. It might not appear to be very dramatic, but it is the result of a powerful momentum, which is extremely difficult to reverse. This book is largely concerned with the nature of this momentum.

In general, economic theory ignores the role of momentum in the economy. Economists typically use the metaphor of a primitive fish market to illustrate how markets work. The fish sellers bring their catch to market. If it is not sold quickly, it rots and loses all value. Buyers and sellers bargain until they find the highest price at which all the fish will be sold. Tomorrow, when the process repeats itself, the price today will be irrelevant (Thornton 1869, p. 47).

If we add even the slightest touch of realism to this example, this brand of economic theory loses its elegant precision. For example, if fish prices remain high for a while, members of the fishing industry may choose to invest in a bigger or a better fleet. Unlike today's price, today's investment, resulting in an expanded stock of fishing capital, will have an incalculable impact.

When one firm invests, it often creates favorable conditions for other firms to invest. For example, Joel Moykyr has described how the growth of Dutch ship-building led to the development of rope and sail-making, which led to wind-driven saw mills, which could make ship building more efficient. These industries gave Holland an edge in trade, which made Holland the most successful economy in the world during the seventeenth century (Moykyr 1990. p. 163).

Moykyr's depiction of the rise of the Dutch economy lacks the minimalist elegance of the classical description of an imaginary fish market, but it offers a great deal more realism. It also illustrates how economic momentum takes hold.

We have no exact idea of the quantitative effects on specific industries, but we do know, as Moykyr's example illustrates, that when a firm erects a new factory, other companies may emerge to service the firm. The growth of these service firms may induce still other firms to locate nearby.

In addition, the growth in the demand from the investing firm may allow suppliers to enjoy economies of scale – meaning a lowering of average cost as the scale of production expands. If these resulting efficiencies lead suppliers to lower their costs, still other firms will benefit, perhaps stimulating even more investment.

Assar Linbeck uses his native Sweden as an example of the cumulative spillover of economic actions. Who could have predicted at the turn of the century that Sweden would be so successful in ball bearings, safety matches, cream separators, automatic lighthouses, telephone exchanges and military aircraft? Sweden had no particular resource advantage that induced it to specialize in these industries. Linbeck gives a simpler answer, 'Some people living in Sweden happened to take initiative' (Linbeck 1981, p. 394).

Economists have long recognized how the cumulative effects of a seemingly small number of such independent decisions can combine to create a major impact. For example, in discussing why industries tend to cluster around a specific location, Alfred Marshall, who more than anyone else was responsible for the formalization of economic theory, wrote, 'When an industry has chosen a locality for itself, it is likely to stay here long: so great are the advantages which people following the same trade get from near neighborhood to one another' (Marshall 1920, p. 271). Unfortunately, neither Marshall nor his successors integrated this insight into their formal theory.

Investment helps to stimulate further investment in another crucial way. When a firm invests it puts money into the hands of its employees and its suppliers. Their spending will create new markets, which will improve the potential profitability of other new investments, possibly setting off a spiral of investment (see Shleifer and Vishny 1988).

The spiral cannot continue indefinitely. Eventually, this happy state of affairs will create a state of overconfidence. Some people will begin to invest foolishly, causing the cumulative causation to work in reverse.

Each market economy develops its own particular pattern of spillovers within the context of boom and bust. Economic historians are familiar with the role of spillovers in a developing economy. We know less about the momentum associated with economic decline. This book explores the nature of this perverse momentum for the case of the U.S. economy.

The pattern that we shall describe is not pleasing. One business's failure helps to drag another into bankruptcy. The government finds itself burdened with the damage created by bankruptcies. Besides increased obligations for welfare and unemployment benefits, the government must cover the pension plans of bankrupt firms.

Soaring government expenses, combined with declining revenues, create spiralling deficits, which raise interest rates. Where interest rates are prohibitive and investors uncertain, business will be slow to create new jobs. Yet prolonged unemployment can make workers unemployable. Certainly, it is associated with almost every measure of crime and disease, creating further demands on the government, which further adds to the demands on government.

Despite the increasing responsibilities of the government, soaring deficits lead to strong pressure to curtail public expenditures. The government responds by diminishing its commitment in crucial areas, such as education and health care, which limits the ability of the economy to produce in the future.

Historically, this process continues until the economy hits rock bottom. At that point, hopefully the economy bounces back and the process begins anew. This rebound is not necessarily a natural phenomenon. Often, it is associated with military adventures. In a nuclear age, this method of economic recovery poses obvious risks.

Economics and Oversimplification

Economists do not generally broach the subject of momentum. They are prone to ignore the complexity of economic processes. Instead, they single out a particular problem, attributing all the ills of the society to a lone cause, as we noted in our discussion of mismanagement.

This habit of reducing the focus of their work to single causes leads to serious errors in judgement. Once economic analysts commit themselves to framing the problem in terms of a single cause, they are prone to proposing to rectify the situation with a simple remedy, whether it be lower taxes or a set of measures to make workers work harder or incentives to increase savings, etc.

Such single-minded prescriptions are wrong-headed. By concentrating on one particular symptom of a complex process, single-minded analysts lose sight of the detrimental effects of the unexpected aftermath of their policy recommendations. They cut themselves off from the possibility of understanding how to improve the process. As a result, single-minded analysis generally deepens the overall problem rather than ameliorating it. In short, complex economic processes require systemic analysis.

In part, the destructive habit of oversimplification is endemic to the discipline of economics. After all, economists purposefully developed their formal theory to allow themselves to make clear and unambiguous predictions about complex economic systems.

The key to this theory was the development of a set of unrealistic assumptions that would ensure that the price system would give the proper incentives to people and firms to do what was best for society. Although this theory was elegant, it required ruling out crucial aspects of the actual economic process, including the spillovers and momentum that we have been discussing.

Economists are only now beginning to think about developing models that will account for the influence of economic momentum, but this work is still in its infancy (see Arthur 1989). Rather than use sophisticated models, I will try to bring together as much as possible of the complex set of forces that are responsible for the economic decline.

Although this work will not be the first to study the contemporary economic mess, it will be unique in attempting to address the complexity of the problems that face us. This caveat extends to my recommendation of measures to boost wages. All measures must be understood in terms of the complexity of the economic process.

I will simplify my task in one respect. Although this decline is world-wide, I will concentrate on the case of the United States.

Summary

This book tells the story of an economy based on self-interest in which the interested parties fail to understand their own best interests. Business perceives its interest to do anything in its power to cut wages. In doing so, it reduces the income of its potential customers. More importantly, it cripples the labour force and thereby undermines its productivity as well as the rate of profit. In contrast to the prevailing opinion about the appropriate level of wages, I will show how a high-wage policy promotes economic growth.

During the early post-war period, both business and the public supported the government's attempt to stabilize the economy. Although stabilization policy helped to reduce the intensity of the business cycle, it also reduced necessary modernization of the economy, preparing the way for an economic decline.

As the decline gained momentum, business as well as the public at large perceived that they would benefit by cutting government. As a result, they helped to create a lax regulatory structure which led to instability and chaos. The government lets the public infrastructure of roads and public works deteriorate enough to hobble the economy. Education suffers, further damaging productivity and profits.

Although business and the public oppose the government in general, they agree that their interests will be served by a huge military build-up. The military expenditures further sap the vitality of the economy, so much so that they ultimately threaten to weaken the military itself.

The build-up of the military dovetails with a program to protect the economy against depressions by maintaining demand for goods and services. Unfortunately, this policy undermines competition and weakens the economy, ultimately leading to a process of de-industrialization.

The revolution in the financial structure of the United States reinforces this process of de-industrialization, leading to an economy that is increasingly built upon low-wage service jobs. The alternative policy that I propose centers on a high wage structure, which has traditionally been the source of the strength of the U.S. economy.

2 The Attack on Labour Accelerates the Economic Decline

The Post-War Labour-Management Accord

During the Golden Age, social conditions on the whole were relatively harmonious, with the obvious exception of violence against blacks. In the North, racial tensions largely reflected the collision between demobilized troops and black workers who had taken industrial jobs. In the South, whites felt threatened by the inevitable dislocations that the imminent destruction of their rural, patriarchal society would cause.

During the initial years of post-war prosperity, the economy was expanding fast enough that wages could grow while profits remained high. Union leaders developed a relatively comfortable relationship with management at the time, especially within the large industrial complexes. They purged their ranks of militants and became active participants in the anti-communist crusade that was at the heart of U.S. foreign policy.

Forces were at work that would eventually undermine this implicit accord between labour leaders and capital. Although management offered workers higher wages, it also claimed the exclusive right to maintain absolute control over work on the shop floor. For example, the 1945 contract between the United Automobile Workers and General Motors included a clear 'right to manage clause,' which read:

> The right to hire, promote, discharge or discipline for cause, and to maintain discipline and efficiency of employees, is the sole responsibility of the Corporation except that the union members shall not be discriminated against as such. In addition, the products to be manufactured, the location of plants, the schedules of production, the methods, processes and means of manufacturing are solely and exclusively the responsibility of the Corporation. (Gartman 1986, p. 278; cited in Lazonick 1990, p. 272)

Later, when General Motors signed its agreement with the United Automobile Workers covering the period between 1948 and 1950, *Fortune,*

30

in an article entitled, 'The Treaty of Detroit,' commented, 'GM may have paid a billion for peace. It got a bargain.' According to *Fortune*, 'General Motors has regained control over one of the crucial management functions in any line of manufacturing – long-range scheduling of production, model changes, and tool and plant investment' (Anon. 1950, p. 53; see also Serrin 1974, p. 170). One estimate put the value of this new found freedom of planning at $0.15 worth of corporate profit per hour (ibid.).

Indeed, the United Automobile Workers union failed to achieve any of its major policy goals in this agreement (Harris 1982, pp. 139 ff; Fairris 1990). Still, many workers, who had only recently experienced the Depression, initially found this deal acceptable.

The Breakdown of the Labour-Management Accord

Wages continued to improve well into the 1960s. Indeed, between 1966 and 1969, unemployment remained below 4 per cent, allowing workers to accelerate the increases in their wages. By the early 1970s, the real value of the average weekly earnings of non-agricultural workers reached an all time high.

Even so, many workers – especially young workers – felt dissatisfied with their work. By the 1960s, many workers found the organization of work alienating. They had become increasingly reluctant to accept capital's pretense of absolute control within the workplace. In General Motors's Lordstown plant, workers wrote on their machines, 'Treat Me with Respect and I will give you Top Quality Work with Less Effort' (Rothschild 1974, p. 119).

Many of the younger workers began to question the value of accumulating more and more possessions. In addition, the birth control pill allowed many workers to avoid some of the family pressures that typically intensify the need for job security (Halberstam 1986, p. 487).

Feeling confident that they could find alternative employment, many of these young workers resisted employers' efforts at maintaining discipline. The auto 'quit rate' at the time was enormous. One study found that more than half of all new unskilled auto workers in 'major northern production centers' leave their job within one year (Rothschild 1974, p. 124).

Among those workers who continued their employment, absenteeism became commonplace. Ford Motor Company claimed in 1970 that absenteeism had 'doubled' or 'tripled' in ten years; that such average figures 'mask[ed] the crippling effects often felt on a key production line' (ibid.).

Douglas Fraser, past president of the United Automobile Workers, used to tell a story about a young employee at the Twinsburg, Ohio stamping plant to illustrate the workers' attitude at the time. This worker faithfully laboured for four days a week, but he never came for the fifth day.

The plant was loathe to fire this worker because labour markets were so tight. In fact, at the time, management was on a seven-day schedule because of widespread absenteeism. Finally, the plant manager confronted the young man, demanding to know why he regularly worked four days a week. The worker responded, 'Because I can't make a living working three days a week' (Halberstam 1986, p. 488).

Absenteeism was not the only symptom of the erosion of shop floor discipline. By 1971, the almost open use of drugs in U.S. factories became a front-page story in the *New York Times* (Salpukas 1971).

A good number of young workers actively rebelled on the job, undermining productivity. Surely, the conduct of the Vietnam War contributed to this spirit of rebellion and a widespread disdain for authority in general. Finally, the conditions of the unions played a significant role.

Many of these workers believed that constructive attempts to create truly democratic unions, which would represent their interests, could not succeed. Without a strong union to express their concerns, they had limited opportunities to make the views felt.

Rebellion on the Shop Floor

In this environment, workers often challenged management's authority on the job, dissipating enormous productive energies. The testimony of John Lippert, who had been a worker in General Motors' Fleetwood plant, is instructive in this regard. He described his fellow workers' vigorous efforts to slow down the assembly line (Lippert 1978). Lippert suggested the intensity of his desire to carve a bit of autonomy on the assembly line by expressing obvious pride in hurrying up his work on a few cars, in order to have 15 or 20 seconds to himself (ibid., p. 58).

Bill Watson, who spent one year in a Detroit automobile factory, offers an even more dramatic example of the lengths to which workers go to assert their independence (Watson 1971). He describes how workers revolted against the production of a poorly designed 6-cylinder model car. In the process, workers and foremen argued over particular motors. Tension escalated.

After management rejected the workers' suggestions for improvements in the production and design of the product, they initiated a 'counter-plan,' beginning by intentionally misassembling or omitting parts on a larger than normal scale. Later, workers in inspection made alliances with workers in several assembly areas to ensure a high rate of defective motors.

Workers went ahead and installed many of these defective motors, thereby requiring that management would have to go to the trouble of removing them later.

Eventually, even more complicated measures were taken. The conflict only ended during a layoff after management suddenly moved the entire 6-cylinder assembly and inspection operation to another end of the plant, presumably at great cost (ibid., pp. 76–7).

In another instance, the company, intending to save money by shutting down their foundry early, attempted to build the engines using parts that already had been rejected during the year. Workers in the motor test area lodged the first protest, but management hounded inspectors to accept defective motors. After motor test men communicated their grievances to other workers, they began to collaborate in intentional sabotage. Inspectors agreed to reject three of every four motors. Stacks of motors piled up at an accelerating pace until the entire plant shut down, losing more than ten hours of production time to deal with the problem. Management summoned inspectors to the head supervisor's office. Inspectors protested that they were only acting in the interest of management.

Watson's third example is the most telling of all. During a model change-over period, management had scheduled an inventory build-up, which was to require six weeks. Management intended to keep 50 people at work on the job. These workers could have earned 90 per cent of their pay if they were laid off. Workers reacted to the opportunity, attempting to finish the inventory in three or four days instead of the six weeks.

They trained each other in particular skills, circumventing the established ranking and job classification system to slice through the required time. If workers had been given the opportunity to organize their own work, Watson claims that they actually could have completed the task in one-tenth the required time.

Management responded harshly, forcing workers to halt, claiming that the legitimate channels of authority, training and communication had been violated. Management was determined to stop workers from organizing their own work, even when it would have been finished quicker and management would have saved money (ibid., p. 80). So much for Pareto optimality!

Watson also described how workers engaged in hose fights and even organized contests to explode rods from engines in the workplace. Watson communicates a sense of intense joy and exhilaration that workers felt from the opportunity to organize their own activity. He applauded industrial sabotage as 'the forcing of more free time into existence' (ibid., p. 80). He explained:

> The seizing of quantities of time for getting together with friends and the amusement of activities ranging from card games to reading or walking around the plant to see what other areas are doing is an important achievement for the labourers. Not only does it demonstrate the feeling that much of the time should be organized by the workers themselves, but it also demonstrates an existing animosity . . . .
>
> While this organization is a reaction to the need for common action in getting the work done, relationships like these also function to carry out sabotage, to make collections, or even to organize games and contests which serve to turn the working day into an enjoyable event. (Ibid., pp. 80–1)

One might argue that the managers that Watson described were unusually short-sighted; however, even when management behaves in a way that we would normally regard as intelligent, management still tries to manage; that is, managers expect to have the power to control the actions of those who fall below them in the hierarchy. This ingrained behaviour would still remain, even where capitalists were not as short-sighted as those that Watson described.

The Social Dynamics of the Economic Decline

In the wake of this combination of labour rebelliousness and wartime tensions, the growth in productivity dramatically slowed and profits fell. We should not be surprised that capital would not stand by idly while workers were asserting their powers. Business was certain that strong measures had to be taken.

The business offensive against labour took many forms. Before discussing some of the more direct weapons that business used against labour, I want to turn your attention to one of the apparently unrelated techniques that business used in its effort to gain the upper hand against labour. Specifically, I want to discuss the Civil Rights Movement. This discussion will highlight the importance of taking a broad perspective in analyzing the decline.

Before explaining the nature of this relationship between the Civil Rights Movement and the offensive against labour, consider the timing of the great victories of the Civil Rights Movement. I cannot accept the Movement succeeded just because a few exceptional people emerged at this particular time. Since the earliest days of slavery, strong and courageous people have stood up for the rights of African Americans.

No, the Civil Rights Movement succeeded when it did, at least in part, because economic conditions were right. Specifically, powerful interests welcomed the Civil Rights Movement, in part I believe, because it helped to undermine the power of labour. I do not mean that the Civil Rights Movement was inherently anti-labour, but it did further some interests that were decidedly anti-labour.

Certainly, the economic conditions of the time helped to reinforce the confidence of people engaged in the Movement. The growing labour shortages of the 1960s were allowing many African-Americans – especially those with better education – economic opportunities that had been largely denied to them before (Smith and Welch 1989). In fact, during 1960s and 1970s, the rise in black wages was more than 10 per cent higher than the gain in white wages (ibid., p. 522). This modest spurt of prosperity created an optimism that eventually burst into a boundless impatience for immediate change among young African-Americans (see Piven and Cloward 1971, p. 223).

Then, by the 1970s the federal government actively began to foster affirmative action. Perhaps the most seemingly unlikely instance was the Nixon administration's proposed Philadelphia plan, which was devised to raise the percentage of minority group members working in six Philadelphia area construction trades (see United States Senate 1970).

Certainly, Richard Nixon was no heady reformer. Indeed, he had some practical goals in mind. First, he could contain some of the demands for reform by offering affirmative action without threatening the interests that he represented. Even better, he could integrate African-Americans into the labour force more quickly, hoping that this increased supply of employable labour would relieve the pressure for higher wages.

Perhaps best of all, the Philadelphia Plan offered the prospect of splitting two of the most powerful voices for reform. Nixon could attack the unions in the name of racial justice, thereby discrediting the unions in the eyes of liberals. Even more importantly, the Philadelphia Plan served to tell both working-class and middle-class whites that African-American progress would come at their expense.

Similarly, I am convinced that the government was as receptive as it was to the women's movement for equally cynical reasons. As in the case of the movement for African-American civil rights, the women's movement had a long and proud history before the dawning of affirmative action. Affirmative action for women conveniently relieved labour market pressure and set group against group.

The Decline and Social Discord

This divide and conquer strategy was largely successful. As the slowdown intensified and unemployment grew, many white workers would blame African-Americans and women for their ills. Rather than working in unison with African-Americans, Hispanics and women, by the 1980s many white – especially white, male – workers shifted their allegiance to Ronald Reagan, who then proceeded to attack the labour movement. The federal government became hostile to affirmative action and most other active measures to bring more blacks and women into better paying jobs.

Within this increasingly acrimonious situation, working people and minorities have had to bear the brunt of the economic decline. Business interests were able to cut into many of the gains made during the early post-war period. Today, affirmative action is all but dead. All that remains is the prospect of further losses and sacrifices until a more co-operative spirit develops.

In general, on the most superficial level, a growing economy generally fosters harmony among groups; a stagnant economy promotes social tensions. In other words, when the economy experiences a healthy rate of growth, employers can afford to be relatively generous. Labour often becomes less rebellious while it enjoys an appreciable growth in its standard of living, although we must understand that the quality of life on the job is an important component of the standard of living.

When we look more deeply, we have to qualify our generalization about harmony. First, once the pace of economic activity passes a certain threshold, social relations actually can become destabilized. During the Vietnam War, the U.S. economy probably exceeded that point.

Second, even when the economy as a whole is growing at a healthy rate, the economic development will be uneven. Some regions and some sectors will not share in the prosperity. Third, some interest groups will still try to manipulate the situation to their benefit, even when the need to do so is less pressing. Finally, at times when economic measures of prosperity may indicate an improvement, deterioration of other dimensions of the quality of life, such as the tensions associated with the hectic demands of urban life, can create discord.

Nonetheless, we will not be far off the mark by generalizing that, once the economy ceases to grow, one group can improve its situation only at the expense of other groups. Politics, as well as social and economic behaviour in general, become more contentious. When an economy deteriorates, people often become disoriented and take their frustrations out in anti-social behaviour.

For example, when cotton prices fell during the early part of the twentieth century, southern whites would lynch Afro-Americans more frequently (Beck, and Tolnay 1990; Myrdal 1962, p. 563). Today, unemployment and urban blight create an even more deadly atmosphere of violence, which is part and parcel of the process of economic decline.

When poor economic conditions persist over an extended period of time, people often come together as they get a better understanding of the roots of their problems. For example, although some people continued to follow demagogues during the 1930s, this tendency was more than counterbalanced by movements based on solid organizing and co-operation.

In conclusion, the decline and social conflict are closely related. Although a co-operative spirit would soften the decline and probably even help to reverse it, we will probably see more and more social discord so long as the decline continues.

How Business Attacked Labour

Although the war in Vietnam was part of the problem facing business, it strengthened business's position in another respect. The posture that the U.S. government adopted during the Vietnam War encouraged business to move manufacturing off shore.

The extensive use of foreign manufacturing operations is a relatively recent phenomenon. We will later see that, in earlier periods, business responded to higher labour demands by introducing labour-saving technologies.

Why had business not taken the path of least resistance and moved its manufacturing operations to low-wage economies earlier? Two problems stood in the way: one was technical and one, political. In the first place, as Alfred Marshall noted in his classic economics text:

> The emigration of capital, with or without its owner, is obstructed by difficulties partly similar to and partly different from those which obstruct the emigration of employment . . . . [T]he tendency of capitalists in general is to prefer investments at home to investments abroad [especially because] information with regard to it is more easily obtained and more easily tested. (Marshall 1920, p. 9)

The development of modern methods of telecommunications during the post-war period largely solved the technical problem, making communication with distant lands no more difficult than placing a phone call down the street. Reports could flow into the front office from foreign operations almost as quickly as if a clerk were bringing them from an adjacent office.

The political problem still remained. How could business be assured that its investments would be safe from unfriendly treatment? Here, the Vietnam War proved to be a crucial watershed.

The Vietnam War was intended to serve as a powerful message to the world. After all, the United States had no important investments in Vietnam, yet it fought with great determination. This show of force demonstrated the resolve of the United States government to protect U.S. investments in the low-wage economies of Asia, just as vigorously as it had in Latin America in the past.

True, Vietnam won the war, but at a great enough cost that few nations would challenge U.S. economic policy lightly. Given this assurance, U.S. business confidently embarked on a policy of moving many of its operations off-shore.

Even without this process of de-industrialization, business was fast getting the upper hand in the United States. Despite labour's often defiant behaviour, even during the Golden Age, the strength of organized labour was already deteriorating, judging by the share of the private workforce under union contracts.

In fact, union strength had been in decline since relatively early in the post war era. For example, the share of wage and salary workers enrolled in unions or employee associations fell from 35.5 percent in 1945 to 21.9 percent in 1980 (Adams 1985, p. 26). In 1953, a record 42 per cent of all manufacturing workers belonged to unions. By 1985, only 25 percent belonged to unions (Craypo 1990, p. 4).

Some analysts contend that the decline in union strength is a natural phenomenon, reflecting changes in the mix of occupations in the U.S. economy, such as the erosion of jobs in basic industries and the surge in service jobs. This explanation appeals to common sense. Services have been growing relative to manufacturing. Unions have more difficulty in organizing service workers than industrial workers. Of course, manufacturing employment has been in decline, at least in part, because business is moving manufacturing off-shore.

Even so, while structural changes are undoubtedly important, economists tend to overestimate their significance. For example, P. M. Doyle attributed 45 per cent of the decline in unionization to such structural changes (Doyle 1985). Richard Freeman and James Medoff went further, suggesting that structural changes could account from more than 70 per cent (Freeman and Medoff 1984).

Jack Fiorito and Cheryl Maranto take issue with those who give excessive weight to the structural explanation of the union decline. They reject the notion that the decline in union strength could be a natural phenomenon. Instead, they make the case that the decline in union strength was the result of a concerted program by business and government to render unions impotent.

Even during the Golden Age, business shepherded anti-union legislation, such as the Taft-Hartley Act, through Congress. The erosion of organized labour's legal rights continued until the 1980s, when the process dramatically accelerated.

Soon after Ronald Reagan took office, he replaced the striking air traffic controllers. This act clearly signaled to business that it could play hardball with labour. In addition, the judiciary has become less favorable to unions in recent years.

The National Labour Relations Board, which has the responsibility to protect workers' rights, also has taken a decidedly anti-union stance in recent years. Even if the union eventually wins an appeal concerning unfair practices, the penalties are so slight that violating the law can be cost effective (Fiorito and Maranto, p. 16).

Fiorito and Maranto cite Freeman and Medoff's own estimate that, in 1980, 'one in twenty workers who favored the union got fired. Assuming that the vast bulk of union supporters are relatively inactive, the likelihood that an outspoken worker, . . . gets fired for union activity is extraordinarily high' (ibid., p. 15; citing Freeman and Medoff 1984, pp. 232–3). Fiorito and Maranto highlight other anti-union tactics, such as declaring bankruptcy to make union contracts inoperative and the use of non-union subcontractors to replace unionized workers (ibid.). In short, the business offensive against labour has succeeded on many fronts.

To the extent that structural forces are responsible for the decline in union representation, we would expect that the relative size of specific industries would vary, but union strength within a given industry would remained unchanged. Instead, Fiorito and Maranto observe that union representation has indeed declined within specific industries (ibid., p. 14). They also note that unions gained strength in Canada, even though the Canadian economy experienced structural changes similar to those of the U.S. economy (Fiorito and Maranto 1987, p. 14).

Building on Freeman and Medoff's own observations, Fiorito and Maranto suggest a different sort of interpretation of organized labour's decline. They point to Freeman and Medoff's own conclusion that structural changes account for less than 3 per cent of the declining rates of union victories in National Labor Relations Board representation elections.

Unemployment and Labour Discipline

The classic method that the government uses for subduing widespread labour unrest is the imposition of restrictive economic policies to create massive unemployment. With the economy growing as fast as it did during the Golden Age, what need was there to slow the economy down? Conditions were so ideal that the economy could provide both high wages and high profits.

As we have seen, the Golden Age did not last for ever. By the late 1960s, the economy overheated while peasant huts were burning in far off Vietnam. The sequence of a long period of relative prosperity followed by the strains of this vicious war had taken its toll. Real wages had ceased growing. Profit rates were falling. A perennial balance of trade surplus had turned into a deficit. The Golden Age had ended and the stage was set for the use of the business cycle to discipline workers.

The economics profession signalled the demise of the Golden Age by electing Milton Friedman to be president of the American Economics Association. Friedman's presidential address, delivered in December 1967 offered a simplistic solution to the economic crisis. If only government would cease its efforts to guide the economy and if the Federal Reserve System would adhere to a policy of increasing the money supply at a predetermined steady rate, our economic problems would disappear.

While Richard Nixon was running for president in the following year, he echoed Friedman's contention that monetary policy was the solution to all of our economic ills. Candidate Nixon declared inflation to be the country's number one problem.

Opinion polls did not support Nixon's view, so he enlisted the Council of Economic Advisors to identify those adversely impacted by inflation. According to the Chairman of his Council of Economic Advisors, Herbert Stein, 'If anyone was being severely hurt, the available statistics were too crude to reveal it' (Stein 1984, p. 149; cited in May and Grant 1991, p. 373).

Indeed, a number of studies indicate that inflation does no harm to the middle or lower classes, although it does have a detrimental effect on the rich (see May and Grant 1991). None of these studies, however, attempted to analyze the role of disinflation in disciplining labour.

Indeed, when Nixon or the business leaders who supported his election complained about inflation, labour discipline was uppermost in their minds. Consequently, between 1969 to 1970, the Nixon Administration engineered a short recession in order to cool the economy – meaning to put labour in its place. Then, on 15 August 1971, President Nixon asked for wage and price controls, with a heavy emphasis on controlling wages (Blinder 1981, Chapter 6). By this time, the public supported wage and price controls because many people associated rapidly rising prices with unfair profiteering.

The Nixon administration's system of wage and price control was not intended to limit profiteering (Blinder 1981, p. 111). Arnold Weber, a labour economist who was the director of Richard Nixon's Cost of Living Council at the time, explained the logic behind these wage and price controls, 'Business had been leaning on [Nixon's economic advisors, George] Schultz and [Paul] McCracken to do something about the economy, especially wages. The idea of the [wage] freeze and Phase II [of Nixon's New Economic Policy, which began in November 1971] was to zap labor, and we did' (Anon. 1974, p. 108; see also Lazonick 1990, p. 281).

Wage and price controls are inconsistent with economic efficiency unless they have the flexibility to adapt to changing economic conditions. Richard Nixon's controls did not have much flexibility, but this inflexibility worked to his advantage. It allowed him to distort the economy to advance his immediate political objectives. After all, Richard Nixon's focus at the time was not economic efficiency. He was far more intent on winning re-election in 1972, as demonstrated by the excesses of Watergate.

Richard Nixon clearly recognized how the economy could be engineered in other ways to further the chances of his re-election. No wonder he proclaimed himself to be a Keynesian at the time, much to the chagrin of his conservative constituency (Buckley 1971).

For example, the president used his unprecedented influence over the Federal Reserve to keep the money supply growing at 7.2 percent from the third quarter of 1971 to the fourth quarter of 1972 (Blinder 1981, p. 33). Federal spending also skyrocketed just before the election. Coincidentally, social security benefits rose significantly in 1971 (Blinder 1981, pp. 142–4). This massive influx of federal purchases, together with a growing money supply and wage and price controls, promised a burst of economic prosperity during the peak of the electoral campaign.

Although these policies won the election, they also undermined wage and price controls by building up tremendous inflationary pressures. With the effective end of wage and price controls in January 1973, business was still dissatisfied with its power *vis-à-vis* labour.

Scorched Earth Economics

In 1979, the Federal Reserve intentionally used its powers to tighten credit to engineer a recession. It had done so five times before since the end of the war and the middle of the 1970s (Romer and Romer 1989, p. 135). Business leaders appreciated that an economic downturn would worked to their advantage. They realized that, with soaring unemployment, labour rightfully fears the threat of termination. Under such conditions, business would in a good position to reassert its authority on the shop floor. For this reason, business leaders welcomed the downturn because they believed that profits could only be preserved by reducing wages.

Certainly, Paul Volcker, Chairman of the Federal Reserve Board, echoed these sentiments in explaining his motives for making credit scarce. He lectured the Joint Economic Committee of the Congress on 17 October 1979, 'The standard of living of the average American has to decline.' 'I don't think you can escape that' (Rattner 1979). Again, economic leaders commended the Haitian path.

Listening to Paul Volcker at the time of the 1980 recession, one would imagine that labour was doing quite well. In truth, the real hourly wage was about fifty cents lower than it had been in 1973.

Presumably, the leadership of the Fed believed that a short recession would tame labour and then allow healthy economic growth to resume. Such was not the case. By this time, the economy had become more fragile. Decades had elapsed without the sort of competitive pressures that could have kept the economy strong. The inflation that Richard Nixon ignited was more virulent than the inflation that Herbert Stein had earlier dismissed as inconsequential. Consequently, the downturn was far more ferocious than anybody had imagined. It was the most massive economic downturn since the Great Depression.

Even as the recession took on more terrifying proportions, Volcker still insisted on holding the course. In further congressional testimony in July of 1981, he complained:

> So far, only small and inconclusive signs of a moderation in wage pressures have appeared. Understandably, wages respond to higher prices. But in the economy as a whole, labour accounts for the bulk of all costs, and those rising costs in turn maintain the momentum of the inflationary process. (Volcker 1981, p. 614)

As late as January of the next year, Chairman Volcker was still unwilling to relent. He told another congressional committee:

> No successful program to restore price stability can rest on persistently high unemployment . . . . The obvious challenge is to shape our policies in a way that can permit and encourage recovery to proceed

while maintaining the progress we are seeing toward greater price stability . . . . But in an economy like ours, with wages and salaries accounting for two-thirds of all costs, sustaining progress will need to be reflected in the moderation of growth of *nominal* wages. The general indexes of worker compensation still show relatively little improvement, and prices of many services with a high labour content continue to show high rates of increase. (Volcker 1982, p. 89)

Although the press saw Volcker as an almost saintly figure, untainted with the self-interest that contaminated most political figures, his recession was a disaster for the country in general, and for labour in particular. Rebecca Blank and Alan Blinder estimate that the substandard economic performance of the 1973–83 decade reduced the income share of the lowest fifth of the population by almost 1 percentage point and raised the poverty count by 4.5 percentage points (Blank and Blinder 1986, p. 207).

Of course, we cannot ascribe the recession to a single individual. Although Paul Volcker was cruelly insensitive to the hardship of unemployment, he was no more so than most business and political leaders. Certainly, business had been clamoring for the sort of policies Volcker carried out. Moreover, as we shall see, market economies require periodic corrections. Although this one was needlessly brutal, it was long overdue.

Recessions are an imperfect instrument for disiplining labour. Although business initially enjoys saving on wage costs as a result of mounting unemployment, recessionary strategies eventually prove counter-productive for business. Business generally remains insensitive to the hardships associated with recessions, until they reach such proportions that business also begins to feel pain. At that point, business demands that steps be taken to get the economy moving once again.

This recession was no exception. By 1982, the economy had reached the point where the recession had become counterproductive in the eyes of business. The official civilian unemployment rate reached nearly 10 per cent. The actual unemployment rate was considerably higher, probably about 15 per cent. Still, the Federal Reserve refused to let up the pressure.

At this point, the recession threatened to turn into a full-scale financial panic. Only when the crisis threatened the values of the loans that the major banks made to Mexico, did business demanded something be done to stimulate the economy. Paul Krugman puts situation in perspective, writing:

By late summer of 1982, the U.S. inflation was subsiding, but the recession seemed in danger of spiraling out of control. The sudden emergence of the Third World debt crisis raised fears of financial chaos. (Krugman 1990, p. 84)

Immediately thereafter, in order to finally bring the economy out of the tailspin of which Volcker was so proud, the Federal Reserve Board began to loosen the monetary reins and the Reagan administration resorted to deficit spending of unparalleled proportions.

A Catastrophe for Labour

Now that the offensive against labour has accomplished its goal, the lack of good jobs appears to be the major source of labour's difficulty (Harrison and Bluestone 1990). Of all new year-round jobs created since 1979, 36 per cent have provided workers with less than half the real income that the average worker earned in 1973 (Harrison and Bluestone 1988, Figure 5.4).

The dramatic collapse of major manufacturing industries is a major cause of this shortage of good paying jobs. For example, Mishel found that production and nonsupervisory workers earned ⅓ less in industries that were growing relative to those that were shrinking. Between 1979 and 1985, expanding industries paid an average of $7.70 per hour and $257.73 per week; contracting industries, $9.93 and $402.30 (Waldstein 1989, p. 24).

Although the absolute size of manufacturing employment has held relatively steady during the economic decline, the number of blue-collar workers has been in rapid decline. In effect, manufacturing has replaced blue-collar jobs with a growing number of administrative and supervisory workers, whose wages on the average are substantially below those of blue-collar workers.

Lester Thurow notes that, between 1978 and 1985, the number of blue-collar workers on U.S. payrolls declined by 1.9 million or 6 per cent, while real business Gross National Product grew 16 per cent (Thurow 1987, p. 334). In 1990, little more than 10 per cent of the existing jobs in the United States were in blue-collar occupations (U.S. Department of Labor 1990, p. 35). Traditionally, these relatively well-paying, blue-collar, manufacturing jobs represented an important bridge that allowed families people to progress from poverty to the middle class.

Within this relatively stable total of blue-collar workers, some important manufacturing industries have declined absolutely. The primary metals sector and the leather goods sector now produce fewer goods than they did in 1970 (U.S. Department of Commerce 1990, p. 745). Since productivity has risen during the last two decades, employment in these sectors has fallen even more than production. For example, the basic steel industry employed 396,000 production workers in 1980. By 1988, all but 215,000 of these employees had lost their jobs. For the primary metals industries as a whole, employment of production workers fell from 878,000 to 592,000, continuing a trend that had begun in the early 1970s (ibid., p. 402).

This de-industrialization wrought havoc in specific locales. For example, since the early 1970s, the number of people who earned their income from steel in the area around Youngstown, Ohio fell from 35,000 to 4,000 (Lynd 1989). Since no new industry has risen to take the place of the steel mills in that region many of these unemployed workers fared badly.

Even if national unemployment rates had remained constant, factories in the high-wage Rust Bowl shut were still shutting down to move to other parts of the country, where unions were weaker and wages were lower. If these workers were to search for jobs elsewhere, they would suffer a double loss. Their new wages would be lower. They would also have to absorb the cost of moving, including the complications associated with selling homes in towns and cities where the population was leaving because of unemployment.

The United States Bureau of Labor Statistics studied the fate of workers who had three or more years of tenure with their employer before losing their jobs between January 1983 and January 1988, due to either plant or business closing or moving, slack work or the elimination of a position or shift, excluding those who were only seasonally unemployed. Even though the economy as a whole was expanding at the time, this survey found 4.6 million workers, who were at least 20 years old and who were displaced during this period (Herz 1990).

The Labor Department survey found that 14 per cent of these workers remained unemployed in January 1988. Another 15 per cent had dropped out of the labour force altogether. The survey also reported that 30 per cent of those who held full-time wage and salary jobs before and after their displacement experienced pay cuts of 20 per cent or more (ibid.).

Many displaced workers also suffered losses of benefits. The survey found that 74 per cent of the displaced workers had been previously covered by some form of health insurance at work before their termination. About 1 in 4 of these workers no longer had coverage by January 1990 (Herz 1991, p. 8). Manufacturing workers seemed to fare especially badly when management eliminates their jobs. Between 1981 and 1985, 10.8 million manufacturing workers lost their jobs. Forty percent of these workers lost their health insurance in the process (Craypo 1990, p. 9; citing Government Accounting Office 1987).

Considering the growing momentum of de-industrialization, we have good reason to be alarmed about what the future holds. Indeed, between 1967 and 1989, almost 93 per cent of all new jobs in the United States were in the service sector (President of the United States 1990, pp. 300 and 343).

The deterioration in the conditions of service employment appears to be continuing, since most of those industries, where workers typically fare well, are the very industries that are now in decline; while industries that generally pay low wages are now expanding.

Although some service workers, such as the merger and takeover specialists, do earn extraordinary wages, the majority of service workers find themselves mired in low-wage, unskilled, dead-end jobs. Half of all full-time retail trade employment pays below $13,000 per year. Even in health care, which we might be inclined to associate with affluent medical specialists, 32 per cent of the full-time workers earn less then $13,000 per year (Waldstein 1989, p. 24).

Adding Insult to Injury

During the 1980s, business in the United States tended to pay far more attention to quick financial profits rather than the long-term rewards for improving production. Given this mind-set, we should not be surprised that business generally regarded labour as a commodity to be purchased as cheaply as possible. Throughout the decade, employers seemed to be in mortal terror of making the mistake of 'coddling' their workers. In reality, they had little to fear. The recession largely achieved its major goal.

Large pools of unemployed workers made business's warnings to potentially rebellious employees thoroughly credible. In the shadow of the threat of unemployment, labour's powers drastically weakened. The recession, together with the long-term process of de-industrialization, hit unions especially hard. The organized labour movement lost 2.7 million wage and salary workers between 1980 and 1984 (Adams 1988, p. 25).

Fearing unemployment many union workers acquiesced in lower wages. A study by the Federal Reserve Board reported that, in 1981 a total of 365,000 union workers, or about 15 per cent of those reaching new settlements in the private sector accepted either first year wage cuts or freezes. In 1982, this number rose to about 2.3 million (Gau 1984, p. 284). Wage settlements in steel, airline, and meat packing called for initial wage reductions ranging from 10 to 20 per cent (ibid., p. 285). When the economy eventually recovered from the recession, labour enjoyed few of the benefits. In fact, the 1980s marked the first economic expansion in fifty years in which wages, corrected for inflation, did not increase. In addition, many workers agreed to changes in working conditions that they had previously resisted.

Instead, the difficulty of earning a living has become so extreme that the poorest fifth of the population must rely on transfer payments from the government for over half of their income. The bulk of these people are not welfare chiselers. In fact, over 40 per cent of these people work, but their wages do not suffice to avoid falling back on welfare (Henwood 1990).

Other workers only avoid welfare by holding multiple jobs. In 1979, 4.95 per cent of all workers held multiple jobs; by 1989, 6.2 per cent (Tilly 1991, p. 10). In 1977, when the conditions for labour were considerably better, more than 33 per cent of multiple job-holders said that they did so out of necessity (United States Department of Labor 1977). No doubt a higher percentage would answer similarly today.

Indeed, since the decline has begun people have been putting in more hours of work. Juliet Schor estimates that in 1987 that the average person in the United States worked 163 hours more than in 1969 (Schor 1991, p. 29). She largely attributes this trend to the need to work longer hours to compensate for falling wages (ibid., pp. 79–81). She observes that production and non-supervisory workers, who make up 80 per cent of the labour force, would have to work 245 hours more each year just to maintain their 1973 standard of living (ibid., p. 81).

The data on falling real wages also do not reflect the decline in the level of benefits that workers enjoy. If the wage data took the account of the declining frequency of benefits such as health insurance and paid vacations, the fall in real wages would be even more dramatic.

Declining job security is another aspect of the deteriorating conditions for labour. For example, many workers cannot find full-time employment. Between 1980 and 1989, the number of contingent workers (part-time, temporary and business service workers) rose 27.5 percent (Belous 1989, p. 9). Most of these part-time workers lead precarious lives. When hard times come for these workers, they have fewer and fewer resources on which to fall back.

Of course, part-time jobs are not necessarily bad. Some of the part-time workers cannot accept full-time work. For example, Victor Fuchs stresses that many women, especially women with children, prefer part-time work – especially in the absence of adequate child care (Fuchs 1989).

In addition, many relatively affluent women actually prefer part-time employment, which represents the possibility of a fulfilling activity rather than economic necessity. Indeed, wives from better-off families tend to work more than those from families that earn less. Not surprisingly, these relatively affluent women tend to contribute relatively less to the family income than wives from poorer families, who typically work out of necessity (Wion 1990).

Despite the case of the affluent women who prefer part-time work, or even the young mothers who do not have access to adequate child-care facilities, we should be clear that workers' needs do not generally determine the growth of part-time employment. Many, if not most part-time workers would prefer full-time employment, especially because, for the most part, part-time employment pays badly.

Part-time labour offers several advantages for business. Because firms can hire and fire them relatively costlessly, these temporary workers shield business from the shock of market fluctuations. Part-time labour is generally cheap labour. Employers turned to part-time workers as a means of cutting overall labour costs, not just wages.

In many cases, firms hire temporary workers to avoid the costs of employee benefits, such as pension plans and medical coverage that permanent workers would enjoy (Thurow 1989, p. 5). For example, a trade publication, *Progressive Grocer*, reported to the industry, where part-time labour as a share of total employment has soared from 35 per cent in 1962 to 60 percent in 1985, 'To cut labor costs by switching to lower-paid part-timers with fewer benefits, the industry's percentage of part-timers had continually grown' (Sansolo 1987, p. 75; cited in Tilly 1991, p. 16).

Only one-third of part-time workers enjoy health insurance from their employers. Only two-fifths of employers of temporary workers have any provision for paid holidays or vacations. Of those that do have such a provision, they generally require temporaries to work about 1,500 hours per year (Belous 1991).

The Disastrous Expansion of Low-Wage Service Employment

The low wages that predominate in the service sector are not preordained. In fact, management created many of these new service jobs in an effort to undermine the wage structure. For example, consider the growth in producer services – services that one firm sells to another. Frequently, these producers service jobs replace positions that were previously performed by workers employed by the firm itself rather than by an outside contractor.

Producer service jobs account for 45 per cent of the total increase in service employment between 1979 and 1986. Of the 25.7 million full-time equivalent jobs created between 1967 and 1985, 26.3 per cent were in producer services, compared to 22.9 per cent in retail trade, 14.6 per cent in health care; 11 per cent in government, and 8.8 per cent in consumer services (Waldstein 1989, p. 20).

Even though workers in the producer service industry often perform the same tasks as workers directly employed in the industry that now contracts out the services, their productivity often differs because of the changing work relations. For example, imagine that a factory that has just installed a sophisticated computer-aided manufacturing system. The firm could let its engineering staff set up the equipment or it could agree to let its engineering staff form a separate company, which it would hire as a consultant. In either case, all the employees would do the same work, but in one case, the engineers would be manufacturing workers; in the other, service workers. This sort of change is becoming quite common in the U.S. economy.

In the case of the engineers in our example, they were once salaried employees. Now they have become entrepreneurs seeking maximum profits. We might expect them to work harder than ever because of the possibility of greater rewards.

For the economy as a whole, such gains from producer services has not been the rule. In fact, as Lester Thurow has pointed out, for the last twenty years, productivity in producers services has actually fallen by an astounding one per cent per year (Thurow 1989, p. 4). The reasons for this decline in productivity are not entirely clear, but we have some idea about the problem so far as low-wage service workers are concerned.

Relatively few of these workers are self-employed entrepreneurs. They are low paid employees with little incentive to excel. Certainly, we know that many of the jobs in the producers service sector are not positions that would be likely to fuel a dynamic high-technology economy.

Still, in many instances, the adverse impact on productivity of service employment has less to do with the sort of service work performed than the treatment of the service workers. For example, one-third of the growth in the producers service employment came in the field of building services, reflecting, in part, a boom in the construction in office space. A more important reason for hiring building service workers is the reduction of labour costs.

Imagine that you run a fine hotel. You would prefer to pay your janitors a low salary and avoid the responsibility of paying for the benefits that unions usually obtain, but a janitorial strike would inconvenience your clientele and threaten your business. If you contract with a building maintenance firm, you avoid any responsibility for the wage rates paid by that firm. Your hands are clean. Nobody can blame you if your workers are underpaid and lack the protection of a union.

Temporary help accounts for another sixth of producers service employment. Temporary work generally pays poorly. For example, temporary operators, fabricators and labourers earned an average of $4.65 (in 1988 dollars) per hour in 1988 (Williams 1989, p. 3). Moreover, these temporary workers do not stay in one firm long enough to develop the sort of job-specific skills that augment workers' productivity and prepare them for better career opportunities. Many are justifiably resentful about their lack of benefits.

Although some temporary workers hope eventually to win permanent employment in their jobs, most do not. We would not expect that such workers would have much reason to feel a strong commitment to their work. Nor would we expect the subcontracted building maintenance workers to have much motivation to excel. Consequently, such forms of service employment can create a drag on productivity.

In France, Germany and Japan, service employees earn wages comparable, or even superior to those of manufacturing workers. For example, U.S. workers in wholesale and retail trade earned 57 per cent that of manufacturing workers; in the case of producers services, 84 per cent; for consumers services, 57 per cent. Only in the transport and communication sector did U.S. service workers earn more than in manufacturing sector. Here the figure was 114 per cent of manufacturing wages.

For Japan, the respective figures for the four different sectors (Trade, Producers Services, Consumer Services, and Transport/Communication) were 81 per cent, 133 per cent, and 78 percent, and 127 per cent. For Germany, the respective figures were 75 per cent; 120 per cent; 71 per cent; 100 per cent (Waldstein 1989, p. 36).

Because European service workers earn more than their counterparts in the United States, their employers take care to make them as productive as possible. In the United States, employers have relatively little reason to devise ways to increase poorly paid workers' productivity.

More importantly, low-wage service workers get little respect for their work. Naturally, they would be less likely to put their hearts into their jobs than many other workers. Not surprisingly, the rate of growth in the productivity of service workers in the United States lags significantly behind the rates found in most advanced European countries.

In fact, the relatively slow growth in service productivity in the United States explains a good deal of the expansion in service employment. If productivity had increased faster, fewer people could perform the same work. For example, Lester Thurow, dean of the School of Management at the Massachusetts Institute of Technology, estimates that, if service productivity had grown at the same rate in the United States as it did in

West Germany, service employment in the United States between 1972 and 1983 would have only increased by 3.6 million instead of the 18.7 million service jobs that the U.S. economy created during that period (Thurow 1989, p. 6).

The penny-wise, pound-foolish approach of hiring more and more low-wage service workers in the United States diminishes the productive potential of the U.S. economy. Individual employers are oblivious to the damage that they are inflicting on the economy. Instead, they revel in the savings that sub-minimum wage workers offer. Within this vicious cycle, those in power do not want to change and those who want to change have little or no power.

How Businesses' Defeat of Labour Impairs the Labour Force

Given the pervasive process of de-industrialization, service-workers – even low-paid services workers – may be deemed fortunate compared to the long-term unemployed. Economists often refer to such periodic bouts of widespread unemployment, such as occurred in the early 1980s, as 'corrections.' These 'corrections' impose enormous costs on the human beings who must bear the brunt of economic inactivity. Eventually, management's efforts to take command of the workplace by using unemployment to gain the upper hand lead to a series of additional costs, which are impossible to measure. To begin with, unemployment is detrimental to the future capacity of the labour force for a number of reasons. Many laid off workers never fully recover from the shock of unemployment.

When unemployment becomes extensive, many people will just give up on the job market. Even more tragically, the job market often gives up on displaced workers.

Given the enormous emotional impact of unemployment – especially long-term unemployment of workers lacking generalized skills – we should not be surprised that unemployed workers' earnings typically never recover after they return to the job market. For example, between 1981 and 1985, 10.8 million manufacturing workers lost their jobs. Of these 10.8 million displaced manufacturing workers, 5.1 million experienced above average durations of unemployment and eventually had to accept lower pay (Craypo 1990, p. 9; citing Government Accounting Office 1987).

The United States Department of Labor study of displaced workers found that 30 per cent of the people suffered pay cuts of 20 per cent or more (Herz 1990, p. 31). Another study, using different data, found that the average worker who experiences involuntary terminations of any kind – not just from the elimination of a job – continues to earn 10 to 13 per cent less than other workers four years after the termination occurs (Ruhm 1991).

Barry Bluestone's analysis gives an even more devastating account of the human costs of de-industrialization. He used the Social Security Administration's Longitudinal Employer-Employee Data file, which contains information on one per cent of all workers covered by Social Security, to track the fate of the workers who once ran the factories in New England. He found that in 1957, the old mill-based industries in New England employed about 833,000 workers. By 1975, 674,000 of these workers had lost their jobs.

Bluestone's study is particularly illuminating because during this period, the New England region experienced a boom in high-technology industries, but this boom did not provide many opportunities for the displaced workers. Only 3 per cent of them found their way into the new high-technology industries in the region. About 16 per cent went into retail or low-wage service jobs (Bluestone 1988, p. 33).

Many of these displaced workers had a stable work record, which should have made them desirable employees. For example, about one-third of the displaced workers in the Labor Department study had been employed by the same employer for 10 years or more. Of those workers, aged 55 to 64, one-third lost jobs that they held for 20 years or more (ibid., p. 24). Unfortunately, the experience of these workers counted for little after their jobs disappeared.

The losses from unemployment continue even after workers return to the labour force. Many unemployed workers accept inferior jobs that do not take full advantage of their skills.

This effect of unemployment is crucial for less educated workers. In our economy, general education only provides certain basic skills. Most important job skills come with work experience. When workers fall into unemployment, they lose the opportunity to gain this experience (Hargraves-Heap 1980, p. 613). Both unemployment and downgrading interfere with the acquisition of job skills.

Economists do not understand the costs of this disruption of the acquisition of job skills very well. Economists are trained to see market arrangements as conducive to an efficient allocation of resources. They interpret the switch to a less desirable job as a rational response to an economic downturn. This theory makes economists insensitive to the economic costs of unemployment because it assumes that people move easily from one job to another with no difficulty whatsoever. In reality, the cost of these adjustments can be significant.

Imagine an expert machinist. The day after this worker ceases to work in her trade, she accepts employment flipping burgers without any intervening unemployment. If, after a short recession, the worker successfully returns to her original job, the traditional economic theory will not be far off the mark. The economic damage from the recession would be limited to the difference between what the worker could produce as a machinist and what the worker could produce flipping burgers during the duration of the recession, plus the difference in the acquisition of job skills.

Now suppose that a strong upturn in the economy creates a shortage of skilled machinists, but the new machinist jobs are in a different region of the country or the new employer does not want to hire this worker only a few years before she is eligible for a pension. Consequently, the ex-machinist's job mismatch might remain permanent, creating an economic loss that exceeds the economists' estimates.

The economic costs will be even higher for an extended recession, because prolonged unemployment can permanently scar its victims. In particular, when a high level of persistent unemployment causes workers to remain inactive or to take jobs for which they are overqualified, their skills will degrade (Cross 1987).

Extended unemployment often results in self-doubts, bitterness and demoralization. Not infrequently, many workers who have remained unemployed for a long period of time will take on attitudes that make them relatively unsuitable in the eyes of their employers. Because employers are unable to identify which of the long-term unemployed have an impaired work ethic, they are understandably hesitant to hire any workers that bear the stigma of long-term unemployment (see Layard 1988; Hargraves-Heap 1980; Jackman and Layard 1991).

In part, such declines in wages represent a downgrading of workers' skills. To the extent that this downgrading occurs, the economy will never adequately utilize the abilities of these workers.

This degradation of workers' skills does not just affect the workers themselves. Alfred Marshall, author of the most influential economics text of the early twentieth century, shrewdly observed that high wages make workers' children and grandchildren more productive (Marshall 1920, pp. 2, 510, and 562). By the same token, prolonged unemployment scars entire families, not just the worker who is out of work and the spouse, but children as well. Obviously, deaths or divorces resulting from unemployment cause children great harm. Even, when the family remains intact, the experience of watching parents suffer the indignities of joblessness damages children. Even if this harm is limited to distracting children from their school work, their future productivity will likely be impaired.

Some of these unemployed workers and their children turn to crime. As a result, security costs balloon and prisons drain off needed government spending. For each one per cent increase in unemployment, we can expect to see 3,300 admissions to state prisons within 6 years (Bluestone 1988, p. 34; and Bluestone and Harrison 1982, pp. 63–66).

Others unemployed workers internalize their predicament, jeopardizing their health. For each one per cent increase in unemployment, we can expect to see 37,000 deaths, 920 suicides, 650 homicides, 500 from cirrhosis of the liver, and 4,000 admissions to state mental hospitals (Bluestone 1988, p. 34; and Bluestone and Harrison 1982, pp. 63–66).

In conclusion, the short-term benefits to business from a higher unemployment in the form of a more tractable labour force, create serious negative effects that can take generations to reverse. Eventually, business itself will be harmed, in part because sales decline with consumer income; in part because business loses the stimulus to invest that a high wage rate provides, – a subject which we will address in detail later. Sooner or later, profits will suffer and business will curtail investment, creating downward economic momentum.

This downward spiral leads to still more sickness and crime. The workers that business rehires when the economy turns up once again will be less productive than they otherwise would have been. Unfortunately, neither government nor business takes this long-term momentum into account when it determines its policies.

Unplanned Fiscal Costs of Labour's Defeat

Full-time workers are also experiencing a significant deterioration in their benefits. Currently 23 million U.S. employees, including many full-time workers, lack health insurance (Summers 1989, p. 178). Those who do have coverage are generally paying more for their insurance.

In addition, the present conditions of workers' pension plans are a scandal (Bloom and Freeman 1992). The number of firms covered by company financed pension plans fell from 50 per cent of all full-time employees in 1979 to 46 per cent in 1988. For all workers, including part-time workers, the decline was more dramatic. In 1979, 43 per cent enjoyed coverage. By 1988, 63 per cent had no pension coverage (Bernstein 1990).

In all likelihood, an even smaller portion of workers will have pensions in the future because the continuing decline in the power of unions is a major cause of the narrowing of pension coverage (Bloom and Freeman 1992). Today, 89 per cent of all unionized workers are covered, compared with 52 per cent of non-unionized workers. As unions become weaker, we can expect pension protection to deteriorate even more (ibid.).

Many of those workers who do have a pension are finding that their benefits are declining or that the plans have become considerably more risky, because firms have used pension money to finance takeovers and other speculative ventures during the past couple of decades. From 1984 to 1980, 2000 large employers milked workers' pension plans of $22 billion (Metzenbaum 1991).

The government is obligated to offer some protection to those workers whose pension plans are in trouble. In 1974, the United States Congress created the Pension Benefits Guaranty Corporation to insure defined benefit pensions, when companies go bust or close down their pension plans. The corporation insures a total of over $800 billion in pensions.

Unfortunately, like so many other parts of the government financial structure, this system stands in need of a major government bail out. Its loss in 1990 was $900 million, taking its cumulative deficit to nearly $2 billion. Among the biggest underfunded pension plans is LTV, Uniroyal, Pan Am and Continental Airlines, Bethlehem Steel, Chrysler and General Motors. In 1990, some $8 billion worth of pensions were in serious financial trouble (Anon 1991c).

The pension crisis is escalating rapidly. By 1991, the level of unfunded liabilities in the defined benefit pension system stood at $40 billion, $10 billion over the level of the previous year (Abken 1992, p. 1).

How much will the government do for these pension plans? How much will the declining state of medical care for the poor evolve into more general public health emergencies that will require increased government spending? Faced with budget deficits, state and local governments are already tapping their workers' pension funds rather than increase taxes. Judging by the federal government's handling of Social Security funds, optimism does not seem to be warranted.

The Haitian Road to Economic Development

Rather than face up to its own failings, business habitually attributes its woes to some external force. We hear continual wailing about government interference, unfair foreign competition, taxes and the like. Perhaps the most popular lament of all is the perennial complaint over excessive labour costs. This destructive state of denial reinforces the prevailing corporate preference for a policy based on the objective of a low-wage structure, which I refer to as the Haitian road to economic development.

We are told that wages must go even lower to make the economy

Table 2.1   Wages and Productivity

Period	Wages	Productivity
All Industries		
1960–9	1.5	2.3
1970–3	1.5	3.8
1974–9	0.0	1.6
1980–9	−0.9	4.0
Durable goods		
1960–9	1.3	2.7
1970–3	1.6	3.2
1974–9	0.0	1.2
1980–9	−1.0	4.7
Nondurable Goods		
1960–9	1.5	3.0
1970–3	1.2	4.9
1974–9	−0.0	2.1
1980–9	−0.5	3.0

Source: Brauer (1991); citing United States Department of Commerce, Bureau of Labor Statistics, Employment and Earnings Handbook of Labor Statistics; BLS, Productivity and Costs, release March 6, 1991.

competitive. Even though U.S. wages are now below those of the prosperous West European economies, we still cannot compete with the Asian economies such as South Korea or Taiwan, let alone Japan?

What level of wages would make labour competitive? Should we then depress U.S. wages still further – below those of Korea or Taiwan? Even if wages continue to decline, we will have to be prepared to hear business leaders complain that wages are too high for American business to compete with the Haitians. Certainly, if low wages were the key to economic success, Haiti would stand out as a role model for economic development.

But, alas, Haiti has no more succeeded than Voodoo Economics in the United States. Haiti remains the poorest nation in the Western hemisphere.

The Haitian road is most dangerous. *High* wages should be part of the solution rather than part of the problem. The provision of high wages and good working conditions are a logical part of a competitive strategy for harnessing workers' creativity to fuel high productivity. We will explore the benefits of high wages later in Chapter 8.

We need only a modicum of common sense to realize the fallacy of attempting to build an economy on the foundation of a low-wage structure.

Indeed, recent history suggests the folly of this strategy. The U.S. economy grew handsomely during the early post-war period, even though wages rose continually.

In contrast, the recent erosion of real wages has certainly failed to reinvigorate the economy. After all, business has enjoyed enormous savings in wages and benefits that in the past two decades. Table 2.1 demonstrates that wages have consistently lagged behind productivity in the United States since 1960. We would expect United States manufacturing to become more competitive if low wages were the key to development.

Instead, manufacturing has withered, especially during the past two decades, while the United States was driving wages down, supposedly to make the economy competitive. This pattern explains why Table 2.1 shows an increase in the productivity and a decline in wages for the latest period. The elimination of unproductive capacity rather than the addition of new and more efficient plant and equipment caused the improvement in the statistical measure of productivity. A continued reliance on this source of productivity increase cannot lead to a stronger economy.

In short, low wages will not save the U.S. economy any more than they will save Haiti. Low wages have never promoted economic development and they never will. Indeed, the experiment in emulating the Haitian road to economic development has been a dismal failure even though the leaders of this country have shown no visible interest in veering from their destructive course.

3 Government and the Decline

Keynes and the Credibility of Government

During the Golden Age, the government seemed to merit the people's trust. The United States had beaten the Depression. It had just won a popular World War. Government policies seemed to be responsible for a good deal of the prosperity at the time.

Economists seemed to have discovered in their Keynesian theory the magic potent that would enable governments to deliver perpetual prosperity. To be sure, John Maynard Keynes was absolutely correct in the context of the Great Depression that massive government spending could pull the economy out of the Depression. Indeed, the war proved him to be correct.

Under the spell of this crude Keynesianism, economic euphoria became commonplace. Politicians echoed the economists' excessive claims about their ability to guide the economy to prosperity. Candidates routinely won elections by promising to end poverty and unemployment.

With the intense antipathy toward the government that prevails today, imagining a time when the government stood in a favorable light may be difficult. However, this present hostility toward the government is part of a larger cycle that has marked the attitude of the people of the United States throughout our history (Schlesinger 1986, pp. 31–43). This sequence of overly optimistic expectations and dashed hopes has repeated itself many times.

Certainly, government planning seemed capable of working wonders during World War I. By the time of the Coolidge administration, laissez faire was in the saddle again. Once the Depression hit, many people in the United States suddenly abandoned their trust in the market, placing their hopes in the government again.

Unfortunately, although the government gave lip service to its obligation to maintain high levels of employment, its failure to take the importance of competitive forces into account contributed to the process of de-industrialization.

The Dark Side of Keynesian Theory: Military Keynesianism

To many business interests in the United States, increased government spending and therefore Keynesianism smacked of socialism. True, Keynes

58

himself was far from being a socialist. He saw himself as devising a strategy to save capitalism from the ravages of the Depression, but this defence of his work could not satisfy many business interests. They were less interested in saving capitalism than in protecting their own opportunities to make a profit. Productive government spending threatened them more than wasteful government spending.

Given the pervasive McCarthyism of the early post-war period, calls for increased government activity presented serious political risks at the time. Many Keynesian economists in the United States soon learned to shield themselves from the charge of socialism by restricting their calls for increased spending to military programs to assist in the fight against communism.

Unfortunately, Keynes's followers willingly distorted his theory. They stripped his theory of all subtlety. They advocated a superficial version of Keynes's theory. Supposedly, all that is required to keep a sagging economy afloat is more spending, no matter what the source. In effect, the leading Keynesians in the United States argued that we can ignore the relative merits of different kinds of spending. Spending of any kind – even wasteful military spending – stimulates the economy under all conditions.

I have difficulty believing that Keynes himself would have sanctioned military Keynesianism (Perelman 1989). Unfortunately, his theory offered little to dissuade these cold warriors. Certainly, he failed to alert economists to the difference between military and civilian spending. Instead, his *General Theory* looked at the economy as a whole.

Although Keynes preferred that the government spends its funds on productive activities (Perelman 1989), his followers took heart from his humorous aside about burying bottles, suggesting that we can disregard the question of who benefits from a particular program. What is good for one person is good for another because a rising tide supposedly lifts all ships.

Within this context, Keynes's theory evolved into a strategy to float our ships on a rising tide of military spending in the name of the sacred creed of anti-communism. Unfortunately, military Keynesianism was never a good idea for a number of reasons, which we shall put off until the next chapter.

We can state here that a rising tide does not lift all ships. An economy develops unevenly. Any policy will hurt some group and help other. Military spending is no exception in this regard. Keynesian theory turned economists' attention from the specific impact of military spending to the beneficial impacts of an increase in government spending as a whole, regardless of its intended purpose.

However, the weaknesses of military Keynesianism made it all the more attractive in some circles. Let us see why this should be so.

The Advantage of Waste

Although military Keynesianism might seem wasteful and even stupid today, during the early post-war period, military spending seemed to serve a legitimate public purpose. Indeed, military spending seemed to be one of the keys to the economic success of the early post-war period. Several decades had to pass to dispel this illusion. Now we can see that military Keynesianism ultimately became an important contributor to the economic decline, although the nature of the impact of military spending is both complicated and controversial.

Military spending drew support from powerful business interests, since business generally favors something akin to Keynes's bottle-burying program over productive investment. Business's attitude made good sense. Suppose that someone proposes to spend money on public mass transportation. The corps of companies that provide private transportation, including the automobile producers and their suppliers, will let out a howl of protest because mass transportation would deprive them of profitable business. Even if they could win the bids to supply the government, changing over into a new line of business would be costly. In addition, private automobiles would provide more spending year after year than mass transportation would. Business interests understandably denounce mass transportation as socialistic and even unamerican.

The military does not displace existing markets. The production of a fighter bomber or an aircraft carrier does not threaten any private seller in the same way as mass transportation might. Instead, it offers an additional market for private business. As a result, we do not hear the private sector shrieking about taxes being wasted on socialistic projects during the debates over military spending, even though the United States Department of Defense is undoubtedly the largest planned economy in the world.

This distinction between the military and civilian sectors is not absolute. Although the peacetime military does not compete with private business, during wars the definition of military production expands to include goods that have use in civilian markets. As a result, we can interpret the cycle of mobilization and demobilization as an experiment to illustrate why business finds peacetime military spending attractive.

For example, as the United States inched toward World War II, business fought vigorously to prevent the government from expanding industrial capacity in strategic industries (Hooks 1991, pp. 98–110). This struggle was especially intense in the steel industry (Vatter 1985, pp. 24–27).

Once the war began, business did an about-face, calling for a rapid build-up in economic capacity. What accounts for this change? Once the war began, greater capacity was no longer a threat to its sales, because business knew that it had a guaranteed market for its output for the duration of the conflict.

During the war, the federal government invested $17.2 billion in capital goods (Hooks 1991, p. 132). Once the war ended, the government tried to transfer military plant and equipment into the private sector. Some observers have claimed that many of these military goods were of little use to the private sector. For example, a significant quantity of the machine tools used to produce military aircraft was sold for scrap (Kapstein 1990, p. 15).

Certainly somebody could have found a productive use for much of the surplus plant and equipment, but the government did nothing to promote a search for the best use. Instead, it developed procedures that impeded small business from purchasing surplus stock, lest they use this surplus capital to compete effectively with existing capital. As a result, a small group of 87 large firms accounted for two-thirds of the $17 billion worth of government plant and equipment that the government dumped (Vatter 1985, p. 65; see also Hooks 1991, p. 158).

Within this context, it appears that business purchased government surplus capital goods where it expected an expansion of capacity. It managed to get government to scrap those goods where it feared that enough capacity would come on-line to create strong competition.

As a result, much of the wartime investment was not put to good use. Hooks cites a United States Senate study, which reported, 'Real property with a net acquisition cost of $9,277,000,000 has been declared surplus. The greater amount of this property was in the form of industrial plants. Approximately $5,479,000 worth of surplus real property has been disposed of and $1,175,000 has been realized from these sales' (Hooks 1991, p. 156).

Allowing surplus goods to be sold to smaller businesses could have made the economy stronger, although it might have inconvenienced some big businesses. Instead, big business emerged from the war with its relative position stronger than ever before while the economic potential of 'surplus' military goods was squandered.

In conclusion, Keynes's theory obscures the role of supply in the economy. Instead, it turns our attention to the need for more spending. It does not help us to see why business prefers military spending to spending on people's real needs. For this reason, military Keynesianism became attractive since one could advocate it without risking the stigma associated with ideas that identified as socialistic.

The Rise of a Garrison State

Although military spending had brought the U.S. economy out of the depths of the depression, many business and political leaders still accepted the pre-Keynesian notion that continued military spending might unleash an unacceptable level of inflation (Gaddis and Etzold 1978, p. 384). This resistance to Keynesian thinking diminished by early 1950, when high-level policy-makers expected an imminent recession or even worse. They cast aside their anxiety about inflation in favor of a program of increased military spending. At the time, Paul Nitze was heading a joint State Department and Defense Department task force.

This group drafted an influential document, known as NSC 68, which became the clarion call for military Keynesianism. NSC 68 proposed an escalation of the Cold War, in part, to stimulate the U.S. economy. According to this document:

> there are grounds for predicting that the United States and other free nations will within a period of a few years at most experience a decline in economic activity unless more positive governmental programs are developed than are now available. (United States National Security Council 1950, p. 410)

Given the risks of a renewed depression, NSC 68 called for a massive military build-up, which could simultaneously fight recession and communism. The authors explained:

> From the point of view of the economy as a whole, the program might not result in a real decrease in the standard of living, for the economic effects of the program might be to increase the gross national product by more than the amount being absorbed for additional military and foreign assistance. One of the most significant lessons of our World War II experience was that the American economy, when it operates at a level approaching full efficiency, can provide enormous resources for purposes other than civilian consumption while providing for a high standard of living. (Ibid., pp. 436–7)

According to Gore Vidal, Secretary of State John Foster Dulles was more explicit about the purpose of NSC 68. He heard Mr. Dulles predict that this policy would lead to an arms race that the Soviets were certain to lose because they were so much poorer. As a result, the Soviet economy would suffer irreparable harm (Vidal 1992, p. 88).

With the acceptance of NSC 68, military Keynesianism had won official recognition, except for Eisenhower's brief warning about the dangers of the military-industrial complex.

The election of John F. Kennedy perhaps marked the high water point in the general confidence in the ability of the federal government to improve society. The experience of the Kennedy Administration symbolized the dominance of military Keynesianism. Kennedy was the first president to be schooled in Keynesian economic theory. According to Seymour Harris, Kennedy's economics instructor at Harvard, despite Kennedy's ambitious plans for social programs, 75 per cent of the increase in government spending during the Kennedy years came from an expansion of military spending (Harris 1964, p. 197).

The Kennedy Administration was infatuated with the prospects for new methods of unconventional warfare. The notion of counter-insurgency also became popular in military circles. As the military constructed new theories about fighting communism in the Third World, it accumulated new weapons to carry out this mission. As a result, some parts of the military welcomed the Vietnam excursion as an opportunity to try out these weapons and these ideas. This enthusiasm for experimentation helped to ensnare us in the Vietnam quagmire.

Successive administrations in Washington convinced themselves that the United States could not afford to lose face in Vietnam. As the U.S. got more deeply enmeshed in the insane logic of the conflict, more and more military spending became imperative. This military spending put an enormous strain on the economy.

This unquenchable thirst for military spending clashed with the economic needs of the country since the economy was already dangerously overheated. In the process, the government had to give up all hope of using the military spending as a flexible policy instrument that could be easily adjusted in light of current economic conditions.

The End of the Excessive Faith in Government Economic Management

Once the decline set in, the economy no longer seemed so manageable. Unrealistic promises of perpetual prosperity came back to haunt these politicians and to discredit their policies.

Now, we look back with amusement at the outrageous confidence of both economists and politicians who convinced themselves that they had mastered the art of steering the economy at will during the early 1960s. Nonetheless, conventional economists still refuse to accept that substantial declines are part of the normal economic process. Instead, most economists regard the serious recessions as unnatural. As a result, when booms turn to bust, economic and political leaders put considerable energy into assigning blame for economic ills. Honest analysis has no place in such an exercise.

The current decline is no exception in this respect. We hear innumerable simple-minded panaceas bandied about. Moreover, the conventional wisdom looks outside of the sphere of business for the roots of our sorry circumstances, except for an occasional tirade against greedy speculators or financial interests.

We have already noted the common tendency to blame labour unions for much of the economy's ills. This outrage against unions pales in comparison to the widespread hostility toward government – a dramatic turn-about from a couple of decades ago, when the government appeared to be the economic savior.

The economic decline alone might not have been enough to undermine popular confidence in the ability of the government to manage the economy. The government's actions brought some of this anger on itself. While the government kept up the pretense of an obligation to minimize unemployment and to promote social welfare, it dissipated much of its spending on military expenditures. Certainly, the conduct of the Vietnam War also did its part to cast the government in an unpleasant light.

Perhaps the straw that broke the proverbial camel's back was President Carter's famous Cardigan Sweater Speech of 18 April 1977, delivered in the midst of the energy crisis. As a candidate, the low-keyed Georgian conveyed an image of managerial competency. If anyone could manage the economy, surely he could. Yet here was the former candidate, now the president, confessing that matters were beyond the control of government.

According to the *New York Times*'s coverage of the address, 'Mr. Carter was deliberately confronting the American people with the harsh news that even in peacetime they must draw limits on their easy-going life-style if they are going to avoid "a national catastrophe" in the long run' (Smith 1977). The next day the *Times* editorialized, 'the President is right, as well as brave, to press this test of Americans' willingness to behave in their long-term best interests.'

Certainly, President Carter was correct in warning the people about the seriousness of the situation. Without a doubt, President Carter was courageous in calling for changes, but he was sadly mistaken if he thought that the people would appreciate his address as much as the editorial writers of the *Times* did. His popularity dramatically plummeted soon thereafter. I do not know if the American public became irritated with him because he was the bearer of bad tidings or people became indignant because he laid the blame at the doorstep of individuals rather than institutions.

In any case, the public did not relish the president's challenge to confront the economic problems facing them as the 'moral equivalent of war.' How could politicians take credit for the Golden Age and then blame the public for the decline?

In one sense, the public was united with President Carter. Although they differed about whether individuals were to blame, both agreed that individual initiative rather than government action was the key to meeting the challenge of the economic decline. Both the president and the public resisted the realization that economic contractions are endemic to a market economy.

The public went much further than the president. Repelled by President Carter's vision of the future and lured by an intensive media campaign, the popular mood laid much of the responsibility for the economic decline on the government's shoulders. Of course, this mood swing began earlier. President Carter himself had campaigned as an outsider who was above the standards which existed in Washington.

Swept up with this antagonism toward the government, a majority of the voting public in the United States enthusiastically embraced a new promise of eternal prosperity under a regime of laissez faire. The seemingly pre-ordained election of Ronald Reagan symbolized this change in the popular mood.

This reaction was not entirely irrational. As economic conditions deteriorated, people who felt the pinch looked for ways to protect themselves. Business is beyond the reach of ordinary people. After all, we cannot force our grocers to sell us food any cheaper. We cannot demand that public utilities lower their rates. Almost everything seemed beyond our control, with one partial exception: the government.

Theoretically, the government is answerable to the people, who can sometimes vote public officials out of office. Indeed, President Carter met this very fate. At this point, the promise of lower taxes sounded very attractive.

The Abdication of Government from Economic Responsibility

In short, the government, in the popular mind, bore a great deal of responsibility for the economic decline. Accordingly, instead of plans for active government policies to manage the economy during difficult times, we hear shrill calls for government policies that would improve the economy by reducing the scope of government.

Given the growing animosity toward government, soon after the beginning of the economic decline, the tax revolt gathered momentum. The scaling back of active government policies had an undeniable appeal. By 1978, the dramatic passage of California's Proposition 13 showed how strongly people felt about cutting taxes.

The arithmetic of the tax revolt can be summed up in two obvious facts. First, the rich usually paid more taxes than the very poor. Second, when governments attempted to balance their budgets by cutting their spending, the poor were unable to protect the modest programs that improved their lives. As a result, the decline in taxes eventually translated to a transfer of income from the most needy to the most affluent. An astounding 74 per cent of all the growth in income during the 1980s went to the richest one per cent of the population. The poorest 40 per cent experienced either stagnant or reduced incomes (Mishel and Frankel, p. 5).

This mix of lower taxes for the rich and fewer government services for the less well-off was an important component of the economic decline. We can measure the impact of this transfer of income with a concept known as the net social wage, which is the difference between the benefits, which the government provides to working-class families (such as Medicaid or Social Security), and the taxes that these families paid. According to three different calculations of the net social wage, between 1980 and 1985 working-class families lost between $100 billion and $250 billion (Miller 1989; see also Shaikh and Tonak 1987; and Tonak 1987).

Initially, government agencies chose cutbacks for the poor as well as wage reductions and higher work loads for its employees as the first means of economizing. The typical affluent tax payer felt little inconvenience from the initial contraction of government programs because government employees bore much of the burden of cuts.

For example, in 1970, the average municipal worker earned 2.06 times as much as the average per capita personal income in the United States. Since the average income is total income divided by the total population including those who do not work, the average worker will earn much more than the average income. As a result, a municipal worker with a child and a spouse who was outside of the labour force enjoyed much less than the average per capita income.

Over time, municipal workers fared considerably worse. By 1980, the average municipal worker earned 1.62 times the average personal income; by 1989, 1.60. In New York City, with its expensive cost of living, the ratio declined from 1.95 in 1970 to 1.72 in 1980 to 1.57 in 1989 (Henwood 1991).

Lower wages hampered government's abilities to recruit and keep good employees. Given a staff of overworked and underpaid employees, government services became less and less satisfactory. Predictably, the regard for government services deteriorated quickly.

Given this popular antagonism toward taxes, government agencies shifted their burdens to others whenever possible. The federal government mandated that state governments take on responsibility for a multitude of programs. State governments, in turn, legislated that local governments take on duties that had previously been the job of the states.

More recently, governments at all levels, have been attempting to pass their obligations on to private business. For example, rather than funding health insurance, government can pass laws requiring private employers to provide health care.

Even where government maintains its responsibility, it often avoids visibility so that a future cohort of politicians will be held responsible for today's problems. For instance, more and more government liabilities do not appear on the federal budget. As a result, the current accumulated federal government debt of $3 trillion in debt pales in comparison to the innumerable unfunded liabilities of the government. Presently, the government stands ready to fund the S&L bailout, the clean-up of toxic waste dumps, and a number of other programs, none of which appear as part of the national debt. The total cost of these liabilities has a present value of about $4 trillion (Webb 1991).

Even though the public has yet to recognize the extent of this 'stealth budget,' except, perhaps, for the costs associated with the Savings and Loan Crisis, the majority of people in the United States should have learned that laissez-faire was even less able to deliver on its promises than the earlier advocates of economic management had been. Although the Reagan era witnessed the spectacular fluorescence of a number of great fortunes, the typical family fared poorly during those years (Mishel and Frankel 1991).

The Nirvana of Deregulation

Of course, tax cuts were not supposed to reduce services. People were promised that tax cuts would only eliminate the fat from government programs. For example, Murray Weidenbaum estimated the annual cost of federal regulations to be $66 billion in 1976 (Weidenbaum and DiFina 1978; cited in Etzioni 1991, p. 387). To put this figure in perspective, keep in mind that the relaxation of regulations of savings and loans industry alone cost the taxpayers many times that amount.

Unaware of the magnitude of the decline's momentum, many economists and business leaders alike blithely promised that tax cuts, together with deregulation, would effectively jump start the stalled economy. Attractive as that strategy sounded in many quarters at the time, it actually intensified the severity of the economic decline.

Indeed, the new strategy of relying on market forces proved disastrous in almost every respect. Deregulation paved the way for the already-mentioned Savings and Loan crisis, as well as numerous environmental catastrophes and a general deterioration of the economy, not to mention the quality of life.

In addition, government service attracted fewer and fewer public-minded people. As might be expected in an age in which the distinction between rapacity and virtue disappeared, people who were intent on their own self-advancement seized upon government service as a means to promote their careers.

All to often, rather than carrying out their responsibilities, public officials used their government positions to ingratiate themselves with the very firms they were charged with regulating, in the hopes that these companies would hire them as soon as they left the government. In the process, violations of the letter as well as the spirit of the law became commonplace, further reinforcing the disrespect for the government.

Surprisingly, the more that laissez faire undermined the economy, the more government fell into disrepute. I do not think that this unquestioning acceptance of laissez faire will continue for long. We cannot say with certainty that people will jettison their faith in the market as suddenly as they abandoned their belief the economic management after the economic decline began, but a good number of many people are now turning from the blind trust in market forces, typical of the 1980s, to a growing cynicism. If this pattern continues, we might soon see the emergence of a new panacea – or should I say snake oil? – that will supposedly cure all of our economic ills. Unfortunately, as we have been arguing, no simple answers are capable of addressing the systemic answers that the U.S. economy now faces.

The Contraction of the Government and the Economic Decline

Conservative pundits greeted the tax cuts with delight for two reasons: First, and most obviously, the wealthy would be the main beneficiaries. Second, the sudden collapse in government revenues would create huge government deficits.

Of course, we are accustomed to hear conservatives railing against huge deficits, but their real target never was not the deficit, but the collection of government programs that aid the poor. We need only note how enthusiastically business embraced wasteful military spending in the early post-war period.

Milton Friedman, the godfather of conservative economics in the United States, illustrates this appreciative attitude toward the huge deficits quite well. He confessed to a gathering of so-called supply-side economists, hosted by the Federal Reserve Bank of Atlanta, 'I would rather have a federal government expenditure of $400 billion with a $100 billion deficit than a federal government expenditure of $700 billion completely balanced' (Bedwell and Tapp 1982, p. 26). Later, Professor Friedman told the readers of the editorial page of the *Wall Street Journal*, whose editors have displayed a consistent antipathy toward government budget deficits, 'We believe that the deficit has been the only effective restraint on congressional spending' (Friedman 1988).

Friedman was not alone in welcoming the deficit. Alan Meltzer, another noted conservative economist, commended the Reagan administration's attitude toward the deficit. He credited the Reagan administration with a policy of intentionally building up the deficit as a deliberate tactic to restrict future administrations from adopting spending programs (Meltzer 1988, p. 538; see also Alesina and Tabellini 1986).

Let us ignore the moral and ethical dimensions of this enormous transfer of income and wealth from the poor to the rich. Instead, I want to draw your attention to the ways that this curtailment of government activity worked to intensify the process of economic decline, which will eventually harm rich and poor alike – although certainly not to the same degree.

I do not mean to imply that government always works to the benefit of all. The government has always been friendly to the rich, but the intensity of this friendship varies from time to time. Nor does the government work with ideal efficiency. We have all heard enough horror stories about ridiculous laws and intrusive bureaucracies that disrupt business to disabuse us of such naivete. Each of us has personally experienced the unnecessary inconvenience of some public regulation. Since most of us are prone to generalize from individual experiences, reining in government might seem to be a perfectly reasonable way of making the economy work better.

Few people at the time recognized how essential some government activities actually were. The cumulative nature of economic process made the benefits of these activities harder to recognize.

In some respects, the detrimental impact of these cutbacks in federal expenditures should be obvious. For example, the federal government policy of curtailing public spending on non-military research and development, will certainly impede efforts to keep the U.S. economy competitive in later decades.

Other aspects of the restricted non-military role for the government will have more subtle impacts. For instance, the combination of tax cuts for the rich together with slashing programs to help the less fortunate members of society has had an enormous impact on the very nature of society in the United States.

The resulting growth of income inequality works to undermine the economy. At one end of the spectrum, the very poor are more and more coming to form a permanent underclass that is ill prepared to contribute to the economy as it now stands. As the underclass expands, it requires more government spending to build prisons and to protect the public health. At the other end of the spectrum, the lifestyles of the very rich, surrounded by an orgy of excessive consumption, hardly offer the best preparation for a productive life.

The contraction of government spending impacts on the economic decline in more direct ways. Let us now turn to the subject of public education, which offers a prime example of the dangers of cutting government spending willy-nilly.

Education, Human Capital and the Economic Decline

Over and above their general faith in the market, economists agree on almost nothing at all. The importance of education is one of the very few areas of agreement. We shall see that the crippling of the educational system has been an important contributor to the economic decline, which promises to create even more damage in the future.

Let us begin our discussion about public education with a brief observation about how economists approach the subject of education. Theodore Schultz earned a Nobel Prize in economics, largely for his economic theory of education. According to Schultz, just as owners of machines earn profits from their equipment, a person's educational experience commands a profit when it is used productively. Schultz called this knowledge-based earning capacity, 'human capital' (Schultz 1961).

The owners of this human capital are not the only ones to benefit from its existence. Society as a whole improves as a result of better education. Many economists are convinced that rising human capital is a major source of the increase in productive capacity in modern economies. For example, Edward Denison estimated that the direct effect of education on the quality of the workforce was responsible for about ⅓ in the total gain in productivity growth in the United States between 1948 and 1982. His estimate does not include the influence of education on improvements in technological progress, management practices, and the development of new products, all of which are important components of productivity growth according to Denison. In comparison, improved equipment accounted for only about 15 percent of the growth in productivity according to Denison's calculations (see Denison 1985).

Although economists agree that education is important, many economists contend that some of the claims made by the human capital school are overblown. Just because individual incomes tend to increase with the level of education does not prove that this income is a reward for education, which has made the person more productive.

After all, children from better off families, who will have easy access to high-salary jobs, will also be likely to get a good education. We can easily imagine a businessman who wants to send his son to college before taking him into his company. In this case, education has not caused the son to be affluent. Instead, this young man's well-being explains his education.

In addition, many employers require college degrees even when such training has little direct relevance to the job. Again, this practice will create a statistical illusion, making those workers with more education appear to be more productive, when, in reality, they are only better paid, but not necessarily more productive (Arrow 1973; Hungerford and Solon 1987).

Bowles and Gintis add that the educational system also devotes considerable energy to make children accept discipline that is unrelated to their ability to be productive (Bowles and Gintis 1987). Nonetheless, nobody can deny that education, training, and work experience can be a powerful force in making an economy more productive.

Despite these caveats, the performance of public education should be a cause for concern. For example, between 1969 and 1980, Standard Aptitude Test (SAT) scores for college bound seniors fell on the verbal sections from 464 to 424. In mathematics, scores dropped from 493 to 476 (National Education Association 1991).

The Decline in Public Education as a Cumulative Process

Despite the widely accepted belief in the importance of human capital, we pay teachers who have a large responsibility for the process of accumulating human capital very little. In fact, public school teachers have long been our lowest paid professionals. In 1988, the median weekly earnings of teachers, who were not employed by colleges and universities, was $487 (U.S. Department of Labor 1989, p. 194).

Correcting for inflation, teachers' salaries have only increased by less than 10 per cent over what they were in 1970 (United States Department of Education 1991, p. 94). Since 1972, starting teachers' salaries are virtually unchanged. Even this insignificant increase teachers's salaries is largely illusory. It is mostly due to the ageing of the teacher corps. In addition, teachers' training has been increasing substantially. For example, the percentage of all teachers with a master's degree or more doubled between 1966 and 1983 (Hanushek 1986, pp. 1148).

In short, teachers' rewards from their human capital have been in decline. The best we can say about our treatment of education is that teachers fared better than the average worker (Hanushek 1986, pp. 1148–49). In contrast, in Japan, teachers enjoy respect and high status, job security and good pay. By law, they must be paid 10 per cent more than top civil servants. They are in the top 10 per cent of all wage earners (White 1991, p. 9).

Even though teachers' wages have not increased, society expects more and more from its school systems. As a result of the decline, by 1987, 20 per cent of the population under 18 lived in families classified as poor (Murnane 1988). Not surprisingly, teacher confront ever more intractable problems.

A 1940 survey of teachers found that their most common problems with students were talking out of turn, chewing gum, making noise, running in halls, cutting in line, dress code infractions, and littering. By 1980, teachers reported an entirely different set of problems. Their greatest concerns were drug abuse, alcohol abuse, pregnancy, suicide, rape, robbery and assault (Anon 1992). No wonder our educational system does not seem to perform very well!

While the decline in public education provides a cautionary lesson about undervaluing government services, we must read this lesson both carefully and critically. At the beginning of this book, we argued against the temptation to associate a single cause with a single effect. We took the position that we must treat the system as a whole. Education is also a prime example of the dangers associated with neglecting to disentangle the complex web made up of the various strands that combine to create the process of economic decline.

For example, in 1969, just as the first symptoms of the decline appeared, scores began to fall on the Scholastic Aptitude Test, which high school students routinely take for admission to college (National Education Association 1991). Since the rate of growth in labour productivity was slowing down at the same time, some people were quick to blame the productivity slowdown on the educational system.

In fact, the cutbacks in education could not have had much immediate impact on education, just as the short-run decline in educational performance (measured by the SAT tests) could not be responsible for much of a decline in productivity.

Consider the consequences for teachers of a cutback in spending on education. As teachers' salaries become less competitive, education will not suddenly collapse. Most teachers are dedicated to their profession. They will continue to teach and to teach well. Still, dedication has its limits. Some teachers will become demoralized over time enough that their work will suffer.

Other teachers may just quit. In fact, about 4 per cent of the public sector and almost 9 per cent of the private sector teaching corps leaves each year. Less than half of these departures are due to retirement, death or some form of disability (United States Department of Education 1991, p. 98).

We should not be surprised by the high attrition rates of teachers. After all, teachers typically have excellent skills that make them very employable in the private sector. Where teachers feel unappreciated or underpaid, they are more likely to move on to better paying jobs. One study of North Carolina teachers found that, for every $1000 increase in starting salary, a typical teacher would remain in teaching an extra 2 or 3 years (Murnane and Olsen 1990).

For a short time, this loss of good teachers can be partially buffered by college students who are already preparing for a career in teaching. Some of these graduates may accept jobs in the public school system, not realizing how grim their future prospects in education will be. Some college students will even continue to work for teaching credentials, mistakenly assuming that the fiscal problems of the school system are temporary. So long as enough students do not recognize the threat to their future professions, schools will still be able to recruit quite a few good teachers.

Over time, more and more college students will respond to the poor treatment of education by choosing other careers. For example, Scholastic Aptitude Tests scores of college freshmen intending to teach was 49 points below the national average of 847 in 1991 (Putka 1991). The cumulative effect of the departures of some good teachers, the demoralization of others, along with the difficulty in recruiting good new ones will cause the quality of the teaching corps to deteriorate, but not immediately.

Just as the effects of a cutback in teachers' salaries will affect teaching over time, so too the consequences of the degradation of the teaching corps for the education process will also be gradual. For seniors graduating from high school just after the initial cuts in educational spending, the impact should be minimal. Most of them have already formed their study habits before their senior year.

For students entering the first grade, their public school education will suffer for over 12 years before they graduate. These students will not escape the impact of a deteriorating education system. In short, we cannot blame the onset of the decline on the failure of education, measured by the pattern of SAT scores.

Test Scores and the Economic Decline

Even if the fall in the SAT scores had preceded the economic decline by a decade, we would still have to be cautious about attributing the decline to the forces that caused the SAT scores to tumble. First, we would have to analyze what the SAT scores actually mean.

John Bishop has pointed out that college-bound students may work hard to get accepted into a good college, but business does not usually reward students for good grades. According to Bishop, young people earn the same wage with a high school diploma regardless of their academic achievement (Bishop 1991, p. 115). As a result, students who do not expect to advance beyond high school have no incentive to work hard in school (Bishop 1991, p. 237). For those workers, on-the-job-training should be of greater concern.

Employers use filters other than education to screen out the workers that they want. For example, Bennett Harrison, writing in 1972, estimated that a high school diploma increased the pay of an unskilled worker from the ghetto by about $150 per year (Harrison 1972). We may ascribe this behaviour among employers either to racism or a presumption that much ghetto education is of little value. Certainly, the stressful conditions of an urban ghetto does make teaching children difficult.

In either case, this low return to education gives ghetto youth little reason to complete school, let alone succeed academically. We should not be surprised if SAT scores among disadvantaged youths should fall or even worse, that more and more of these young people fail to take the test at all, because they have abandoned all hope of pursuing higher education.

In addition, some of the initial fall in the test scores reflected a success of sorts rather than a failure. When a small proportion of students expected of get a college education, only a relatively elite group of high school students took the test. As more and more students set their sights on a college education, some less prepared students began taking the test, dragging down the average score. This factor explained about ½ of the fall in the test scores (Baily 1981).

By 1980, as a smaller proportion of students was taking the test, test scores began to improve once again, but they have never reached the 1969 levels.

Even though the fall in SAT scores gives us cause for concern, we should realize that measuring educational achievement by SAT scores can be misleading. The SAT scores may only be indicative of the educational experience of the minority of students who plan to attend college, but they are irrelevant to the majority that do not expect to pursue higher education.

The Cost of Crippling Public Education

Although the erosion of the public school system is not the sole cause, it is a major contributor to the economic decline. According to John Bishop, by the mid-1970s, the effects of the educational decline, reflected in the falling SAT scores, had time to work their way through the system. He estimates that by that time, the reduction in SAT scores reflected a setback in educational achievement equivalent to a drop of one and one quarter grade levels per student (Bishop 1989, p. 179).

According to Bishop, if the rate of gain in the education of new high school graduates that prevailed between 1948 and 1973 had continued, then by 1989 workers would be 2.9 per cent more productive than they are today (ibid., p. 180). Consider the following example of the consequences of the crippling of public education:

In New Jersey, all freshmen entering public colleges and universities are tested in basic skills. Of the approximately 30,000 students who took the tests in 1981, only 38 percent were fully proficient in computation at a sixth grade level, and [another] 35 per cent failed to demonstrate a competence at this minimal level. Most discouraging of all, even the 7,000 students who had taken college preparatory courses in mathematics – algebra, geometry, and advanced algebra – did poorly. Only 4 percent of these were judged fully proficient in algebra and nearly two-thirds failed that portion of the test. Results for the test of verbal skills were hardly more encouraging. Off all the students who took the tests, 28 percent were rated as proficient, about 44 percent were lacking in one area (reading, vocabulary, grammar, writing) or another, and 28 percent failed in all areas. (Madison and Hart 1990, pp. 26–27)

Poor education, together with limited possibilities for job experience, undermine productivity. Firms have difficulty in finding workers with adequate skills. The experience of Nynex, the New York telephone system, may suggest the depth of the problem. In 1987, the company had to test 60,000 applicants to hire just 3000 employees. 'There are lots of people who still want jobs, but they're dropouts who aren't qualified,' said Howard

Hartman, New York Telephone's director of employment (Bernstein 1988, p. 105).

The crippling of public education threatens society with a bitter irony. The initial impetus to cutting public education was the popular pressure to cut tax rates. However, money spent on public education may actually reduce tax rates in the long-run. After all, more productive workers earn more. Consequently, they will pay more taxes, lowering the tax burden for other rate payers.

In addition, poorly educated citizens impose more costs on society. The growing number of children who fall through the cracks of the public education system are more likely to require public assistance of all sorts or to become ensnared in the criminal justice system. Between 1980 and 1987, the federal prison population rose by an astounding 83 per cent (Aschauer 1990b, p. 30). To put it bluntly, prisons are more expensive than schools. In short, the initial reduction in taxes may ultimately lead to a much higher tax rate. Such is the logic of the economic decline.

The erosion of the performance of the educational system will help to ensure that the decline will continue. For example, in Britain, where the decline has been underway longer than it has in the United States, researchers have found that poor job skills are responsible for most of the disadvantages of British industry relative to that of Germany (see Green and Mayes 1991; and Daly, Hitchens and Wagner 1985).

Even though the initial verdict, that failure of the educational system (measured by the decline in the SAT tests) was responsible for the decline, was too hasty, we must recognize that it had a grain of truth. Although the deterioration in public education is not necessarily the primary cause of the economic decline, it has been an important contributor to the decline.

Now that the schools are failing to do the impossible, the public is becoming disillusioned with the public school system. Powerful forces are attempting to exploit those feelings in a move to privatize education. Although privatization might be an effective means to both cut taxes and channel hefty profits to the providers of educational services, in a privatized educational system, poor children will far no better than they do in a privatized medical system.

We cannot predict the likelihood of privatization. One hopeful sign appears. Now, more than a decade after the passage of Proposition 13, business has suddenly become alarmed about the quality of the educational system that trains the labour force. For example, in 1987, the Committee for Economic Development, an organization of major corporations, published its report, *Children in Need: Investment Strategies for the Educationally Disadvantaged*. It concluded:

Children of the poor have always been less likely to complete their education. However, in an earlier era of industrialization our nation could tolerate a sink or swim attitude toward those in school. Not only could industry absorb massive numbers of unskilled laborers, but the nation's economy thrived on the endless supply of labor available . . . . [I]f present trends continue without corrective actions, American business will confront a severe employment crisis . . . . Our industries will be unable to grow and compete because an expanding educational underclass will be unable to meet the demands of such jobs. (Committee for Economic Development 1987, pp. 4–5; cited in Hillard and McIntre 1991, p. 111)

Enlightened business leaders should have seen what was afoot long ago. Instead they ignored the rot that was eating away at the school system, revelling in the short-term benefits of tax cuts. They must realize that, just as the gutting of public education was a cumulative process that built up over an extended period of time. Consequently, the rebuilding of the educational system will require a long-term commitment. Whether these business leaders or those who are intent on privatization will prevail is an open question.

Even if we begin to commit more public money to eduction, we will probably do so with the unreasonable expectation that the schools can improve in short order. Stop and go spending policies are always inefficient. We may very well find ourselves facing another round of tax cuts aimed at the elimination of pervasive waste.

How the Economic Decline Reacts with the Education System

We should not be surprised to learn that the economic decline exacerbates the decline in education. Because of the problems associated with the decline, education is less effective than it would otherwise be.

According to UNESCO, the United States is relatively generous, spending $3,232 per child enrolled in school in 1986. Spending per child enrolled in school varied widely, from $1922 in Japan to $4,026 in Switzerland, compared with $2084 for France and $1941 for West Germany (Shrag 1981).

International monetary comparisons are always tricky. Does Switzerland really spend twice as much as Japan to educate a child? Peter Shrag attempted to put this data into context. He notes that schools in the United States have to bear burdens that are not educational in nature because of inadequate social spending outside of education, Japan's savings in school expenses rest largely on a higher student-teacher ratio, which a more cohesive society makes possible. German children have universal health insurance. French children benefit from a high quality day-care center. Other western nations have family leaves (Shrag 1981).

As a result, the money spent in education in the United States is less effective than it would otherwise be. For example, good public transportation eliminates the need for school buses. Better health care, nutrition, children's services and support for families could lift enormous burdens from the schools (Shrag 1981).

The rise in poverty has been especially detrimental to education. Each year, the United States is becoming increasingly like a typical Third World economy. More and more children cross over the poverty line. Among children under 18 year of age, 19 per cent are impoverished. For black children, the figure is more than 43 per cent (Mishel and Frankel 1991, p. 175).

Poverty creates problems and distractions that make such children harder to teach. In total, about ⅓ of all students in elementary public education in the United States are educationally disadvantaged (Levin 1989, p. 52). To make matters worse for the school system, more and more children in the school system come from non-English speaking families.

These changes in the student population make the teachers' job more difficult. Nonetheless, we still expect more from our teachers than ever before. Over and above educating students in mathematics and language skills, we call upon our schools to help in coping with drugs, teenage pregnancies, AIDS and other social ills stemming from the economic decline. The complexity of the educational challenge in the midst of an economic decline makes education expensive.

Of course, privatized schools could save a great deal of money by filtering out the more difficult children, saddling society with an even greater problem.

The Deterioration of the Public Capital Stock

The deterioration of the nation's infrastructure – the name that economists give to the stock of bridges, highways, sewer systems, public transportation networks and other such publicly owned physical plant and equipment – is another important element of the economic decline. Like public education, it is a cause as well as a result of the decline.

The passage of Proposition 13 signaled the severe political difficulties that were to come. The public was convinced that, since the government wasted much of its money, curtailing taxes would eliminate waste, leaving vital expenditures intact.

George Peterson tracked the dramatic decline in public support for spending on infrastructure by following the record of state and local elections for approving bonds for infrastructural development. He found that during some years, public only approved 30 per cent of the value of all such bond issues during some years in the 1970s (Peterson 1990, p. 122).

As public resistance to taxes intensified, public officials sought to curtail spending in ways that would not create an immediate outcry. Public investment was a natural target. According to one study of 42 city budgets for the period, 1978 to 1979, fiscally distressed cities engaged in considerably lower capital and capital maintenance expenditures (Baumgarner, Martinez-Vazquez and Sjoquist 1991).

Although the infrastructure is of vital importance in making the economy work well, when spending on the infrastructure ceases, some time may pass before serious problems emerge. Who would notice if the maintenance on a sewer system were put off for a year or if nobody resurfaced a road?

Given this mood, a dramatic curtailment of public capital spending occurred. Gross capital investment fell from 27 per cent of total state and local spending in 1965 to 14 per cent in 1977. In New York City, annual capital appropriations fell by nearly 70 per cent between 1974 and 1978 (Bahl 1984, p. 78). Total public net capital investment, which totaled $63 billion in 1964 fell to a mere $12 billion by 1982 (Du Boff 1989, p. 7).

In the mid-1960s, the ratio of non-military government capital investment to gross national product peaked at 3.9 per cent. By 1986, the ratio had collapsed to about one per cent of gross national product (Aschauer 1990a, p. 9).

We can see the impact of this curtailment of spending on public capital in comparing the path of public and private capital per worker during the post war period. In 1950, the level of infrastructural capital per worker was around $8500 in 1982 dollars. By the early 1970s, it had climbed to $15,000, only to fall back down to $13,000 by the end of 1987. At the same time, the dollar value of private plant and equipment per worker continued to expand from about $16,000 in 1960 to $34,000 at the end of 1987.

The Social Cost of Deteriorating Public Capital

As the tax revolt gained momentum, so too did the growing recognition in more enlightened circles that the condition of the national infrastructure was getting out of hand. While the public might not have noticed the immediate effects on the infrastructural system at first, years of skipping necessary expansion or maintenance eventually caused the system to fall apart, eroding the productive capacity of the economy.

Only three years after Proposition 13 passed, the Council of State Planning Agencies brought out a shocking study, entitled *America in Ruins*, which thrust the urgency of the deterioration of public works into the public eye (Choate and Walter 1981). Although this study received a flurry of attention in the press, it had little impact on public policy. Instead, the deterioration of the public works accelerated during the 1980s. Eventually, even the general public began to recognize the need for more infrastructural spending.

Despite the obvious importance of the infrastructure and the growing public support for alleviating the problem, politicians became convinced that their careers would suffer if they championed the development of improvement in the infrastructure. They only brought projects before the public which they thought would win overwhelming public support.

As a result, between 1984 and 1989, 80 per cent of infrastructure bond proposals on a value basis were approved at public ballot, even though a number of states require more than a majority for approval. Since 1984, the average bond proposal commanded more than 66 per cent voter approval, confirming that the politicians' excessive timidity has blinded them to a public awareness of the crisis in the nation's infrastructure (Peterson 1990, p. 122).

The longer we wait to confront the infrastructure problem, the more difficult and the more expensive our actions will be. According to the authors of *America in Ruins*, Pat Choate and Susan Walter, the 42,500-mile Interstate Highway System was deteriorating at a rate requiring reconstruction of 2,000 miles per year. They expected that the cost of maintaining the existing level of service on non-urban highways required more than $700 billion during the 1980s. One of every five bridges in the United States stood in need of rehabilitation or reconstruction. They predicted that 756 urban areas with populations exceeding 50,000 would require more than $75 billion to $110 billion over the next 20 years. According to their calculations, over $25 billion would be required to meet existing water pollution control standards. New York City alone needed more than $40 billion to repair its basic public works (ibid.).

Today, after another decade of neglect, the situation had become far worse than when Choate and Walter first issued their warning. The Federal Highway Administration has estimated that 23 per cent of the nation's 575,000 bridges are structurally deficient and more than 25 per cent of the interstate highway has deteriorated (Malabre 1990).

To make matters worse, the public capital stock was hit from both sides. While spending fell, the demands on the public capital stock have grown dramatically, in part, because the economy expanded. For example, between 1960–5 and 1980–5, the economy grew by 80 per cent although the public capital stock remained virtually unchanged (Du Boff 1989).

Perhaps more ominously, the mission of the public stock has been expanding. For example, in 1964 the public gave little thought to the clean up of hazardous waste sites. Today, we realize that even multibillion dollar budgets are hopelessly inadequate for protecting the public from hazardous wastes.

Consider the problem of landfills. In 1978, the United States had 20,000 municipal landfills; by 1986, less than 6,000. Florida, Massachusetts, New Hampshire and New Jersey are expecting to close *all* their landfills in the next few years (Aschauer 1990b, p. 27; see also Malabre 1990a). Obviously, we must find a better way of handling our wastes without any further delay.

Transportation and Public Capital

Even when the costs of an inadequate infrastructure are not as dramatic as an unregulated toxic waste dump, the decaying infrastructure imposes significant costs on people and businesses. For example, the U.S. Department of Transportation estimates that in 1985, total vehicle delays on highways exceeded 722 million hours. If improvements are not made, we can expect to experience 3.9 billion hours of delays by 2005 (Aschauer 1990a, p. 3; citing United States Department of Transportation 1990).

The United States Department of Transportation estimates the total annual cost of traffic congestion at $9 billion (ibid.). This estimation certainly understates this cost. Traffic delays create stress and anger. Economists do not count convenience or inconvenience in calculating our economic welfare, but ordinary people do.

Traffic delays and detours impose other costs. For instance, while stuck in traffic, our vehicles wasted nearly 3 billion gallons of gasoline, almost 4 per cent of the national consumption of gasoline (Aschauer 1990a, p. 3). The resulting pollution threatens our health and imposes economic costs, such as damage to plants and animals.

John K. Mldainov, Deputy Commissioner of Transportation for the State of New York State, offered another example of the costs of a deteriorating infrastructure. The New York City Board of Water Supply owned an old bridge over Traver Hollow. When this bridge was declared unsafe, the residents of Olive in Ulster County had to take a 20-mile detour. Some bought a second car. Mldainov said 'They'd drive to one side of the bridge, walk across it and pick up the second car' (Dione 1981).

Environmentalists might applaud inconveniences to the private automobile, which might pressure people to use public transportation as an alternative, but the public transit systems have fared far worse than the roads and highways. For example, New York City's public transit system was in such disrepair in 1980 that it stood in need of an estimated $5 billion to prevent further erosion (Anon. 1981, p. 137). Consequently, people have been abandoning the New York City subway, turning to their cars instead. As a result, in 1980, subway use fell by 2 per cent. Consequently, automobile traffic to Manhattan increased by 3 per cent that year. Not surprisingly, the average speed on 5th Avenue fell by 26 per cent during that same year (Chall 1981).

Daniel Chall, an economist with the Federal Reserve Bank of New York, possibly because he personally experienced the inconvenience of the New York City subway system, estimated that an extra 5 minutes per trip for each subway rider in New York was equivalent to a loss of 41 million hours of work each year, or an annual average of $166 million loss per year (Chall 1981). Unpredictability adds even more to the extra cost of commuting due to the deterioration of the subway system. Chall estimated that, if commuters had to suffer two random delays of 25 minutes, one morning and one evening each week, the economic loss would be twice as large as the $166 million (ibid.).

I could not begin to calculate the full costs of the evisceration of the New York subway citizens. Certainly, the stress and frustration from clogged streets exacts an enormous toll. The typical New Yorker must pay a considerable price for this stress. The damage to human health from increased automobile fumes must be taken into account. Such medical costs alone could have eaten up a considerable part of short-run savings from scrimping on the public transit system.

The deterioration of the subway system imposes still other costs. People who fear delays on their trips home will leave work earlier. Others will arrive later than they should. Because the absence of one worker may disrupt the work of several others, the cost to employers will significantly exceed the wage that the absent worker would have earned during the time that she or he was waiting on the subway. To cut down on the losses that the inefficient commuting system imposes on their business, some firms are now requiring that their new employees must be Manhattan residents (ibid.).

Chall lends support to Peterson's charge that politicians have failed to act on the public's desire for more infrastructure spending. Chall speculated that the delays are so frustrating that the typical subway commuters would probably prefer to have their city income taxes doubled rather than having to put up with delays in commuting (ibid.).

Residents of New York are not alone in their dissatisfaction with their public transit. Respondents to the Census Bureau's Housing Survey typically place public transportation at the top of the list of 'inadequate neighborhood services.' In the 1973 survey, 36.1 per cent of the owner occupied households and 24.3 per cent of the renter-occupied households reported that public transportation was inadequate to meet their needs; in 1983, the respective figures had risen to 51.1 per cent and 32.9 per cent (Aschauer 1990b, p. 28).

In one way or another, we are all paying a price for the deterioration of the infrastructure. Just as in the case of education, we hear frequent rhetorical flourishes about the importance on investing in the future, while the deterioration of the system continues apace.

Inadequate Infrastructure and the State of the U.S. Economy

Many business interests also began to recognize that the damage caused by the foolish policy of trying to economize on the national infrastructure threatened its economic position. For example, the deterioration of our roadways also cut into business profits. The United States Steel Corporation depended upon a bridge that was found to be unsafe for heavy vehicles. As a result, trucks had to take a detour of almost 20 miles, increasing the company's transport costs by $1 million per year (Vicker 1981).

Some economists are now becoming convinced that the deterioration in our public capital is the major cause of the economic decline. David Aschauer is the most prominent proponent of this view. Indeed, the data seems to bear him out. Figure 3.1 shows the rates of growth of labour productivity for seven nations – Japan, Canada, West Germany, France, Italy, Canada, the United Kingdom and the United States – together with their share of their gross national product devoted to public investment (Aschauer 1990a, p. 17 and 1988, p. 197).

The pattern in Figure 3.1 is striking to say the least. Countries that devote the most to public investment show the highest rate of labour productivity growth.

Aschauer's time series data for the United States suggest that deterioration of the infrastructure alone is responsible for as much as 60 per cent of the recent fall in the rate of productivity growth (Aschauer 1988a; see also Aschauer 1988b; 1989a; 1989b; 1990a; 1990b; and 1990c). Building on Aschauer's work, Alicia Munnell estimates that investing in enough public

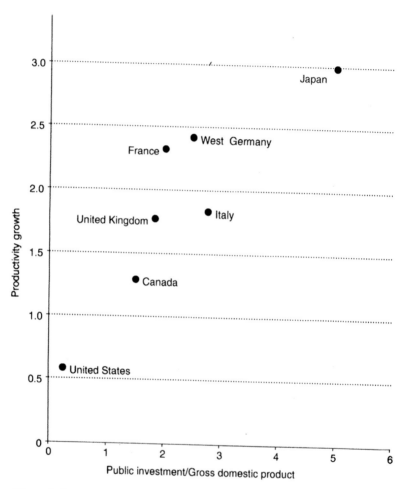

Source: Aschauer 1990, p. 17 (Economic Policy Institute)
A cross-country comparison of average annual growth rates of labor productivity with the ratio of public investment to gross domestic product indicates that, over the period 1973 – 1985, nations which invested more in their public capital stocks saw productivity gain.

Figure 3.7   Cross-country comparison of productivity growth and public investment to GDP ratio

capital so that the stock of public capital per worker would grow at the same rate as the stock of private capital per work would practically double the annual growth of labour productivity to 2.1 per cent (Munnell 1990). According to Aschauer's estimates, a dollar spent on public investment might be as much as four times as potent as private investment (Aschauer 1990a, p. 24).

Aschauer estimates that a $500 billion increase in the 1988 public capital stock would have boosted gross domestic non-farm business production between 14.0 and 14.8 per cent, equivalent to $479 to $509 billion. In other words, the investment in infrastructure would have almost repaid itself in a single year. In effect, this estimate assumes that all infrastructure expanded proportionally, even though Aschauer finds that only certain kinds of infrastructure, such as roads and water treatment plants, make a great contribution to productivity. Since this core infrastructure is what matters, the increase in the relevant capital stock would only have to be $275 billion, that the economy will return nearly $2 in output for each $1 of infrastructure investment (Aschauer 1990b, p. 34).

Infrastructural Decline as Part of the General Decline

Although Aschauer's work does a great service by highlighting the role of the infrastructure, we should be skeptical about attributing the economic decline to any single cause, whether it be the crumbling of the infrastructure, education, the military, or any other problem. In reality, the decline is the result of a complex process. The erosion of infrastructure is an important part of the process, but it is only part.

Not surprisingly, many economists have challenged Aschauer's results. One common line of reasoning suggests that Aschauer's concern with the rate of growth of infrastructure is misleading because the need for investment in school construction and highways had been largely met by the 1970s (Tatom 1991, p. 14; Rubin 1991; and Hulten 1990, p. 105). Overcrowded schools and congested streets seem to discredit this critique of Aschauer.

Aschauer's critics have also charged that his measure of falling public capital per worker is faulty because a greater proportion of the population is now in the workforce (Tatom 1991). Aschauer could rightly respond that private capital per worker has continued to increase despite rising labour force participation rates.

Henry Aaron centered his criticism of Aschauer on the fragility of the statistical methods that Aschauer applied (Aaron 1990). Among other things, when Aaron added the seemingly irrelevant value of the yen against the dollar to Aschauer's model, the statistical importance of public investment dropped considerably. Of course, the value of the yen is not entirely irrelevant since the decline of the U.S. economy has done much to increase the value of the yen.

Aaron massaged the model in other ways, which also diminished the estimated contribution of public investment. In this way, he satisfied himself that Aschauer had given too much weight to public investment.

In all fairness, Aschauer used standard economic procedures. Aaron's complaints about Aschauer's work could just as easily be levelled against almost any article you find in a modern economics journal. Unfortunately, we only find such critiques when an economist commits the heresy of suggesting that market solutions might be inadequate.

Aaron raised another question that Aschauer himself attempted to address: How do we know that increasing productivity might not cause public capital to rise, in effect reversing the direction of causation (Aschauer 1990b, p. 43)? We have suggested a similar phenomenon, in which the economic decline led incomes to fall, creating popular pressure for tax cuts, which, in turn, restricted spending on public capital.

This broader approach to the infrastructure problem also reinforces Aschauer's case for a massive commitment to rebuilding society's public capital stock. A substantial part of public capital goes to increase amenities like the environment (see Eisner 1991, p. 49). The stress of traffic jams and the unpleasantness of public transportation should remind us of the non-economic benefits of public capital. Counting these amenities as part of the productivity of public capital would substantially increase Aschauer's measure of infrastructural productivity.

Future Infrastructural Needs

Arnulf Gruebler proposes that Aschauer may be altogether wrong for still another reason. Gruebler suggests that the sort of infrastructure that is falling into disrepair today may not be appropriate for the future economy. In this vein, he postulates a general theory of infrastructure, in which today's transportation infrastructure becomes tomorrow's recreational infrastructure. According to his optimistic scenario:

> The horse has disappeared as a means of transportation but is presently used for recreational purposes. Former canals, riverport and dock sites become preferred leisure and residential areas, railway lines are being turned into bicycle tracks. (Gruebler 1990, p. 288)

A humorous example lends some support to the idea of unexpected reshuffling of leisure and infrastructure. Princeton and Cornell were scheduled to compete in a swimming meet, but a blizzard precluded travelling. The teams agreed to race against each other without leaving their campuses. Each team swam in its home pool, while the coaches relayed information about their respective team's performances over the phone to determine the winner of each match (Anon. 1991b).

While increased information can reduce the need for transporting some manufactured goods, and bicycle tracks can improve the quality of life, we are far from ready to abandon all of our railway lines or highways. For example, motor freight carriage climbed at a 4.5 per cent annual rate between 1960 and 1987 (Aschauer 1990b, p. 28).

True, we need a different sort of infrastructure, not more of the same. With our increasing reliance on information, many experts are suggesting that a national fiber optic system represents the national highway system of the future. Certainly, we would be foolish to strangle our cities with still more freeways. Nonetheless, the infrastructural problem remains a serious threat to our economic well-being.

The challenge of providing an appropriate infrastructure will be all the more difficult. First, we will have to develop new forms of public capital to meet our needs. Second, to the extent that we have to create entirely new systems, the cost will be far greater than incremental additions to the existing infrastructural system.

Unfortunately, such concerns seem to lay far off in the future. Public officials in the United States still seem to be blissfully blind to the importance of infrastructure in economic performance. In fact, in one case, the United States is government is behaving as if it believed that making foreign nations spend more on infrastructure would somehow give the United States a competitive edge.

In 1989 during bilateral trade negotiations, the U.S. government pressured the Japanese to agree to increase its spending on infrastructure. In fact, the Japanese spend a much greater portion of their Gross National Product on infrastructure, but because of high population density, inadequate infrastructure remains one of the greatest weaknesses of the Japanese economy.

In the face of pressure from the U.S. negotiators, the Japanese acquiesced, promising to spend an additional 0.8 per cent of their Gross National Product on public works. To put this demand in perspective, the United States only spends about one per cent of its Gross National Product on non-military public capital.

The U.S. negotiators mistakenly reasoned that, if the Japanese had to spend more money on infrastructure, the Japanese saving rate would decline making their economy less competitive. Of course, this strategy is utterly self-destructive. By demanding that the Japanese devote more to public works, while the United States continues to neglect its own infrastructure, the U.S. negotiators are all but guaranteeing that the U.S. economy become even more uncompetitive relative to the Japanese economy (Kanabayashi 1990).

The discussion of the state of the public capital stock provides a clear perspective on the pattern of the cumulative process of the economic decline. First, as the economy deteriorates, profits fall. In response, wages drop. People attempt to resist the decline in their economic well-being. Desperately, they search for a solution. In this case, they get tax relief. Government responds by cutting back on investment in public capital, in the process intensifying the economic decline.

Ironically, today the public strongly supports spending on only one form of public capital – prisons to house the people who fall between the cracks of our crumbling economy. For example in fiscal year 1988, the United States spent more than $19 billion on corrections, just about equal to the capital expenditures for all primary and secondary schools (U.S. Department of Justice 1990, p. 2; U.S. Department of Education 1991, p. 37).

Yes, the education figure only reflects capital expenditures, while the corresponding corrections figure includes all kinds of spending. Capital spending for prisons was approximately $1 billion. Nonetheless, something must dreadfully wrong when we put so much money into prisons, while our schools go unfunded.

The Erosion of the Stock of Public Data for the U.S. Economy

In one sense, fears about the deterioration of the stock of public capital in the United States may even be too conservative. Economists now regard information and knowledge as capital. Accordingly, public information is public capital.

In its zeal for cutting back government spending of all kinds, the Reagan Administration foolishly scrimped on both the quantity and the quality of economic information that the government collects and disseminates. The savings on data collection were trivial.

For example, early in the Reagan Administration, the Bureau of Labor Statistics discontinued its spot market commodity price index, which has been available to the public since 1940. In this case, Commodity Research Bureau of Analysis Corporation, a subsidiary of Bache Halsey Steuart

Shields Inc. decided to maintain the index for its own use. William Jiler, head of the Commodity Research Bureau said, 'I don't know how much the BLS [Bureau of Labor Statistics] is saving by dropping the index, but I figure it costs us next to nothing to turn it out – about a half hour a day of one person's time' (Stollman 1981; see also Malabre 1988).

Since 1965, annual federal outlays for collection and analysis of statistical data have fallen by $4 million, or about 10 per cent (Malabre 1990b). Another source estimates that the real resources that the U.S. government spends on the collection and processing of statistical data has remained virtually unchanged (Juster 1988).

A recent article illustrates the benighted logic behind the reduction of spending for the collection of public capital. Stephen Gillespie compared the cost of assembling public data with the public's willingness to purchase it. True, few firms or even few economists would be willing to spend more than $18,000 to purchase a tape from the Commerce Department with all the raw data used to produce the Producers Price Index. Most economists are only concerned with the final product. Similarly, few economists need to subscribe to the Commerce Department's monthly publication, which includes the index, since they can readily find it in their university libraries or even more commonly in computer data bases (Gillespie 1990).

Rather than being 'overproduced,' as Gillespie charges, we shall see that the needs for spending on public data are increasing; that cutting back on the collection of public data may be even more destructive than curtailing investment in the infrastructure.

First of all, the cost of producing this data is increasing. As a result, the same number of dollars provide less information. Consequently, the quality of the data would be declining even if the structure economy were relatively stable. However, rapidly changing economic conditions require substantial improvements in the collection of public data. These structural changes make the deterioration of the public data stock even more severe than it would otherwise be.

For example, international transactions have become a more prominent part of the U.S. economy. In addition, service employment is becoming more important than manufacturing. This movement from the production of goods to a concentration on services makes the construction of data considerably more difficult (Stout 1989). Unfortunately, the government has failed to develop data sources that could aid in understanding such changes in the U.S. economy. To make matters worse, the Census Bureau's reports are now voluntary. Companies routinely fail to fill out these reports to save money (Stout 1989). In short, significantly more effort needs to be devoted to improving the public data base if we are going to get a handle on how the economy is performing.

Many people are now coming to recognize the dangers inherent in such false economies of cutting back on vital economic data. For example, the commissioner of the Bureau of Labor Statistics, Janet L. Norwood, noted that 'the economy is so much more complex, you really need better data than we have ever had' (cited in Gleckman 1991, p. 113). Similarly, Alan Greenspan, Chairman of the Board of Governors of the Federal Reserve System has warned, 'The economy has been changing faster than our ability to measure it' (ibid., p. 112). In addition, Michael Boskin, head of the Bush administration's Council of Economic Advisors, fretted that 'The quality of the statistics as a whole is a serious problem.'

Drs Boskin and Norwood could not complain too emphatically since some years before President Reagan had made their employer, George Bush, the person responsible for the elimination of paper work. Indeed, Mr Bush took great pride in the economies that he helped to introduce in areas such as in the collection of public data during his tenure as Vice President.

The Strategic Importance of Public Data

Public data serves three purposes that neither President Bush or Stephen Gillespie acknowledged. First, it represents an important component of the intellectual infrastructure. Hopefully, economists' study of this data could add to our understanding of the economy. Second, this data assists business in making decisions. Business has to plan for an uncertain future. The quicker business can respond to new economic conditions, the more stable and the more productive our economy can be.

Finally, and most importantly, public officials take action on the basis of this data. In the words of Michael Boskin, 'We make everything from budget policy to trade policy to monetary policy based on these numbers' (Stout 1989).

Decision makers in the U.S. government adjust their economic policies according to their reading of the Department of Commerce's Index of Leading Economic Indicators, yet this data is embarrassingly flawed. For example, 5 of the 11 components of the Index of Leading Economic Indicators monitor manufacturing. Manufacturing, alas, is suffering a serious decline. The service sector, for better or worse, is coming to dominate economic activity in the United States. Because of this emphasis on manufacturing, the Index of Leading Economic Indicators is relatively insensitive to conditions in services (Malabre 1990b).

One could rightly argue that the collection of data on services is maddeningly difficult. Rather than make an effort to improve its data, the Reagan Administration eliminated important data. For example, one of the 11 components of the index is the index of initial claims for unemployment insurance. Initial claims do not give much indication of future economic trends. The government only uses this statistic because it had discontinued other labour-oriented indices, which would be a more appropriate indicator. Lacking any alternative, the Commerce Department had no choice but to make do with this inferior statistic (Malabre 1990b).

Saving a few dollars on the collection of data can result in billions of dollars lost as a result of public officials making decisions based on misleading information. For example, in the fourth quarter of 1989, the economy was declining at a troubling 3.1 per cent; however the Commerce Department had initially estimated that the rate of decline was about one-half as steep. After looking at the misleading Commerce Department statistics, the Federal Open Market Committee decided not to lower short-term interest rates at a critical 27 March 1990 meeting.

According to a *Business Week* report, Federal Reserve officials insist that they received no 'false signals' from the data. 'And no one will ever know if the Fed would have cut rates in the spring of 1990 had it known how serious the slowdown was.' Had the Federal Reserve Board taken more prompt action, the recession might have been far less severe (Gleckman 1991, p. 112).

Recently, the business press recognized the serious danger of an inadequate statistical data base. They are calling for a determined effort to improve the state of the public data. For example, in a special issue of *Business Week* with the lead story entitled 'Are We in a Recession?' the editors warned:

> In today's volatile economic climate, inadequate information can have a devastating effect on the decisions of policy-makers, businesses, and the financial markets. It's long past time the government jettisoned economic models that lump together silicon wafers in a category of manufactured goods that is dominated by bricks and cinder blocks.
>
> As the economy teeters on the brink of a recession, Congress should consider the extent to which the nation's economic predicament is the result of decisions made on the basis of inadequate and faulty data. It's a problem that could be fixed for a relative pittance. (Editors of *Business Week* 1990a)

The terrible state of the public data base moved the American Economic Association, a group that is not known for calling for government action, to appoint a committee including representatives from business to make recommendations for improving government data collection. The committee's preliminary report concluded:

> the statistics now collected by the government provide a weak basis for understanding and choosing among policies, and are likely to be increasingly inadequate to meet policy needs in the future. (Juster 1988)

In contrast to the United States, where firms must rely on public data for much of their information, in Japan, the government works actively to create semi-public information, which business can use, but which is unavailable to the rest of the world. The Japanese method of collecting information is extremely efficient. According to one scholar:

> the system of industrial policies in post-war Japan . . . has been a very effective means of collecting, exchanging and propagating industrial information. Government officials, industry people, and men from governmental and private banks gather together and spend much time discussing the problems of industries and exchanging information on new technologies and domestic and overseas market conditions . . . . Probably information related to the various industries is more abundant and [more] easily obtainable in Japan than in most other countries. Viewed as a system of information collection and dissemination, Japan's system of industrial policies may have been among the most important factors in Japan's high rate of industrial growth. (Komiya 1975, p. 221; cited in Vives 1990, pp. 17–18)

The continual erosion of our stock of public data will, no doubt, put the U.S. economy at an even further disadvantage relative to some of its more successful competitors.

4 The Role of the Military in the Economic Decline

Military Spending as Class Warfare

In contrast to the curtailment of public investment in productive infrastructure, the military has continued to grow by leaps and bounds since the Camelot days of the Kennedy administration. Today, the extent of military spending in the United States today is almost incomprehensible. By 1990, the Military Industrial Complex was employing about 6.5 million military and civilian personnel – about 1 of every 10 workers – in more than 135,000 factories (Melman and Dumas 1990). According to the conservative estimates of the Office of Management and Budget, national defence made up 26 per cent of the fiscal 1990 budget.

Paul Murphy, an independent budget analyst, warns that these official figures are misleading. In the first place, the social security trust fund does not belong in the budget. The Johnson administration first included it in 1969 specifically to dilute the percentage of the budget used for Vietnam. Supposedly, this budgetary manipulation would give less ammunition to the peace movement. By subtracting the trust funds from the budget, national defence amounts to 32 per cent of government spending. Counting military aid to foreign governments plus NASA and other military spending by related agencies brings the military's share to just over 50 per cent. Murphy's estimate of the military's share of net interest on national debt in 1990 comes to $119 billion. These additional estimates bring the defence budget from $296.3 billion to $423.5 billion. Adding Veterans Administration benefits brings the defence share to a staggering 54 per cent of federal spending (see Cwiklik 1990).

No matter whether we see the military as a cancer eating away at our economy or as a crutch to keep it upright, we still must confront the question – why then would our society, with so many pressing needs that remain unmet, devote such an inordinate amount of its resources to building means of destruction rather than means of production?

We can begin with the proposition that military Keynesianism was never intended just to increase the overall economic or political power of the United States. It was expected to change the distribution of power within this society.

We have already discussed how business found military spending attractive because it did not threaten existing markets. Increased military spending has had a more direct impact on the working people in the United States. Pumping up military spending does not simply mean an expansion of overall government spending, as crude Keynesian theory suggests. Some of the expansion of military spending comes at the expense of civilian programs.

Business obviously appreciated that military spending competed for funds with social programs. Its leaders feared that many, if not most, popular social programs undermine the work ethic.

Because working-class people are often patriotic, military spending remains relatively popular with them. Knowing this, business interests welcome expansion of military spending, trusting that it will siphon off funds from these other programs that it opposes. In this way, business delights in inducing labour to join in an effort to undermine labour's own interests.

For example, already, back in 1949 while the country was still debating about the peace dividend of the day, *Business Week* explained to its readers why it found military spending to be preferable to social programs:

But there's a tremendous difference between welfare pump-priming and military pump-priming. It makes the government's role in the economy – its importance to business – greater than ever.

There's a tremendous social and economic difference between welfare pump priming and military pump priming . . . . Military spending doesn't really alter the structure of the economy. It goes through regular channels. As far as a business man is concerned, a munitions order from the government is much like an order from a private customer.

But the kind of welfare and public works spending that [President] Truman plans does alter the economy. It makes new channels of its own. It creates new institutions. *It redistributes income.* It shifts demand from one industry to another. It changes the whole economic pattern. That's the object. (Anon. 1949, p. 20; emphasis added)

President Truman's successors also used military spending to affect the balance of power between labour and capital every bit as much as they intended it to influence the balance of power among nations. For example, Max Frankel, Washington Bureau Chief of *The New York Times*, clearly expressed the strategy of using military spending to restrict social spending after the Nixon administration proposed a massive defence build-up. In discussing the trade-off between defence and social aims, Frankel observed:

> the conservative dream of depriving Washington of the funds for vast new social programs is close to realization. [Increased defence commitments] for reasons that are vigorously asserted but in no sense explained or measured against the risks of frugality in other parts of the budget . . . and the two big rounds of tax cutting since 1969, in which liberal Democrats joined enthusiastically, have now left the budget $20 billion short of money that might have been invested in health or education or the cities or transportation.
>
> The President welcomes this fact and notes approvingly that current programs and current tax rates will leave only $5 billion in loose change for the budget writers of 1976 – a margin that, experience suggests, will almost certainly disappear altogether . . . . For the next President, this means that there will be no special dividend for great new initiative for either peace or prosperity. (Frankel 1972; cited in DuBoff 1989, p. 10)

Sometimes it seemed that no program could win support in the Congress without first demonstrating that it was essential to the national defence. The interstate highway system was, probably with good reason, seen as part of the national defence. With modern highways, the military would be able to move troops and materiel from one end of the country with ease.

The School Lunch Program, established in 1946, years before NSC-68, was the classic case of the need for a military rationale to win support for a government initiative to help the civilian population. Much of the initial support for the program was due to the persuasive testimony of Major General Lewis Hershey, Director of the Selective Service Commission. The general told congressional committees that, during the World War II, poor nutrition accounted for many of the rejections of young men by local draft boards (U.S. House of Representatives 1989, p. 53).

Although the military rationale occasionally does help to pass beneficial social programs, such as the school lunch program, the high priority given to the military has typically worked to the detriment of social programs. When military spending competes with social programs, the military usually proves victorious in the halls of Congress.

Symbolic of this state of affairs, the Reagan administration budgeted $154 million for military bands in 1987 compared to $145 million for the National Endowment for the Arts – well before that agency became controversial (Anon. 1986b). How did our priorities become so skewed?

Workers' patriotic support of military spending continues to harm their own economic interests. A number of studies have concluded that military spending creates fewer jobs than comparable forms of spending, although this assertion is difficult to prove conclusively (see Adams and Gold 1987; Gold 1990). The reason for the lower employment effects of military spending is due to the type of labour that defence industries hire. In part, military spending creates less employment because of the peculiar wage structure in defence industries.

For example, hourly wages in defence-intensive manufacturing industries in 1983 ran $2.80 higher then the average for all manufacturing industries (Adams and Gold 1987, p. 35). Military spending typically leads to a demand for a combination of highly paid workers (such as the scientists and engineers as well as highly paid executives and lobbyists) in private employment and low paid government workers in the public sector (Blank and Rothschild 1985, p. 694).

The Benefits of Military Power

Although this lavish military spending harms workers, military force does serve a useful function for certain groups in our society. To begin with, the military actively supports the interests of corporations and wealthy individuals with important stakes in the less developed nations of the world. By threatening to use massive violence against almost any political movement that might be inhospitable to the needs of business, the worldwide U.S. military presence augmented profits for many individual corporations.

Certainly, judging by the history of the deployment of the military, the armed might of the U.S. has been directed more at Third World countries than at superpowers. Frequent interventions in the Third World protect U.S. markets and sources of raw materials. In the words of Ronald Reagan, 'Our industries depend on the importation of energy and minerals from distant lands. Our prosperity requires a sound international financial system and free and open trading markets' (Reagan 1984, pp. 1–2; cited in Riddell 1988, p. 62).

Tom Riddell reported that according to Howard Morland, a military analyst, 37 per cent of the U.S. military budget was directed to Soviet containment and another 45 per cent supported U.S. military capability in the Third World (Riddell 1987, p. 6). However, at least some of the 37 per cent directed at the Soviet Union served to make the Soviets leery about lending support to Third World liberation movements.

The massive military build-up was instrumental in bringing about the collapse of the Soviet Union. Although the leaders of the United States never openly admitted how harmful military spending was to the U.S.

economy, they realized how it undermined the Soviet economy, where the military consumed as much as one quarter of the gross national product (Silk 1985; Epstein 1990; Marshall 1987, p. 484). As Judy Shelton wrote in *The Coming Soviet Crash*:

> For a while it almost looked as if Soviet claims about the efficiency of a state-managed economy would turn out to be correct . . . . After World War II, the country moved to build huge factories and construct massive dams and railroads. Projects were built to take advantage of huge supplies of natural resources and to increase manufacturing output. By the 1960s the Soviet Union was starting to close the gap with the United States – not just in terms of economic productivity, but in military armaments as well. (Shelton 1989, p. 178)

Although they did not seem to relish the need to expand their military, the Soviets felt that they had no choice. In the words of Mikhail Gorbachev:

> I shall not disclose any secret if I tell you that the Soviet Union is doing all that is necessary to maintain up-to-date and reliable defences. This is the duty to our own people and our allies. At the same time I wish to say quite definitely that this is not our choice. It has been imposed on us. (Gorbachev 1987, p. 218)

The Soviet leader acknowledged the underlying basis for the U.S. stance on the arms race, noting: 'United States foreign policy . . . is based on . . . the belief that the economic system of the Soviet Union is about to crumble' (ibid., p. 220).

Like his counterpart in the United States, Gorbachev seemed assured that the Soviets could continue to escalate their military spending without harming their own economy. He bragged, 'A tenth of the U.S. investments would be enough to create a counter system to SDI (the Strategic Defense Initiative)' (ibid., p. 234).

Returning to the analysis of Judy Shelton:

> In the end, Kremlin authorities could not bring themselves to cut back on the Soviet Union's nuclear arsenal, their main claim to global status and the source of Soviet influence around the world. To build up the military, the other sectors of the Soviet economy were being squeezed harder and harder. Fixed capital investment was slashed, and consumer needs

were give short shrift. By the early 1980s, defence was claiming more than one-fifth of total Soviet production and soaking up an inordinate proportion of Soviet economic capabilities. (Shelton 1989, p. 179)

From the standpoint of the U.S. economy as a whole, the cost of this military force far exceeds any profits that might result from the military threat against progressive movements in the Third World. For example, the military's Rapid Deployment Force was supposed to protect the supply of Middle Eastern oil. Richard Heede and Amory B. Lovens estimated that diverting the funds budgeted for supplying this operation for one year would free up enough money to develop a well-designed weatherization program capable of eliminating all Mideast oil imports (Heede and Lovens 1985).

Why bother to expend funds on the military in order to get a lesser amount in return in the form of profits? The reason is not difficult to fathom. Business pays for a relatively small part of cost of the military, but reaps the bulk of the benefits. In this respect, we might see the military as a siphon to draw wealth from the country as a whole to direct it to a relatively small segment of society.

The Economic Failure of Military Keynesianism

Many experts contend that the object of this military spending is not military prowess, but the creation of a healthy economy by virtue of military Keynesianism. Some commentators revel in the notion that wanton spending on the military spending is something akin to Keynes' scheme for burying bottles: it might be wasteful, but it keeps the economy going.

Of course, all spending is not alike. For example David Aschauer estimated that $1 spent on the military increases economic output by $1. A similar investment in core public works will result in $4 (Aschauer 1990d). Still, political leaders never sold the public on military Keynesian as such. Instead, they played on the people's patriotism and implicitly promise that the government could manage the economy into prosperity.

The military did seem to be an excellent vehicle for pursuing Keynesian economic policy. Keynes himself insisted that government spending should not just grow willy-nilly. It should be flexible. When the economy falters, increased government spending should take up the slack. When the economy threatens to overheat, government spending should subside, releasing pressures that build up when the economy grows too fast. In this way, economic policy makers supposedly can guide the economy to prosperity.

Military spending seemed to be ideally suited to meeting Keynes's goal of allowing flexibility in government spending. Since military spending is less controversial than other forms of public spending, the government can quickly beef up the military when the economy threatens to sink into a recession. Once the economy needs to cool off a bit, it can reduce military spending by drawing attention to peaceful overtures from the other side.

Howard Sherman made some interesting calculations that illustrate how the government attempted to use military spending to control the business cycle in the United States. According to his calculations, in the average peacetime expansion between 1949 and 1980, military spending fell by an average 0.14 per cent per month. In the average contraction, it rose 0.19 per cent a month (Sherman 1983, p. 382). Although other forces do influence military spending, all in all, the evidence does suggest that the state did attempt to use defence spending to stabilize the economy (see Griffin, Wallace and Devine 1982).

As Keynesian policies in the United States became closely entwined with the Cold War, military spending seemed to be able to accomplish what had hitherto eluded the alchemists: they seemed to succeed in changing the lead of war into the gold of business; namely profits.

In reality, military Keynesianism was less successful than it initially seemed to be. Yes, the economy was more stable in the post-war period than before (Balke and Gordon 1989; but also see Romer 1989). How much credit does military spending deserve for this stability?

In reality, military Keynesianism is not quite as flexible as it seemed to be. In fact, it was probably destabilizing. Although military spending is theoretically capable of kicking the economy in the right direction, the economy cannot react instantaneously. To increase military spending, government first stirs up hysterical fears which are difficult to contain later.

To decrease military spending, it tries to put the public mind at ease. The government can engineer these mood swings, but such changes are impossible to fine tune. More often than not, overreaction will result. Overly abrupt changes in military spending will destabilize the economy.

Certainly, military spending turned out to be far less effective as a counter-cyclical tool that it first appeared to be. To begin with, in the immediate post-war period, the economy was so strong that it was not particularly vulnerable to down-turns. As a result, the economy at the time did not pose a severe challenge to military Keynesianism.

As the decline took hold, the deficiencies of military Keynesianism became apparent. For example, when Michael Edelstein included the 1980s in his analysis, he found no evidence that defence spending worked counter-cyclically (Edelstein 1990).

Robert Gordon reached a similar conclusion, a decade earlier in his analysis of the role of fiscal policy as a tool of economic stabilization. According to Gordon, '[I]n the broadest sense fiscal policy has been the most important *destabilizing* influence in the postwar economy' (Gordon 1980, p. 121). Gordon found that fiscal policy in general was not the problem. He identified the culprit as the huge swings in military spending. He explained:

> In the first postwar decade the enormous magnitude of the rise and sub- sequent fall in defence spending was the dominant feature of aggregated demand fluctuations, and the expansion of spending for the Vietnam War in 1965–68 destabilized the economy again. By a narrower criterion that takes defence spending as exogenous and outside the purview of discretionary stabilization policy, however, fiscal policy deserves relatively high marks in the 1947–57 decade. (Gordon 1980, p. 121)

In short, the overall record of military Keynesianism is not a happy one. Although an intense burst of military spending did succeed in pulling the U.S. economy out of the Great Depression, the conditions created by the Great Depression made that initial success possible. Over time, as the economy became more fragile, military spending proved to be less and less capable of infusing any vigor into the economy.

The rise of military spending illustrates a pattern that recurs in this book: a remedy for an economic problem (in this case the purported cure for insufficient demand served its purpose) creates a host of other ills, which required new remedies, which brought on new infirmities. In short, the U.S. strategy of promoting economic strength by military spending turns out to be self-defeating.

The Changing Nature of Military Spending

During World War II, the Middle West was known as the arsenal of democracy. This region built military hardware with labour-intensive technology similar to that which was used to produce automobiles and trucks. Over time, as the military technology became more sophisticated, an increasing share of the Pentagon budget went to new industries that specialized in military production.

In the process, an increasing share of the defence budget went to hard- ware instead of wages. This trend has probably accelerated in recent years.

Between 1973 and 1984, the share of spending on durable goods in defence industries rose significantly. As a result, after employee compensation as a percentage of total defence spending reached a high of 49.8 per cent in 1973, it fell to 35.2 per cent by 1984 (Blank and Rothschild 1985, p. 679).

James Cypher interprets this change in mix of defence spending to be a transformation of the nature of military Keynesianism. While the initial form of military Keynesianism included low unemployment as one of its goals, this new variant, which he terms, 'Redistributive Militarism,' down-played the importance of employment, focusing more and more on the profits from lucrative defence contracts (Cypher 1991).

According to Cypher, redistributive militarism transferred income from those in the bottom 80 per cent. He concluded, 'increasingly lax procurement practices . . . permitted both higher profit margins and a greater volume of business for arms contractors – thus increasing the *mass* of profits' (Cypher 1991, p. 609).

During the 1980s, massive military spending became far less effective in generating jobs. For example, by the mid 1980s, unemployment remained around 7 per cent even though the government was running huge deficits of well over $200 billion.

Of course, millions of people still owe their livelihood, directly or indirectly, to military employment. If military spending were to be eliminated overnight, massive disruptions would certainly occur, probably enough to send the economy into a tail spin.

In conclusion, military Keynesianism has run its course. Even if military Keynesianism had served a purpose earlier, it now appears to be incapable of stabilizing the economy. Despite its enormous destructive potential, military spending has lost its economic punch.

The Question of Spillovers from Military Research and Development

Defenders of military Keynesianism contend that their policies have not harmed the economy. Even if military Keynesianism might have failed as an economic stabilizer, they allude to a slew of economic benefits spawned by the scientific advances that the engineers and scientists developed in the course of their military research projects. Certainly, defence spending funded many of the most important new products that we see around us today.

For example, most of the major advances in the computer industry have been products of military research (see Flamm 1988a and 1988b). One

MIT scientist estimated that about ½ of the $400 billion United States computer industry could be traced to the $1 billion that DARPA (Defense Advanced Research Projects Agency) had invested over the last 25 years. Even seemingly non-lethal computer components owed their existence to military funded research. For example, the ubiquitous computer mouse – popularly associated with the user-friendly, entrepreneurial spirit of Apple Computer – developed out of a DARPA grant to Xerox (Flamm 1988a, p. 24).

We should not be surprised that military research and development has contributed to the development of new technologies. Judith Reppy estimates that defence projects employ 42 per cent of the scientific personnel in the United States (Reppy 1985, p. 11). Considering the enormous resources that have been devoted to military research, the question about the contributions of military research should be rephrased: could these military researchers have made even more valuable contributions to the U.S. economy if they had worked on civilian projects?

In general, the answer is positive because military research is less significantly fruitful than civilian research. Reppy identified several barriers that prevent military projects from yielding benefits comparable to civilian research (Reppy 1985, p. 12).

First of all, most military projects are shrouded in secrecy. This restriction of the free flow of ideas cripples the scientific potential of military research. The major benefits from science come from communication and the cross-fertilization of ideas (Nelson 1990, p. 129). Commercial developers also want to restrict the use of their 'intellectual property,' but at least when they seek protection from the patent system the must reveal their discoveries (Scotchner 1991).

Secrecy is doubly damaging because the bulk of the ultimate benefits from science come from uses that the original researchers had never envisioned. For example, the computer was initially designed as a tool to calculate the trajectory of artillery shells. Howard Aitken, one of the early pioneers in developing the computer, was confident that his invention would be of limited use. He predicted, 'If it should ever turn out that the basic logics of a machine designed for the numerical solution of differential equations coincide with the logics of a machine intended to make bills for a department, I would regard this as the most amazing coincidence that I have ever encountered' (Cerruzzi 1986, p. 197).

In fact, every major corporation, as well as many small businesses, employs the computer today for the very uses that Aitken once dismissed as impractical. Computer technology became as advanced as it is today only because hackers and hobbyists, academic and commercial researchers of all kinds were free to explore the potential of this technology once it was released beyond military circles.

Regulations compound the problem of secrecy. To prevent large military contractors from using Pentagon research contracts to subsidize their civilian work, regulations require the artificial separation of large firms into military and civilian divisions. Again, this arrangement hampers the process of cross fertilization. For instance, returning to our example of the computers, this separation would prevent people interested in office automation to become familiar with the work of people building specialized machines to calculate the trajectory of artillery shells.

In addition, the military usually concentrates on developing specific products rather than processes that would be applicable in civilian projects. This specificity restricts the potential benefits to other sectors of the economy. For example, military projects often require electrical components that are 'hardened' so that they can continue to function during a nuclear attack. Learning to 'harden' electronic components does little to help most U.S. business compete.

To make matters worse, many modern military products are just unsuited to the civilian sector. For example, the early jet engines that the military used had obvious civilian benefits. Once military planes entered the world of supersonic speeds, 'they began to assume performance and cost characteristics that were inappropriate for the cost-conscious world of commercial travel.' Similarly, communications satellites initially had great civilian spillovers, but the special requirements of contemporary military satellites are inappropriate for commercial communications (Mowery and Rosenberg 1989, p. 148).

Finally, bloated military prices discourage civilian applications (Reppy 1985, p. 12).

Even if the benefits of military research could easily spill out into the civilian sector, the military fosters a perverse institutional framework that discourages efficient use of resources. As Seymour Melman has observed, defence contractors are cost-maximizing rather than cost-minimizing (Melman 1983).

Unfortunately, even if we suddenly decided to rearrange our priorities, our scientific establishment is ill prepared for civilian research. The decades during which science has been overly committed to military missions will take its toll for decades in the future because the mind-set common to military research is inappropriate for civilian missions.

For example, the U.S. national weapons laboratories have been trying to forge an alliance with industry to develop new programs (see Carey 1990). This endeavor has not been very successful. *Business Week* editorialized:

Naturally, lab directors are arguing fiercely that their scientists could clean up the environment, boost U.S. industrial competitiveness, and educate a nation . . . . But the truth is that they haven't been very adept at transferring their research, such as the expensive studies on alternative energy in the 1970s, to the private sector . . . . Let's not waste money on vague hopes. (Editors of *Business Week* 1990b)

In conclusion, although military research has paved the way for many important civilian applications, had this same research occurred outside of the military industrial complex, the benefits would have been many times greater.

In fact, today we may well be witnessing a reversal in the direction of spillovers. The business sector is probably less dependent on advances in military technology than the military is on new civilian technological breakthroughs. If this hypothesis is true, then the gutting of the economy might eventually undermine the U.S. goal of maintaining military leadership in the world.

The Pernicious Influence of Excessive Military Spending

We better be quick about developing new methods of harnessing creativity. So long as the bulk of our creativity goes for military purposes, our economy will continue to decline. After all, military spending is, by its very nature, wasteful because military suppliers have no incentive to economize. They operate on a cost-plus basis. The more they spend, the more profits they earn. Without competitive checks and balances, the military industrial complex will adhere to its cost maximizing practices (Melman 1983, p. 4).

The enormous amounts of money involved in military contracts, together with the lax supervision of defence practices, invites abuse. In addition, especially in more recent times, arms suppliers have richly rewarded high ranking military officers with generous contracts upon their retirement. Within this context, we should not be surprised by the familiar horror stories about the military spending $500 for a toilet seat.

Nonetheless, the sensational nature of these examples make these expenses seem as if they were exceptional. In fact, all the sophisticated weaponry in the U.S. arsenal is grossly overpriced. For example, Melman estimated that the cost per pound of a B-1 bomber was about $4,400 (Melman 1983, p. 81; also see Fitzgerald 1989), making the plane literally worth more than its weight in gold.

True, these planes had a considerable amount of sophisticated electronics, but were these really so expensive that each single pound of a B-1 bomber cost about as much to build as the retail price of a small automobile? Not surprisingly, few major military suppliers are capable of competing in civilian markets and civilian producers in the United States. have become less competitive relative to competitors from other countries, where the defence industry is more modest.

The relationship between defence spending and the declining competitiveness of industry in the United States is not hard to understand. Since the military suppliers need not worry about economizing, they have been able to attract a disproportionate share of the best and the brightest engineers. In this sense, we cannot measure the cost of the military build-up simply the adding up the money that the military consumes, since many of the resources that the military obtains are strategic resources, especially skilled technical labour.

Traditionally, in Germany, Japan, Britain and France, military and colonial service was a principal route for social advancement. In the United States, it was business and industry. Today, in the United States, the defence sector provides the most attractive opportunities for advancement and high earnings, while our competitors are turning toward business management (Dertouzos 1989, p. 25).

David Halberstam's five-year comparative study of Ford and Nissan demonstrated dramatically how the Japanese company was able to draw upon the best talents in the nation while in the United States, defence industries lured away the most promising people (Halberstam 1986, p. 726). In this sense, we are witnessing a distressing reversal in the relative positions of the military in the U.S. economy and in those of economies its major competitors!

To make matters worse, the practices associated with doing such profitable business within the military industrial complex may contaminate other sectors of the industry given the mobility of technical and management personnel in the U.S. economy. In this vein, Michael Edelstein concludes that the main flaw in expanded defence spending is its detrimental impact on the human element in the economy (Edelstein 1990, p. 436). Accordingly, we can conclude that the quality, as well as the quantity, of military spending has eroded the productive potential of the U.S. economy.

How Military Spending Might Actually Harm the Military

Since military power ultimately depends upon economic strength, sooner or later, this erosion of economic vitality will undermine the military itself.

Consequently, military Keynesian may well turn out to be a failure in terms of militarism as well as Keynesianism.

Of course, the United States still has the strongest military in the world, but the basis for this military prowess is rapidly eroding, since the cutting edge military technologies of today result from technological developments from previous decades when the United States was dominant in the commercial sector. For example, *Business Week* concluded immediately after the war against Iraq:

> The hardware doing so well in the Gulf is the product of the '70s and early '80s, when military applications were the cutting edge of technology. Now, commercial developments in high-speed computers, composite wings, fiber optics, and flat-panel computer displays drive military applications. This means that the nation with the most advanced commercial uses may enjoy the greatest military spin-offs.
>
> Others worry that when hi-tech manufacturing moves abroad, research and engineering with potential military use move as well. (Magnusson *et al.* 1990, p. 18)

The continuing emphasis on military spending in the United States allowed U.S. corporations to seek lucrative defence contracts, while abandoning the consumer sector. At the same time, Japanese corporations steadily sought to perfect their production for the consumer sector.

Yet, research and product development in the commercial sector is central to progress in military applications. For example in the low-technology washing machine market, the Japanese are replacing mechanical parts with semiconductors. This technique makes their products both quieter and less expensive (Florida and Kenney 1990a, p. 117). It also gives the Japanese valuable experience in producing and designing semiconductors, so essential to a modern military.

As U.S. firms continue to abandon the consumer sector, they will progressively lose their expertise in cutting edge technologies. The Semiconductor Industry Association, a not-disinterested party, has been quick to recognize the threat, warning, 'Our international competitors are far ahead of us in developing advanced electronics applications via the consumer market segment. We as an industry, and as a country, must pull together quickly . . . before our competitors have an insurmountable lead' (Semiconductor Industry Association 1989, p. 12; cited in Florida and Kenney 1990a, p. 116).

As a result, with the continued collapse of consumer goods production in the United States, more and more of the hardware essential to new military technology will come from foreign suppliers. This arrangement poses two sets of additional problems. First, the U.S. military may not always have adequate access to these supplies when a problem arises. Second, and more important, as engineers in other nations perfect these technologies, they may well accumulate the expertise to surpass our own military engineers (ibid.).

So in the end, military spending – at least carried to excess – may be a sure route to long-run military weakness!

The Class Nature of Military Keynesianism

Excessive military spending is a cancer, eating away at the U.S. economy. Today, as the Cold War draws to a close, we watch the spectacle of the military desperately searching for a rationale for increased spending (Cypher 1991). The military offers to fight the war on drugs, say in the Jungles of Peru. It offers to maintain the capacity to quickly put down Third World insurgencies. Most of all it promises to spend a great deal of money, which we can ill afford.

Checking the expansion of military spending is no easy matter. Some groups have significant stakes in military Keynesianism over and above its effect in holding labour in check. Certainly, a small group of influential arms merchants has parlayed the naivete, patriotism and anxiety of the citizens of the United States into a magnificent stream of profits with the willing and the able assistance of politicians who either fear being honest with the public or who directly benefit from the largesse of the arms merchants.

Military spending has many advantages for business. To begin with, as we have already noted, military spending avoids competing with private business. In addition, business generally favours military more than civilian projects, in part, because military spending tends to help business more than labour, especially in the age of redistributive militarism. Given a national fervor for a strong military presence and a guaranteed profit from the government, business has no reason not to be happy with the financial fruits of military Keynesianism.

Of course, business is not united in its support of military Keynesianism. The meat axe approach to setting national priorities characteristic of the military contributed to the further deterioration of the economy. Only now, after decades of neglect, some progressive business leaders are coming to recognize the importance of increased spending in areas such as education.

We cannot ignore the military's own interest in the rise of military

Keynesianism. Although we commonly think in terms of a homogeneous military-industrial complex, the military has its own specific interests to pursue. Gregory Hooks demonstrates that the military has frequently been successful in pursuing its goals that did conflict with those of business (Hooks 1991).

Certainly, the military is as generous with itself as it is with its suppliers. Although the enlisted personnel do not live lavishly, the military tries to make everything as comfortable as possible for its constituency of high-ranking officers. Lester Thurow observed that the United States supported as many generals and admirals in the late 1980s with an army of only 2 million uniformed troops as it did in World War II with 12 million troops (Thurow 1987, pp. 339–40). Although business continually censures wasteful government bureaucracies, it has never evidenced much concern about waste and corruption in the military,

Others are not so deeply wedded to military Keynesianism: for example, many liberal policy-makers who accepted military Keynesian out of pure expediency. Such people hoped to avoid confronting the deeper problems in our society. Instead, they opted for a quick policy fix that could indirectly correct some of the ills of society without stirring up the enmity of the powerful and without challenging the comfortable views of the well-indoctrinated masses.

We have an enormous challenge facing us if we are to get a handle on the military budget. Recent trends give little cause for optimism.

As the economy fell into a decline, the military and the Keynesian dimensions of military Keynesian separated. The military gained prestige while winning easy victories in Grenada, Panama and Iraq. While the military won public favour, the economic decline soured the public on other forms of social spending. In this sense, the success of military Keynesianism in its goal of undermining social programs exceeded the wildest expectations of the early post-war leaders. Today military Keynesianism is dead; only militarism remains.

5 Keynesian Policy, Monetary Policy, and the Weakening of Competition

The Logic of Keynesian Policy and Cumulative Economic Processes

In this chapter, we will look in more detail at John Maynard Keynes's doctrines, which form the theoretical base for the Economic Management School. We shall see that, while Keynesian policies can stimulate the economy relatively quickly, in the long run they can cause serious damage.

Let us begin with the positive contribution of Keynesian economic policies. Certainly, Keynes was correct in his understanding that investment can set of a spiral of economic growth. Economists do not know precisely how much cumulative economic growth will occur as a result of a new investment. Instead, they have to make rough estimates of the statistical relationship between capital investments and the size of the economy. Still, even using a crude approximation, the results are striking enough to confirm the importance of capital investments.

Lawrence Summers, writing in a volume dedicated to Robert Solow, has observed that for the period 1952 to 1987, an investor who owned shares in a hypothetical mutual fund, which owned the entire corporate sector, would have earned an average return of 7.7 per cent, an amount which is not far from the average accounting rate of profit of 9.6 per cent for the corporate sector as a whole (Summers 1990, p. 119). Summers reminded us that Solow's own estimate of the benefit to society as a whole from capital investment was about 23 to 25 per cent for the United States in 1954 (Solow 1963, p. 92).

Technically, an economist would not want to look at average profits, but the marginal profit rate – what a firm could earn by investing one more dollar. We would expect this rate to be below the average rate. Similarly, we would want to get a handle on the rate of growth for the entire economy resulting from one more dollar's worth of investment. Unfortunately, neither the private nor the social rate of return is known, so we have little choice but to use Summer's average estimates as rough proxies.

Summers concluded that this discrepancy between the accounting rate of profit and Solow's estimate suggested that about half of the benefits from investment accrue to the firm that actually makes an investment and plant and equipment. The other half benefits society as a whole rather than the investing firm.

Summers' interprets this situation to mean that the average firm that invests in new capital captures about half (9.6 per cent) of the fruits of the investment. Society as a whole earns about 23 to 25 per cent on the same investment. Why then does society as a whole benefit more than twice as much from a new investment than the firm that makes the investment does?

To begin with, new investment often incorporates new technologies. The new technologies that one plant introduces, frequently become common knowledge, helping to boost productivity in other nearby plants (see Paul Romer 1987; Nelson 1989).

In addition, the primary investment of one firm can create profitable opportunities for others. As a result, when one firm invests, other firms are likely to respond to an initial investment with investments of their own to supply the new demands of the initially investing firm. This pattern of new investments, incorporating new technologies, can create a cumulative spiral of investment.

Given the situation that firms earn less than one-half of the total benefits of their investments, we should expect that firms would systematically underinvest. If this hesitancy to invest could be broken and firms would invest more, business as a whole would be better off, as Keynes understood.

Unfortunately, firms will not invest as much as would be optimal for society, because each individual firm only takes its own profit into account when it makes its investment decision, ignoring the benefits that other firms reap from the cumulative spiral that investment can initiate, creating what economists refer to as a coordination failure. In other words, if each firm agreed to increase its investment proportionately, all firms would be better off. In a market economy, firms have no way of making such an agreement. Keynesian policies (meaning policies that other economists interpreted as being Keynesian rather than policies which Keynes himself advocated) were intended to break this log jam by stimulating investment one way or another.

The Contradictory Nature of the Business Cycle

At first, the logic of stimulating the economy with Keynesian policies seems impeccable, but, alas, no simple policy rule can make the market perform as well as it could if decision-makers could somehow deliberately co-ordinate their actions. Keynesian policies are no exception. We shall see that, while stimulating investment has undeniable benefits, especially in the short-run, Keynesian policies are beset with contradictory influences that more or less reflect the contradictory nature of competition itself.

A market is an extremely complex form of social organization, fraught with contradictions. Early economists, such as Adam Smith, revelled in these contradictions. Writing at a time when market forces were mistrusted, Smith delighted his readers by pointing out the paradox that people who followed selfish motives supposedly could benefit society as much as if they were driven by generosity.

Today, when much of society holds market forces in high repute, economists are loathe to point out the contradictions inherent in the market. Instead, mainstream economists present markets as wholly harmonious affairs even though the competitive forces that Smith can and often do turn destructive. History shows us that time and time again, economic competitiveness often becomes so intense that firm after firm withers until the downward momentum becomes sufficient to cause a general depression.

In short, depressions and competition are parts of the same process. Each of these parts has a two-fold nature. Competition can appear benign at times; at other times, destructive. Similarly, depression has a positive and a negative side.

The negative side of depressions is self-evident. We know that depressions are terrible events that wreak havoc on a good part of society. Worse yet, depressions can persist for decades on end. In addition, in light of our earlier discussion of the cumulative nature of economic processes, we know that depressions can permanently scar the productive capacity of the labour force and impede economic growth over long periods of time, long after the depression itself has expired.

Still, depressions also serve a positive – even a necessary – purpose within a market economy. Recall our discussion about how the Great Depression to laid the groundwork for the Golden Age.

Mainstream economists studiously avoid the complexity of the competitive process by treating contradictory elements of the market as separate and unrelated forces. They treat business cycles 'like tonsils, separable things that might be treated by themselves, [rather than] . . . like the beat of the heart, of the essence of the organism that displays them' (Schumpeter 1939, i, p. v).

For example, mainstream economists restrict their depictions of competition to its positive effect in spurring business to become more efficient.

They rarely point out the destructive side of competition. Instead, they separate their discussions of competition and depressions and subsume the negative side of competition within their analysis of depressions. Acknowledgement of either the positive side of depressions or the negative side of competition is all but unknown.

Economists facilitate this habitual fragmentation of the their analysis of the contradictory forces of competition by splitting their theory into two subjects: micro-economics (how competition affects an individual firm or household) and macro-economics (how the economy as a whole works). Economists rarely discuss how these two branches of economics are related.

Not surprisingly, this fragmented analysis misleads economists into recommending disastrous policies. For example, most conservative economists would have us believe that the post-war prosperity should be the norm for a capitalist society. They insist that trusting our fate to market forces would allow us to enjoy a rapidly growth standard of living without interruption because competition will lead business to make the correct decisions.

Although Keynesian macro-economics teaches that government should act to maintain sufficient aggregate demand, it still accepts that competition will lead firms to make the proper decisions within that framework. In short, both contemporary conservatives and Keynesians emphasize the positive side of competition without taking the negative side into account.

Almost all mainstream economists treat depressions as abnormal events that only occur as a result of some act of mismanagement. In no case do they acknowledge that depressions are a normal part of the competitive process and that they have both a positive and a negative side. We will see that by assuming away the necessity of depressions, these economists recommend policies that pay no heed to the need for capital renewal.

Keynes's Heresy

Keynes delighted in posing his theory in a shocking manner. In terms of the conventional conservative economics of his day, his theory was indeed quite heretical. The full extent of Keynes's heresy went unrecognized, probably because his book was macroeconomic in nature. More importantly, despite his desire to tweak his contemporaries, Keynes's policies appeared less heretical than they were because they seemed so commonsensical given the extreme conditions that existed at the time.

We can easily understand why, given the enormous costs of the Great Depression, Keynesian policies seemed reasonable enough at first.

Disregarding the excessive emphasis on military spending, the avoidance of recessions seemed to improve the immediate economic welfare of the citizenry. After all, during the Great Depression, when he was writing, competitive forces had gathered so much momentum that Keynes had good reason to doubt that the economy could correct itself and emerge from the depression. The odds were high that popular pressure would cause capitalist societies to rise up abandon the market altogether and to turn to an alternative form of economic organization – either fascism or socialism.

Given this perspective, Keynes virtually ignored the positive aspects of competition. Unlike most mainstream economists at the time, Keynes concentrated on the negative side of competition by focusing on slumps, where competition is most intense. Keynesian economists still generally reject the belief that competitive forces necessarily induce business to act in a way to promote prosperity.

Where mainstream economists emphasize the theory that competitiveness is essential for promoting efficiency in a market economy, Keynes countered that in practice, normal competitive processes can get out of hand and throw an economy into a depression. Keynes taught that when times are tough and competition is fierce, overall investment will be limited.

Keynes was convinced that the momentum of the Great Depression was so strong that few managers would have any interest in expanding their productive capacity. He believed that, rather than building up their firms to weather the storm of competition, those who controlled the major companies would just let them run down rather than make any attempt to modernize their operations (Perelman 1989, pp. 18–20). Consequently, during the Depression, competitive forces become so strong that the economy was likely to remain stagnant for long periods of time.

Knowing that the level of investment would remain weak during a depression, Keynes was intent on designing a quick means of stimulating enough investment to blunt the enormous competitive forces that the depression had unleashed. Policies to expand demand and to shield business from competition were just what the economy needed to break out of the depression at the time. Keynes's precise policy recommendations remained exceedingly vague, but regardless of the specifics, he never doubted the need to frame measures to stimulate the expansion of investment of any kind whatsoever (Perelman 1989).

Keynes gave absolutely no indication of the positive effects of depressions and competition, within the context of a market economy. Instead, he took pride in his heresy and mocked the callousness of the 'austere and puritanical souls [who] regard [the Depression] as an inevitable and a desirable nemesis on "overexpansion" as they call it' (Keynes 1931b, p. 349). He complained:

> It would, they feel, be a victory for the mammon of unrighteousness if so much prosperity, was not subsequently balanced by universal bankruptcy. We need, they say, what they politely call a 'prolonged liquidation' to put us right. The liquidation, they tell us, is not yet complete. But in time it will be. And when sufficient time has elapsed for the completion of the liquidation, all will be well with us again. (Ibid.)

Keynes's attitude is not surprising. After all, the negative aspects of depressions are so glaringly obvious and painfully tragic that most people are inclined to overlook the positive side of depressions, especially in the midst of the havoc of an economic crisis.

To the extent that Keynesian policies succeeded in stimulating investment, shortening or even precluding depressions, the mass of U.S. economists deemed Keynesian policies to be a success. Indeed, by the 1960s, the majority of economists in the United States embraced Keynesian policies. Recall that even President Nixon proclaimed himself to be a Keynesian.

Unfortunately in their zeal to stave off depressions, Keynes and his followers, as well as the bulk of the economists at the time, believed that appropriate government policies would guide the economy along a path of permanent prosperity. They failed to realize the complex relationship between competition and depressions.

Nobody seemed to notice that Keynesian policies, which are ostensibly designed to fight depressions or recessions by expanding demand, are more or less equivalent to a reduction in overall competitiveness.

Keynesian Policies and Replacement Investment

Keynes helped to obscure our understanding of the consequences of this reduction in competitive pressures by ignoring the positive side of depressions. Keynes added to the confusion by failing to take the importance of capital renewal into account. Instead, he lumped all investment together (see Perelman 1989).

Keynes must have known that depreciation charges cover the vast majority of all investment, suggesting that replacement investment is the dominant form of investment. Still, he assumed that capital replacement occurs automatically when a capital good reaches a given age, regardless of economic conditions (Perelman 1989).

You might wonder anyone should care about the distinction between replacement investment and investment in general. In fact, inadequate replacement investment is one of the keys to the economic decline.

In the long run, modernization is crucial for the health of a competitive economy. In general, widespread replacement of existing plant and equipment is the key to modernization. However, modernization generally requires strong competitive pressures. As we have already noted, Keynesian policies undermined replacement by effectively limiting competitive pressures.

Economists often refer to the expansion of capacity as capital widening. Their term for making existing capacity more efficient is capital deepening. In effect, the concept of capital widening is meant to suggest the accumulation of more of the same sort of capital. In contrast, capital deepening suggests making capital more efficient rather than increasing capacity. Of course, capital widening in practice is not absolutely distinct from capital deepening. Still, we know that firms emphasize widening during expansions and deepening during recessions.

Keynes's practice of ignoring the distinction between capital widening and capital deepening was appropriate to his own objective. Writing his *General Theory* in the midst of the Great Depression, he was engaged in the urgent task of finding short-run measures that could prevent the capitalist system from self-destructing.

Common-sense also seems to support Keynes' approach. A buoyant economy should encourage the purchase of new capital goods, which should promote economic efficiency because they embody the most modern technologies. Economists and policy-makers alike failed to recognize the fallacy of this common-sense approach. The root of their failure was their fragmented understanding of economic processes. To understand the nature of a market economy, we need to recognize the positive function that depressions serve as well as the negative consequences of a prolonged absence of a depression.

Specifically, during expansions, firms tend to expand capacity rather than to make the existing capacity more productive. In contrast, during depressions firms will tend to increase efficiency, often by replacing older plant and equipment with newer, more productive capital goods. In other words, what investment that firms do make during slumps will frequently be capital deepening, although, as Keynes understood, hyper-competition can immobilize the investment process.

Substantial capital deepening does not generally occur during expansions. When times are good, firms prefer to reduce their investment in the replacement of existing capital goods so that they can devote more resources to the expansion of capacity. Over time, in the absence of a depression, the capital stock will age and the economy will weaken.

Neither Keynes nor his followers acknowledged the importance of the down-side of the business cycle. Considerations of modernization were understandably extraneous to Keynes' immediate objective of beating the depression. Certainly, the Great Depression had become too severe for Keynes to find much satisfaction in the knowledge that strong competitive pressures can eliminate obsolete plant and equipment. Instead, Keynes was concerned with the immediate problem that excessive competition was immobilizing an economy.

Long after the depression had passed, Keynes's followers continued to fail to recognize the importance of strong competition in promoting capital deepening. We can ascribe this reluctance to address the down-side of the continual application of Keynesian policy for several reasons. First, the fragmentation of the analysis of competition obscured the connection between depressions and competition.

Second, Keynes taught economists to focus on investment as a whole, thereby obscuring the crucial role of replacement investment (Perelman 1989). In addition, economists were disinclined to examine the role of replacement investment because they became infatuated with the undeniable short-run benefits of promoting investment by stimulating the economy.

Perhaps the most important reason for ignoring the role of replacement investment is psychological. Nobody can anticipate when new technology or market conditions will make a new investment obsolete. In other words, once you allow a consideration of replacement investment, you introduce uncertainty into economic theory. This uncertainty ruins the neat and tidy theorems which economists love. As a result, economists chose to ignore reality in order to perfect their theory. In the case of the study of replacement investment, this choice has proven to be disastrous.

Capital Widening versus Capital Deepening

In this section, I will elaborate on the theory of capital deepening, a subject of the utmost importance. Consider what happens when an economy fails to engage in capital deepening over an extended period of time. A typical firm may plan to invest a great deal, convinced that the demand for its product will continue to expand.

Although, its investment may be substantial, management will not be likely to invest much in modernizing existing capital goods under these circumstances. After all, why divert investment funds to replacing older, less-efficient plant and equipment? Even if the firm's old capital goods are only moderately profitable, they can still contribute to the firm's total earnings. Firms will prefer to use their investment funds to purchase new capital goods to expand the productive capacity of the firm without scrapping existing capital goods.

Now imagine a firm that has just emerged from a depression. Suppose that its capital stock is entirely new because it has just replaced all of its old capital goods during the depression. The firm may continue to invest in new capital goods, but now this investment will be for capital widening instead of capital deepening. One year into the expansion, the capital goods which the firm owned at the end of the depression will have aged by one year. The only new capital goods that the firm owns will be its expansion investment for that year. After two years, the firm will own a substantial amount of two-year-old capital goods, some capital goods that are one-year old and its new expansion investment for that year.

This example shows how the capital stock typically ages between the end of one strong recession and the beginning of the next. In other words, without some strong market pressure, firms will continue keep their increasingly obsolete capital goods in use, long after they should have been scrapped or even better, diverted to more appropriate alternative uses. These market pressures can come from two sides: either competitors force the firm to lower its price or suppliers will demand more for their goods and services. Since wages are typically the most important cost, higher wages are a particularly effective means to compel firms to upgrade their old capital stock.

The ageing of capital goods is not the only economic problem associated with the absence of strong competitive pressure. Where competition is lax, firms will tend to get careless, investing unwisely in plant and equipment as well as generally adopting inappropriate business practices.

Part of the problem is psychological. During boom times, managers and investors of all kinds generally interpret their good fortunes to be the result of their own intelligence and hard work. They fail to recognize that the boom owes a great deal to the restructuring that had previously occurred when the economy was struggling during a depression or a recession. Even more ominously, they are generally blind to the fact that booms create the seeds of their own destruction.

This uncritical arrogance leads many managers and investors to overestimate their own abilities. They sink funds into foolish projects fully expecting great rewards. Without the market discipline imposed by strong competitive pressures, wasteful business practices will become increasingly common (see Perelman 1987).

To the extent that firms continue with capital widening without much capital deepening and to the extent that they continue to pursue inappropriate business practices, the economy will become increasingly vulnerable. If this process goes too far, the economy may become incapable of withstanding a severe blow. Should an oil shock occur or should foreign competition suddenly become more fierce, such an economy can swiftly collapse.

Even in the absence of Keynesian policies, competitive pressures will be weak during economic expansions, yet these competitive pressures are needed as an incentive to achieve efficiency, just as mainstream economics teaches. In this sense, periodic recessions and depressions act as an economic immune system. They discipline the economy by weeding out inappropriate business practices or even inefficient firms. They allow the economy to correct itself before it becomes too fragile.

In conclusion, depressions and recessions are absolutely necessary for capitalist economies. They are a crucial phase in the process of modernizing market economies and helping to keep them efficient. Without them, the economy will become weak and inefficient.

After the crisis passes, when business becomes vigorous once again, business will be in the fortunate position of enjoying a strong demand for its products together with a low production cost structure. The stage is then set for a profitable boom, such as the one the United States experienced during the Golden Age, but such expansions are destined to be temporary, not eternal as the Keynesian theorists had imagined.

Keynesian Policies and the Ageing of the Capital Stock

I want to avoid any misunderstanding. My point is not to single out Keynes or the Keynesians. All mainstream economists fail to accept the contradictory nature of market economies. All refuse to accept that markets necessarily impose pain and hardship on society. By failing to come to grips with the realities of the markets, they leave us unprepared for the inevitable.

In general, Keynesian policies were preferable to the dogmatic laissez faire ideology of the Chicago School. Still, we must realize from our discussion of the contradictory influences of Keynesian policies, that policy-makers are caught on the horns of a dilemma. Without Keynesian policies, firms are likely to under-invest systematically to the detriment of society as a whole. Yet, these same Keynesian policies create a long-run tendency for firms to keep existing capital equipment in place rather than investing in modernization.

Policy makers find themselves in another damned-if-you-do, damned-if-you-don't situation. While Keynesian policies can increase efficiency in the short-run, the same policies also impair efficiency in the long-run by inhibiting the replacement of existing investments.

This dilemma is a direct result of the contradictory nature of markets, but economists have systematically avoided facing these contradictions. Instead, they concentrate on one side or the other of markets, leaving themselves unprepared for the consequences of the policies that they recommend. Keynesian economists were not immune to this failing, but then few economists during Keynes's lifetime were sensitive to the long-term risks of Keynesian policy.

Keynes's followers, especially those in the United States, deluded themselves into believing that their master had left them with a blueprint for running an economy. These disciples took up their master's impressionistic call and transformed it into an ambitious blueprint for permanently eradicating the business cycle.

For the Keynesians, the economist's task was to arrange policies that would steer the economy away from depressions and recessions. For the most part, they recommended that the government administer the proper dose of government spending, mostly for military purposes. In the glow of post-war prosperity, everything seemed to be going according to the economists' plan.

The corrosive influence of this military Keynesianism went unnoticed. Influential economic advisors were no more aware than the typical citizen of the hidden dangers that were accumulating during the first decades of Keynesianism.

The Keynesians also overlooked the contradictory nature of expanding demand. In particular, they did not realize that the expansion of demand required the weakening the forces of competition, thereby making the economy more fragile. In effect, military Keynesianism represented the worst of all possible policy mixes: it simultaneously weakened both competition and the industrial prowess of the industrial structure.

Of course, even Keynesian economists realized on an abstract level that, in a market society, competition prods business to find new and better methods of production, but they were oblivious to the converse proposition – that the absence of the pressures associated with hard times removes much of the incentive for modernization (Perelman 1989). Instead, they saw their policies in the narrow context, in which increasing demand would benefit the economy by stimulating investment.

Perhaps Keynesians assumed that appropriate anti-trust measures alone would ensure sufficient competition. At least, to the best of my knowledge,

Keynesian economists gave no hint that they recognized that their policies could eventually undermine the economy by eliminating the periodic depressions that force the modernization of plant and equipment.

This failure to recognize the long-run consequences of attempting to do away with recessions altogether was a serious, though understandable, blunder. During the early days of Keynesianism, this failure to recognize the necessity of downturns in a market economy was to be expected given the enormity of the Depression. Tragically, decades after the immediate threat of the Great Depression had faded away, few economists realized the importance of depressions within market societies.

I am convinced that, by blunting the force of economic downturns for decades, Keynesian policies may have eventually done as much harm as good, but we lack the data to make a precise judgement. Instead, we must speak in qualitative rather than quantitative terms when faulting Keynesian policies for letting inappropriate investment practices become common since no exact measures for appropriateness exist.

Peter Bernstein does provide some calculations that do suggest how Keynesian policies protected inappropriate investments until the economic decline set in. Bernstein takes the trend in the ratio of corporate dividends to the value of the capital stock as evidence of the problem. He notes that this ratio had traditionally been fairly constant because of management's policy of paying out a fixed fraction of true capital value as dividends. This policy changed in the wake of the oil shock. Bernstein concludes:

> [This movement reveals] market and management judgments that a sub-stantial part of stated corporate assets are worthless . . . . [As a result of this revaluation, the ratio] dropped abruptly in 1969 and . . . [has] remained depressed ever since. This suggests that many management errors have occurred during the heavy capital spending years that preceded the oil shocks of the 1970s. (Bernstein 1983, pp. 31–2)

Louis Schorsch points to the practice of the U.S. steel industry as a specific example of the sort of management errors that became obvious with the onset of the crisis accompanying the oil shock. In a well-run industry, management would concentrate investment where it could be most productive. The steel industry did otherwise. Schorsch claims that among major steel manufacturers in the United States, 'without strict cost controls, investment tended to be dispersed throughout the Corporation, each plant getting its share' (Schorsch 1984, p. 36).

Once the industry began to face crisis conditions, it had to pay the price for its previous, wasteful investment patterns and the delay of scrapping.

It had to expend huge amounts of money to replace and upgrade obsolete plant and equipment. As a result, the U.S. steel industry spent as much for investment between 1965 and 1979, when very little capacity was added, as it had during the previous 15 years, when capacity increased by more than one-third (Adams and Mueller 1982, p. 119).

The steel industry, as well as Bernstein's data, lends support to our contention that market societies need depressions, or at least hard times. Otherwise, business will accumulate an inefficient capital stock and industry will become increasingly inefficient.

Monetary Policy and Capital Renewal

Although Keynes was mistaken in overlooking the importance of competition in fostering capital replacement, the framers of U.S. monetary policy were equally wrong in failing to recognize their own responsibility for inhibiting capital renewal. While Keynes correctly emphasized that low interest rates would promote investment, monetary authorities and financial interests favour high interest rates because of their obsessive fear of inflation. In their view, money must be kept tight in order to maintain a sound financial system.

The Federal Reserve Board prides itself in its generally rigid opposition to policies that could moderate interest rates. The Fed takes the position that, maintaining low interest rates would create dangerous inflationary conditions. It contends that market forces must determine the appropriate interest rates. If the market requires interest rates to be high, no harm is done. Higher rates of interest will only discourage those projects that promise a relatively low rate of profit.

The Fed has generally been successful in fighting government efforts to moderate the rate of interest, except during World War II. At that time, the federal government required the Fed to keep interest rates low in order to minimize the cost of financing the military, but the Fed did not do so willingly (Lucia 1983). Finally, in 1951, after a long struggle with the Treasury, the Federal Reserve Board was relieved of the obligation to keep interest rates down.

The Fed saw its 1951 accord with the Treasury as a victory for economic rationality. The Fed contended that removing the controls on interest would not harm the economy since high interest rates would threaten only less profitable investments. Instead, by requiring firms to make investments that pay the highest rate of return, the market disciplines investors to move their capital to those activities that are the most productive.

Because this theory fails to distinguish between the rate of savings and total savings, it leads to the fallacious conclusion that a higher rate of interest automatically encourages saving, by creating a larger pool of funds for future investment. In reality, total savings are the product of the savings rate and the level of national income.

John Maynard Keynes' great work, *The General Theory of Employment, Interest and Money*, showed the fallacy of this emphasis on saving. He demonstrated that, although savings rates might be higher with a higher interest rate *for a given level of economic activity*, higher interest rates are likely to lower the level of economic activity, so much so that total savings may fall as a consequence of raising interest rates.

Low interest rates have other desirable consequences, but the Federal Reserve Board's almost pathological fear of inflation obscured these benefits. First and foremost, low interest rates reduce the cost of capital and thereby make business more willing to undertake investments, especially long-term investments. Obviously, no rational firm will want to invest in a project that will earn an expected rate of profit that is less than the interest rate.

Interest rates also affect the kind of investment that firms undertake. Later, we will discuss how high interest rates are dangerous because they encourage risky behaviour. We will also see how high interest rates lower the share of investment devoted to replacement investment.

Because of the failure to understand the contradictory nature of markets, the Federal Reserve Board won its battle to keep interest rates high. In so doing, the Fed made a substantial contribution to the unravelling of the U.S. economy.

The resulting combination of high interest rates together with a blunting of competitive forces probably represented the worst possible policy mix. The absence of competition would ensure that firms would have little need to replace their capital goods. High interest rates would make such investments uneconomical, if not unaffordable. The following sections will explore the implications of this disastrous policy mix of high interest rates together with the relative absence of competition.

High Interest Rates and the Economics of a Short Time Horizon

All economists accept that high interest rates will inhibit investment. Some, like those economists associated with the Federal Reserve Board, look with favour on this effect, assuming that high interest rates will only restrict the least efficient investments. Mainstream economists rarely realize that high interest rates will restrict replacement investment more than investment in general.

While Keynes forcefully brought into public view the fallacy of trying to use interest rates to stimulate saving, no economist was capable of bringing the relationship between replacement investment and the interest rate to the attention of the world before George Terborgh, an economist employed by a machine tool builders association. Terborgh attempted to alert economists to the effect of the interest rate on replacement investment, but his work never attained the influence that Keynes' opus magnum enjoyed. Even today, few economists demonstrate an awareness of this consequence of high interest rates.

Terborgh went beyond merely showing how requiring investments to earn a higher rate of return inhibits investment. He demonstrated how it also distorts the pattern of investment. We can illustrate this distortion by considering the speed with which firms expect to get their money back, known as the pay-back period. James Malcolmson has demonstrated that this shift in perspective is legitimate by proving mathematically that requiring an investment to earn a high rate of return is more or less equivalent to expecting an investment to repay the outlay in a short period of time (Malcolmson 1969, pp. 207–209; see also Magaziner and Reich 1981, pp. 110 and 160).

What could be wrong with creating a filter that tends to select only those investment that can repay themselves in a short time? Are not these just the sort of investments that will ensure that the economy will be run with new and modern equipment?

Terborgh proved that concentrating on those investments with the highest rate of return has just the opposite effect of what you might think. Consider the following warning supplied by an industrial expert as the United States was just emerging from the Great Depression:

> The practice of expecting all new equipment to pay for itself out of savings in from one to three years, or at the very longest in five years, does not have the effect of keeping plants up to date. In fact, it often has exactly the opposite effect . . .
>
> It is not unusual to find equipment 20–30 years old still in operation because new equipment will require from 7 to 9 years in which to pay for itself. This does not lead to low cost production . . .
>
> The shorter the time allowed which the savings must pay for the cost of equipment, the more obsolete will be the equipment that it replaces. (Gaylord 1940, p. 52)

Terborgh, perhaps the most outspoken opponent of investing for a quick return, was even more dramatic. For Terborgh:

A short pay-off period betokens a stodgy conservatism, willing to protect its aged mechanical assets by a Chinese Wall. For the short pay-off requirement is a barrier of the most formidable character to the replacement of equipment . . .

The shorter the pay-off period required of the challenger, the larger the next-year advantage over the defender that is necessary for replacement. (Terborgh 1949, pp. 194–5)

Terborgh and Gaylord turn our attention to the fact that high interest rates discourage capital replacement. They warned that, behind the Chinese Wall, to return to Terborgh's metaphor, an economy that places an excessive importance on a quick pay-back will gradually slip into uncompetitiveness because of a neglect of strategic investments that cannot pass the test of a high rate of return. We shall now pursue this argument in more detail.

The Economics of the Chinese Wall

Analyzing the economics of Terborgh's Chinese Wall helps to throw light on an important dimension of the overall process of economic decline. The key to this problem is that the Chinese Wall will be more of a hurdle for long-lived investments than for short ones. Let us think in terms of rates of return on investment instead of pay-back periods. Now imagine two firms contemplating $100 investment projects that are to last 2 years. The first firm expects to earn at least 10 per cent per year for its investments; the other, 3 per cent. The first firm will reject all projects that fail to pay at least $121 after 2 years. The second will consider any project that returns more than $106 in two years.

For twenty-year investment projects, the disparity for the two firms is far greater. The first firm will not consider any projects that yield less than $673 in twenty years. The second needs a payoff of only $181 (Dertouzos *et al.* 1989, pp. 59–60). In effect, higher interest rates tend to discourage longer-term investment.

Let us turn to a more concrete example to illustrate the difference between long-lived and short-lived investments more concretely. Suppose that you have an old factory that is rapidly becoming obsolete. When a machine breaks down, say a fuse burns out, fixing it can be very cheap, yet without the repair, the factory might not be able to produce anything at all.

The replacement of the fuse is a form of replacement investment, but it is a very different form than the reconstruction of an entire factory.

It represents the minimization of replacement investment consistent with keeping the plant running.

In the case of the installation of the new fuse, even if the factory is relatively unprofitable, earning a mere $100 per year, replacing a 10 cent fuse would be very profitable investment, representing an astounding 10,000 per cent rate of return. Most people would jump at the opportunity to make comparable profits.

In contrast, building a new factory from the ground up would be very expensive. Certainly, it would earn a lower rate of return than 10,000 per cent!

How does the example of the fuse square with the common sense idea that an economy will be most efficient when all firms invest to earn the highest possible rate of return? In reality in a changing world, the strategy of investing for the highest immediate rate of return is flawed. In a competitive economy with continual technical change, our obsolete factory will become increasingly obsolete, eventually going bankrupt. We are faced with the paradox that a firm that can earn a rate of return of 10,000 per cent on its investment will eventually fall victim to new plants that earn considerably less on its investments.

Again, James Malcolmson's mathematics are relevant to the discussion. Just as the post-war economy began to peter out, he offered a theoretical proof of Terborgh's notion. He demonstrated mathematically that, when investors only put their money in investments that can repay themselves quickly – following the quick pay-back rule – they will invest less in long-lived capital goods than would occur in a theoretical economy in which investors had perfect certainty about the future. This distortion becomes more pronounced when capital depreciates at a high rate and when the discount rate is high (Malcolmson 1969).

In effect, keeping a patchwork of old equipment together with bailing wire and a rubber band only seems to be the most profitable use of capital. This illusion is a figment of the accountant's craft. In the example of our old and outdated plant, the rate of return on investment seems to be high only because management sees the old capital as costless since its value had already been depreciated away (see Edwards 1955). Because profits are calculated on the basis of the sum of the investment outlay and current costs – and the investment outlay is nil where all the capital has been depreciated away – profits will often appear to be high in outdated operations, even when bankruptcy is near at hand. Obviously, something is amiss in this situation.

The theoretical analysis that lay behind Terborgh's warning about the economy disintegrating behind a Chinese Wall dates back as far as the nineteenth-century economist, John Rae (1834; see also Perelman 1983, Ch. 6). Unfortunately, it has was not widely understood then any more than it was in Terborgh's day.

Certainly, Terborgh's metaphor did not sound very convincing to readers in the United States at the time. Despite the conventional wisdom that the economy would suffer a serious recession with the post-war demobilization, pent-up consumer demand carried the U.S. economy into the early phase of the post-war boom.

The excessive fears of recession gave way to an equally unjustified tide of confidence – if not overconfidence. After all, the United States had just won the war. Its economy was the strongest in the world. This confidence in the economy seemed to be warranted at the time. Indeed, the United States was about to enjoy two decades of unparalleled prosperity. Nobody seemed to be in a mood to pay attention to Terborgh's sour note.

Today, Terborgh sounds more prescient. Because the conventional economists failed to take Terborgh's point into account, the Federal Reserve Board did not realize that raising the rate of interest would create a profound change in the type of investments that firms would undertake, encouraging firms to make short-run incremental investments while discouraging them from making long-run investments. The habit of expecting high rates of return compounded the decline.

This problem has an ironical overtone. The business community is in the habit of blaming much of the nation's woes on labour's expectation of a high wage. Supposedly, high wages discourage investment. In fact, as we shall see, high wages encourage needed investment, prompting firms to rebuild their factories rather than just to change blown-out fuses. High wages, in this sense, can foster competitiveness.

In contrast, the expectation of a high rate of return, rather than high wages, is a major cause of inadequate investment, just as Terborgh warned. This problem is especially severe in an economy where investors habitually expect to be able to make a quick pay-off. Unfortunately, managers who attempt to act on the need to invest for the long run tend to be punished in the market place where stock holders want high dividends right away.

Managers soon learn that discretion is the better part of valor. Better to construct a Chinese Wall than to build a strong economy.

The Costs of an Ageing Capital Stock

Let us consider how the existence of an ageing capital stock leads to a progressive deterioration of the economy. Anne Carter's study of structure of industry in the United States throws some light on this phenomenon. She used a mathematical technique, known as input-output analysis, to analyze government data in order to estimate the technological characteristics for each industry in the United States in 1947.

Within this framework, Carter estimated the quantity of inputs that would have been required to produce the same goods and services that the United States produced in 1958, assuming that the economy would be using 1947 technology instead of the technology which was actually used in 1958. Although much technical change occurred during this period, according to Carter's calculations, the 1947 technology actually turned out to be superior to the 1958 technology in 14 of 76 sectors (Carter 1970, pp. 171–2).

What could explain the apparent superiority of 1947 to 1958 technologies? Ryuzo Sato and Rama Ramachandran hinted that the decline in efficiency may be related to the ageing of the capital stock in these 14 industries. They noted that replacement in these 14 industries was less vigorous than in other industries (Sato and Ramachandran 1980, p. 1007). Consequently, much of the 1958 technology in these industries might simply be the 1947 technology after 11 years of operation.

Consider what happens to an industry without significant capital renewal. Recall our earlier discussion about the nature of investment during an expansion. We saw that firms tend to install new investment alongside the old facilities instead of replacing existing investments with more efficient plant and equipment while the economy is growing. Consequently, much obsolete plant and equipment operate, or at least stands ready to operate, alongside modern operations. For example, in the U.S. automobile industry during the late 1960s, the productivity per employee of the top quarter plants was 2 ½ times as productive as the lowest quarter (Melman 1983, p. 184; see also Hulten 1992, p. 965).

Such disparities in productivity became even more extreme during the 1970s as a result of the continued deferral of scrapping of capital goods. Over time, the absence of capital renewal will operate as a drag on the economy.

For example, as much as 50 per cent of the railroad track in the United States is estimated to be defective. Because of the sorry state of the railroad system, in 1976 trains had to reduce speed on more than 15 per cent of total track, sometimes to as low as 10 miles per hour (Etzioni 1991, p. 384; citing United States Department of Transportation 1978, p. 15).

The ageing of the capital stock helps to explain how the rate of productivity growth in the U.S. economy plummeted during the 1970s, despite widespread evidence that the rate of improvement in new capital goods has accelerated in recent decades (McHugh and Lane 1987). In effect, the enormous accumulation of old and outdated technologies was so great that the addition of these modern technologies was unable to increase the average productivity by much.

Frank Gollop attempted to warn a congressional committee of the dangers of a long period of inadequate capital replacement. According to his description, '[T]hroughout New England, . . . you see very, very old buildings, but sometimes fairly modern equipment. The conveyor takes the product of this new equipment on floor one up to floor four. Why isn't there a new building?' (U.S. House of Representatives 1981, p. 471).

Gollop's question is not trivial. Frequently, different capital goods are organically related. The commitment of fixed capital to one technology often makes the adoption of later technologies less economical. More often than not, firms resist scrapping a wide range of plant and equipment to build a new 'green field' operation. Instead, they tend to jerry rig various vintages of plant and equipment together in a predictably inefficient manner. Sydney Pollard termed this practice, 'patching' (Pollard 1982, p. 132).

The Economics of Patching

Now we can return to Terborgh's paradox. Although investment in a temporary patch seems to promise a high rate of return, continued patching will eventually result in a catastrophe. For example, Gollop noted the grave consequences that excessive reliance on patching will produce: '[I]t often postpones the introduction of new process technology . . . . Old equipment is kept in use, old methods are followed, and the advantages of new equipment and techniques are foregone with consequences for both future costs and product innovation' (ibid.).

Although patching is not unique to buildings, patching structures can create obvious inefficiencies over time as gradual changes in technology occur without much comparable alteration in the plant. In the end, the firm will be left saddled with an inefficient layout, which can disrupt the process of production (U.S. House of Representatives 1981, pp. 19 and 47; see also Schmenner 1980, p. 104).

Such cumulative obsolescence can occur relatively fast, even for structures. A survey of plants with more than 100,000 square feet in the North Central United States, which closed between 1 July 1977 and 1 September 1980, found that about half the idle plants had been constructed after 1947 (Institute of Science and Technology 1984, pp. 6–7). Of the 56 plant closings analyzed in the study, more than one-third had been demolished or abandoned or were still on the market.

Norman Robins, research manager of Inland Steel, pointed out some of the inefficiencies of working with an outmoded plant. He recalled:

> I was in the Fukuyama plant last year, and one of the most impressive things about it was the lack of truck and train traffic. Inland's plant, on the other hand, was begun in 1902 and undoubtedly was not conceived at that point in time to grow to the size that it has since become. Presently there are blast furnaces in two locations and a new one being built in a third location, steelmaking at four different locations and a great deal of material handling and transportation required to move steel through the finishing facilities. (Robins 1979; cited in Mueller 1984, p. 56)

Don Barnett, previously chief economist for the U.S. Iron and Steel Institute, offers another graphic example of the consequences of maintaining obsolete equipment in the steel industry. Although the Japanese steel industry is reputed to be the most efficient in the world, he calculated that the efficiency differential was limited to a small part of the overall production process. For most processes in manufacturing cold-rolled steel, the labour requirements were about equal in Japan and the United States, except for three specific processes: the production of coke, production of iron in blast furnaces, and the casting of semi-finished shapes according to his estimates for 1977 (U.S. Senate 1982, pp. 33–37).

In all three cases, the problem seems to be related to an ageing capital stock. In the first two processes, the labour requirements were closely related to the age of the equipment utilized. In the third case, modern continuous casting technology is especially hard to install in the aged structures that are typical of the U.S. steel industry at the time of Barnett's study.

Although the dangers of protracted patching are so great that a number of economists have proposed that war-time destruction of a nation's capital stock ultimately gives that nation an economic advantage, we must be careful not to give the impression that uncritical scrapping of existing plant and equipment is an appropriate strategy. For example, in a later publication, Barnett along with co-author, Lewis Schorsch, asserted that reluctance to invest by the steel industry may have been rational (Barnett and Schorsch 1983, p. 179). The authors contended that new greenfield plants would not significantly lower costs.

We should take the conclusion of Barnett and Schorsch with a grain of salt. Their calculations assume a much quicker write-off than is typical for the steel industry, which is notorious for its exceptional dependence on old capital (Barnett and Schorsch 1983; see also Magaziner and Reich 1981, pp. 110 and 156).

In any case, the broad picture about the ageing of the capital stock in the United States does seem to be a matter of record. The United States began the post-war period with enormous advantages. As we discussed earlier, our major foreign competitors laid in ruins. The U.S. capital stock was relatively new. Business had clean balance sheets, relatively free from debt.

Under these conditions, a regime of military Keynesianism could show relatively good results for a comparatively long period of time. By the late 1960s or early 1970s, while Keynesian economists were basking in their apparent success in eradicating the business cycle, a facade of decades of prosperity had masked over the emerging weakness. In the absence of strong competitive forces, the capital stock aged and the economy weakened.

Investing for Rapid Pay-back during the Depression

The emphasis on a quick pay-back from investments predates the Federal Reserve Board's 1951 Accord with the U.S. Treasury Department. According to E. M. Richards, who was chief engineer for Republic Steel of Youngstown, Ohio, the high pay-off rule was originally associated with the extreme capital rationing that became common during the Depression:

> This practice started about twenty years ago . . . but was not generally adopted by other industries until the beginning of 1932, when the extreme curtailment of all capital expenditures became almost imperative. Since then it seems to have become almost universal practice . . .
>
> Under normal business conditions, it is felt that an improvement should pay for itself in three years or less. In a severe depression, where the conserving of cash is paramount, companies are inclined to work on the basis that an improvement must pay for itself in one year. (Richards 1933, p. 499)

In May of 1930, Frederic V. Geier, a vice-president of the Cincinnati Milling Machine Co. delivered a paper entitled, 'Amortization of Machine Tools', to the Machinery Builders Society of New York, reporting on a questionnaire sent to 800 large U.S. manufacturing companies. He reported that none would buy equipment with a pay-back period of more than five years; 43 per cent insisted on two year pay-back (Wagoner 1968, p. 134).

This anecdotal evidence is consistent with our limited knowledge of replacement practices during the depression. Since the steel industry was especially uncompetitive, it felt less need than most industries to respond to competitive pressures throughout the depression.

Note that Geier's survey includes 800 companies. This high number would include many medium-size firms. Since he merely reported the share of firms that gave a particular response, this survey probably reflects the practices of medium-size firms. Recall that we had earlier suggested that in the early years of the Depression, large and relatively competitive companies, intent on maintaining their level of employment relatively steady, would have good reason to make extensive long-term investments in order to meet competition without cutting wages and employment. Richards's recollection, that the short-payback rule became common after 1932, squares with our previous discussion of the two stages of the Great Depression.

In conclusion, although the Great Depression created untold damage, it did succeed in inducing many businesses to modernize the stock of capital in the United States. Unlike the steel industry, most had to adjust to strong competitive pressures during the Great Depression. Consequently, many firms weeded out much of their inefficient plant at the time.

On the Ageing of the U.S. Capital Stock

By the end of the Great Depression, the capital stock in the United States was very new. Recall Staehle's estimate that, by 1939, one-half of all equipment that had existed in 1933 had been replaced (Staehle 1955, p. 127). In 1940, only 28 per cent of all of the machine tools in the United States were 10 years old or more (Noble 1984, p. 8). This state of affairs did not last long because of the absence of competitive pressures, and if Richards is correct, the increasing reliance on a short pay-back rule.

By 5 October 1955, *Business Week* lamented that 43 per cent of all of the machine tools in the United States were ten years old or more (Phillips 1958, p. 149). The *Business Week* staff continued with its theme of the ageing capital stock. Dexter Keezer, head of the McGraw-Hill Economics Department, told the *Detroit News* on 9 February 1956 that $125 billion, an amount equal to a quarter of the valuation of the existing capital stock, would be required to put the nation's industrial equipment in 'first class condition' (Phillips 1958, p. 149). In 1958, Mr Keezer returned to the subject again:

[I]n terms of antiquity and degree of obsolescence . . . less than one third of it [has been produced] since 1950. Yet the years 1950–1958 comprise a period when rapidly changing technology has made older

Table 5.1   Age Distribution of Machine Tools in the United States
(in percentages)

Year	Under 10 years old	10–20 years old	More than 20 years old
1963	36.0	43.3	20.7
1968	35.6	41.0	23.4
1973	32.9	38.7	38.4
1976–8	30.5	35.2	34.2

Source: National Machine Tool Builders Association 1982–1983, p. 259.

Table 5.2   International Distribution of Machine Tool Ages (percentages)

Country and Year	Under 10 yrs. old	10–20 yrs. old	More than 20 years old
U.S. '76–78	31	35	34
W. Germany '77	37	37	26
U.K. '76	39	37	24
Japan '73	61	21	18
France '74	37	33	30
Italy '75	42	30	28
Canada '78	47	35	18

Source: National Machine Tool Builders Association 1982–1983, p. 259.

equipment obsolete . . . . [A] 1958 metal working tool is about 54 percent more productive than one that could be purchased in 1948. A combination of new freight cars and modern freight yard equipment can reduce operating costs up to 50 percent. New instruments that automatically direct the flow of chemical (or other raw material) processes can often reduce costs enough to pay back the cost of the controls in one year. These savings are rarely possible in older plants. (Keezer 1958, p. 23; cited in Baran and Sweezy 1966, p. 96)

Business Week was not alone. Angus Maddison speculated in 1964 that the U.S. capital stock had aged more than its European counterparts (Maddison 1964, p. 93).

The U.S. capital stock seems to have continued to age long after Keezer had issued his warning. Unfortunately, much of the data on the age of the capital stock is relatively impressionistic. The usual economic data bases do not help much in getting a fix on the degree to which the capital stock consists of obsolete plant and equipment (see Miller 1990; Perelman 1989, p. 109). However, we do have some information on the machine tool sector.

Seymour Melman notes that only 31 per cent of machine tools in use in the United States in 1976–8 were ten years old or less (Melman 1983, p. 6). In the United States automobile industry in 1978, 76 per cent of the machine tools were ten years old or even older (Melman 1983, p. 184).

An international comparison of the age of equipment in the machine tool sector of the major capitalist nations indicates that ageing of capital goods still might be a greater problem in the U.S. than elsewhere.

The steel industry also showed dangerous signs of ageing. Given the lack of competitiveness, which has characterized the United States steel industry, we should not be surprised about the ageing of the capital stock in that industry. By 1979, 33 per cent of steel production facilities were more than 20 years old; 12 per cent dated back more than 30 years (Melman 1983, p. 189; see also Barnett and Schorsch 1983, esp. p. 91).

Although we do not have good data on the age of capital goods for the economy as a whole, we do know that a smaller and smaller portion of investment funds have been devoted to the acquisition of long-lived capital goods. Economists usually attribute this phenomenon to high interest rates, the degree of economic uncertainty, or taxes. In contrast, I have been emphasizing the absence of strong competitive pressures during the Golden Age. Later we will pay attention to another strategic factor in the ageing of the capital stock: low wages.

The Short Pay-back Period and the Decline in U.S. Competitiveness

Some years ago, Martin Weingartner came to the defence of the quick pay-back rule (Weingartner 1969). He argued that a quick pay-back can make sense for the individual firm by providing flexibility. Just think of the risk that a firm faces when it commits itself to an expensive investment in a durable capital good, especially when that good has a purpose that is specific to the firm. In the words of John R. Hicks, 'an entrepreneur by investing in fixed capital gives hostages to the future' (Hicks 1932, p. 183). Keynes himself amplified this point, speculating:

> Investment based on genuine long-term expectations is so difficult to-day as to be scarcely practicable . . . Furthermore, an investor who proposes to ignore near-term market fluctuations needs greater resources for safety – . . . a further reason for the higher return [expected from long-term investment]. (Keynes, 1936, p. 157)

Keynes' observation is important. Writing in the midst of the Great Depression, Keynes was pointing out that excessive risk (at that time stemming from the heightened competitive pressures of depression) would destroy the confidence required to allow firms to invest in expensive long-lived capital goods.

Here we come back to the central problem that Keynes faced. Think of the short pay-back rule as a partial withholding of investment. Under this rule, firms will only consider those investments that promise an immediate return. Given the uncertainty of economic conditions, each firm might rationally refrain from investment, but when all firms do so, the economy as a whole suffers. So too do the individual firms that refused to invest. Had they been able to work out a common agreement to invest, these same firms would have benefitted.

Our analysis of replacement investment takes us one step beyond Keynes. We can see that, although the quick pay-back rule allows individual firms to maintain their flexibility, the short pay-back rule also condemns an economy to eventual uncompetitiveness, because the short pay-back rule effectively rules out extensive replacement investment.

Indeed, some authorities associate Japan's recent economic success with the low rate of return required to justify investment projects to be adopted in that nation (Leontief 1981; and Magaziner and Reich 1981, p. 160). For example, U.S. companies expect to earn their money back in 4.5 years; Japanese firms, in 12 (Magaziner and Reich 1981, p. 351). I should mention that recent financial pressures in Japan are causing the Japanese to adopt a more short-term planning horizon.

The reasoning of Bernard Butcher, Vice President of Dow Chemical, illustrates the destructive logic behind the quick-pay back rule. He explained why his firm avoids building new plants from the ground up by saying, 'These incremental expansions don't cost much and *you don't have to be thinking in terms of three years from now*' (cited in Naj 1988; emphasis added).

The devastating consequences of this strategy of piecemeal investment might not appear for years. For example, although industrial buildings do not physically decay very fast, they become obsolete after an extended policy of minimum alterations in plant. After a sequence of several such changes, the poor layout of the plant will eventually undermine productivity (Institute of Science and Technology 1984, p. 19).

A short pay-off criterion will be self-reinforcing. The restriction of long-lived investment eventually leads to lower profits although the rate of profit may be higher. For instance, in our earlier example of the replacement of a fuse we saw this combination of a relatively small total profit with a very high rate of profit. As the profit base shrinks, business will find itself with fewer funds than it would otherwise have. Given this shortage of investable funds, business will set its sights on a still shorter pay-off period.

A short pay-back criterion may even encourage business to put off needed maintenance, the costs of which will not be felt until some time in the future. For example, a *Wall Street Journal* article concerning the takeover of Cities Service by Occidental Petroleum reported:

> [I]n the worksheds and offices nearby, Cities Service roughnecks talk of the changes. Spare-parts inventories and preventative maintenance have been reduced, they say. As aging underground pipes in the oil field's water injection system fail, geysers of water sometimes shoot 20 to 30 feet into the air. 'We replace the section that's broken and wait for the next one to blow,' a worker explains. (Rose 1984)

We should be grateful to this anonymous worker for providing us with a telling metaphor for our economy: We [try to] replace the section that's broken and wait for the next one to blow.

Crisis and Competition in the U.S. Economy

By the time the problems associated with an obsolete capital stock came to light, the crisis had already gathered substantial momentum. Unbeknownst to the leaders of the U.S. economy, fundamental forces were at work, which were altering economic relations. The balance of power between labour and capital, as well as the balance between the United States and the rest of the world, was shifting.

At first, the crisis appeared in the form of what seemed to be unique and seemingly unrelated incidents. Given this mind-set, relatively simple and direct measures seemed to be appropriate. For example, when the government finally recognized that foreign competition was becoming a serious problem during the 1970s, it merely attempted to moderate the force of foreign competition by stimulating the economy with monetary and fiscal policy.

Unfortunately, domestic business enjoyed only part of the benefits of attempting to stimulate the economy with monetary or fiscal policy. A substantial part of the demand stimulus encouraged the purchase of imported goods, providing foreign producers with an even stronger beachhead in the United States.

The government also attempted to blunt the force of foreign competition through trade agreements, but these too proved to be an inadequate solution. Nor could devaluing the dollar stem the tide of foreign imports.

The dramatic oil shocks that rocked the economy during the 1970s should have immediately jolted business into realizing the seriousness of its situation, but they did not. Once again, the leaders of the U.S. economy attributed economic ills to external events. The popular mood created an image of evil Arabs who were supposed to have caused much of problems of the times.

Eventually, in some quarters, the combination of the oil shock and the military defeat in Vietnam, together with the heightened political and economic militancy of the period, brought on a delayed recognition of the gravity of the new state of affairs. In this context, de-industrialization became a common term in economic and business circles.

The hideous neologism, de-industrialization, did have the advantage of suggesting a generalized, although incompletely understood, force. It evoked a mood in which simple measures would no longer appear to be inadequate.

Still, most of the business community, as well as the economics profession, failed to realize the consequences of the decade-long blunting of the forces of competition. When the oil shock hit the U.S. economy, it revealed or at least it began to reveal, what could no longer be entirely hidden: a substantial portion of the capital stock in the United States consisted of obsolete plant and equipment, which could no longer add much to the productive potential of the economy.

Within this context, some economists have suggested that the oil shock literally wiped out the value of a substantial portion of the capital stock of the U.S. economy. They reasoned that many capital goods, installed during a period when low energy prices prevailed, were designed to take advantage of inexpensive energy (Baily 1981a; and 1981b; see also Gibbons 1984; and Klein 1983, p. 54). As energy prices rose, a good deal of this equipment suddenly became economically inefficient and its value diminished accordingly.

Ernst Berndt has discounted the importance of the oil shock. He contended that, because energy prices are a relatively small fraction of manufacturing costs, they should not be a major determinant of the level of productivity in the U.S. economy (Berndt 1980). Robert Pindyck and Julio Rotemberg have shown why Berndt's reasoning does not necessarily hold (Pindyck and Rotemberg 1983).

Still, I believe that we should always be careful about attributing the decline to any single cause. I remain convinced that the surge in oil prices in the 1970s was symptomatic of other far reaching changes in the political economy of the United States and the rest of the world (Wolfe 1981; and Bowles, Gordon and Weisskopf 1983).

The Overhang of Phantom Capacity

Even the massive oil shock proved to be insufficient to cause management in many industries to recognize that its capital stock was inappropriate until the crisis threatened to get out of hand. For example, Gordon and Veitch noted that the airlines did not ground their 707s until four years after the second oil shock (R. J. Gordon and Veitch 1984, p. 19).

As usual, the steel industry provided another excellent example of the inability of management to realize the importance of keeping the capital stock in good order. Some of its 'dinosaur' steel plants took longer to retire than the relatively new 707s did (ibid.). Conditions became so desperate in the steel industry that, despite its belated attempts at modernization, a substantial portion of the U.S. steel capacity still had to be scrapped. Between 1977 and 1984, the industry abandoned 25 million short tons of capacity – 16 per cent of the industry total (Anon. 1984).

Paul Davidson referred to such obsolete capital goods as 'fossils of many past investment errors' (Davidson 1972, p. 135). I prefer the term 'phantom capacity' because these obsolete capital goods give an appearance of a productive potential that does not exist.

The people of U.S. economy paid a high price for the errors of its leaders, who imagined that they could build a solid economic structure on a foundation of old and obsolete capital stock. As we have been insisting, over time, the absence of strong competitive forces led U.S. business to allow its capital stock to age almost without interruption until the Volcker recession, which briefly reinvigorated competition during the early 1980s.

The absence of competition explains this build-up of phantom capacity. As the economy took on more and more of this phantom capacity, it became more fragile and less able to withstand shocks. We saw some evidence of this growing economic weakness in the calculations by Tom Michl and Thomas Weisskopf, mentioned in the first chapter. Both suggested that the capital structure seemed to become less efficient as the decline progressed.

In general, however, when the government stands by and lets a depression or a recession occur, government leaders count on hard times to drive labour costs down. This recession was no exception. We have seen that the intent of Paul Volcker during this recession was not to make the economy as a whole competitive, but only to single out labour. Nonetheless, the hard times of the 1980s do seem to have been unique, because of the extent to which labour has been almost alone in absorbing the shocks to the system, while business was left relatively unscathed.

In general, when an economy slows down, unemployment generally increases before most business feel the pinch. When the slowdown reaches that level, business typically calls upon the government to get the economy moving again. Despite the best efforts of the government, the economic slowdown typically accumulates enough momentum to make business become serious about efficiency, but by the time the Volcker recession hit, business was quite vulnerable.

Had the resulting recession been allowed to run its course, the results would have been disastrous for U.S. business as well for labour. In effect, the more Keynesian policy succeeded in taming the business cycle, the weaker business became. Most industries in the United States today would have difficulty surviving the competitive forces that are an integral part of a healthy capitalist economy.

Now the day is coming when business will have had to pay the price for decades of the luxury of an absence of competition. Of course, if business is able to withstand such a blow, it will emerge stronger than ever.

We do not know how much of a shock business can take. Once the Volcker recession had done its job of taming labour, the government leaders realized the magnitude of the competitive forces that it unleashed. The Federal Reserve Board loosened its monetary controls and the Reagan Administration began a more vigorous regimen of military Keynesianism than any of its predecessors had ever imagined.

The Elimination of Phantom Capacity

In contrast to the experience of the earlier downturns of the post-war period, the shock of the recession of the early 1980s was severe enough to force business to scrap considerable amounts of obsolete plant and equipment, even though the government moved to cut short this recession. This statement remains at the level of generality because we do not have data on the scrapping and upgrading of installed plant and capital. We can only infer how much of this scrapped plant and equipment constituted phantom capacity and how much phantom capacity still remained.

One shred of evidence about the effectiveness of the recession in eliminating phantom capacity, concerns a measure that economists use, called, 'the capacity utilization ratio.' This measure is intended to indicate how close an economy is operating to its optimal level of production. During the 1950s, annual capacity utilization rates exceeded 85 per cent in five years; in the 1960s, six years; in the 1970s, only two years. In the first four years of the 1980s, annual capacity utilization failed even to reach 80 per cent (President of the United States 1990, p. 351).

Although some of this trend may be explained by fluctuations in the business cycle, I am convinced that gradual accumulation of phantom capacity is a major cause of the declining frequency of peak capacity utilization rates. Let me explain.

Economists theorize that production costs decline as a firm increases its output up to a point near full capacity because fixed costs are spread over a larger output. Eventually, as output expands further, the firm reaches a point where costs increase because it runs up against difficulties in expanding output. For example, it might have to pay overtime wages or machinery might break down from overuse. In fact, capacity utilization rates seem to be better predictors of inflation than the commonly used indicator of unemployment rates (McElhattan 1985).

In a competitive economy, capacity utilization would be a poor indicator of inflation. When capacity utilization is very high, costs will be falling. In a competitive economy, we would generally expect to see prices declining along with costs. Prices should only begin to increase when the economy reaches a point near full capacity.

We have been making the case that, beginning in the late 1960s, with the onset of the economic decline, competitive forces have been on the upswing due to greater foreign competition. If that hypothesis is correct, we might expect to find a diminution of the tendency for prices to rise as the economy well before the economy begins to reach full capacity. As we noted in the previous paragraph, as competition increases, prices should not begin to accelerate until the economy reaches a point near full capacity.

We should expect that, as competitive forces increased, the capacity utilization rate would have to come closer and closer to 100 per cent before prices would begin to rise. In fact, the opposite tendency seems to have been at work. During the mid- to late-1960s, prices did not begin to accelerate until the capacity utilization rates reached the mid-80s; in the mid- to late-1970s, by contrast, prices began to accelerate at only about 80 per cent of capacity (Woodham 1984).

Why should prices begin to increase at a lower capacity utilization rate during the late 1970s? I attribute this trend to the existence of phantom capacity. During the early post-war period the government shielded the U.S. economy from strong competitive forces. Over time, more and more capital goods ceased to be very productive, falling into the category of phantom capacity. Management could prevent phantom capacity from becoming a larger share of the capital stock by a commitment to replacement investment, but throughout the post-war boom, management gave little indication that it had much of an inclination to maintain a healthy capital stock.

According to this scenario, a substantial portion of the reported capacity of the U.S. economy could constitute phantom capacity. Suppose that phantom capacity represented 5 per cent more of the reported productive capacity in the 1970s than it did in the 1960s. I consider this number to be a substantial underestimate. In that case, other things being equal, during the 1970s, prices would begin to rise when the capacity ratio stood at about 80 rather than the mid-1960s when the mid-eighties was the point where prices would escalate.

If, however, competitive pressures were stronger in the 1970s than in the previous decade, we might suspect that the increase in phantom capacity as a share of reported capacity might be even greater than 5 percent. In the wake of the strong recession of the early 1980s, business scrapped considerable phantom capacity. As we would expect, from that time on, prices began to accelerate at a higher capacity utilization rate than before, although, of course, other explanations are possible (e.g., McElhattan 1985).

Creative Redeployment of Old Capital Goods

Although the continued inappropriate use of old capital goods in outmoded production processes results in a progressively weakening economy, we should be wary of being overly critical of the use of old capital goods. Words of caution about the dangers of inappropriate use of capital goods remain tautological until we define the term, 'inappropriate.' Given the almost universal condemnation of the investment practices of the steel industry, the Barnett and Schorsch analysis of the futility of investing in modern steel industry capacity suggests how almost any hypothesis about capital obsolescence is subject to dispute.

Just because capital goods are old does not mean that they are obsolete – although they may be obsolete for their current use. With care and ingenuity, innovative managers can turn old capital goods to new uses for which they are absolutely appropriate. Indeed, many old capital goods are quite suitable to uses for which they were not necessarily designed. For instance, in my own neighbourhood, farmers use old tractors, which they consider to be uneconomical for plowing and harvesting, to carry irrigation pipe.

Given this perspective, the fact that many of the plants studied in the survey of plants in the North Central United States stood idle or even no longer existed did not demonstrate the absolute absence of an economic potential. Instead, the underutilization of these plants stood as a bleak testimony to a failure to recognize that potential.

For example, one group of analysts combined a detailed architectural study of old industrial buildings with relevant economic analysis to investigate the possibility of alternative uses for such buildings. These analysts were not recommending patching. They were suggesting a complete redeployment of the factory. The same characteristics that made these buildings obsolete for their initial uses might make them ideal for others.

For example, some of these buildings were abandoned because they were multi-storied, making them inappropriate for an assembly line process. Yet a multi-storied lay-out can well suit the gravity feed and batch milling of pharmaceutical powders (Institute of Science and Technology 1984, p. 19). Indeed, many old industrial plants near Boston now house some of the prestigious high-technology companies that had sprung up in the region.

In fact, with enough ingenuity such plants can even successfully accommodate traditional smokestack industries. For instance, General Motors profitably renovated its half-century old Baltimore manufacturing plant with a 1500 person retrofit team using a winding roller-coaster-like assembly line (Zaslow 1985, p. 9c).

Where old capital stock becomes inappropriate for a particular use, specialists often cannibalize it, selling off individual components for alternative uses. Creative redeployment can significantly upgrade the value of capital stock even for sophisticated multinational corporations. For example, in 1961, 'Lockheed Aircraft Corporation's outer space research [was] . . . depending to a large measure on a 52-ton generator that formerly fed power to the inner reaches of Boston's subway system' (*New York Times*, 3 June 1961; cited in Waterson 1964, p. 91). This 40-year-old generator, used 'on such projects as Agena B satellite vehicles and advanced versions of Polaris ballistic missiles' cost about one-tenth as much as a new unit (Waterson 1964).

In a more recent example of such ingenuity, Williams Cos. converted its obsolete natural gas pipelines into an underground corridor for fibre-optic cable. In doing so, it saved itself the need to purchase right of way and dig trenches. In areas where the pipelines were still in use, the above-ground cable was still protected since contractors rightly feared disturbing the cable for fear of explosion. 'The next best thing to being inside a pipeline,' Mr. Williams says, 'is to be alongside a pipeline.' Today Williams Telecommunications Group owns 4600 miles of cable and 800 miles of microwave line. Presently, Williams Cos. is the fourth largest U.S. telecommunications service after AT&T, U.S. Sprint, and MCI (Pentzinger 1988).

These examples are worth mentioning only because this sort of creativity, which is common in a traditional environment, is so rare among modern corporations. These examples also serve to remind us that our references to the ageing of the capital stock do not refer to a chronological age of plant and equipment. I have only been using the term 'ageing' as a short-hand expression to refer to the economic dangers that occur when an economy relies on old plant and equipment for *inappropriate* uses.

In conclusion, the utilization of old equipment may just as well signify creativity as an economic failure. The Lockheed generator and the Williams Cos. pipeline discussed above represents excellent examples of such creativity.

The Elimination of Productive Capacity

While we might applaud the elimination of phantom capacity, the cleansing of the economy comes at a high cost. To begin with, when firms shut down factories or go out of business altogether, innocent people bear much of the burden. Workers and their families suffer. So do people who count on the business of the plant or of the laid-off workers. To make matters worse, plant closings are typically clustered in economic crises, when the unemployed have the least opportunity of finding alternative employment.

Ideologues of laissez faire counsel us to trust in market forces. We are supposed to believe that when the crises cut a swath across the economy, that the efficient firm that falls will be the exception that proves the rule.

The evidence from the economic decline suggests a less sanguine understanding of crises, suggesting that crises are not precise affairs. Instead, they attack both sick and healthy firms.

During the early post-war period, prosperity in the United States was synonymous with manufacturing. As profits fell and wages rose during the decline, U.S. business began to shed much of its domestic manufacturing activity.

We have seen that the ageing of the capital stock set the stage for what came to be known as the de-industrialization of the U.S. economy. Few, if any observers, realized that the foundation of the manufacturing system in the United States was crumbling beneath their feet.

Part of the problem was the growing penetration of imports, but de-industrialization can occur in a closed economy without any exports or imports. Hanns-Joachim Rustow has convincingly shown how easily competitive pressure can create a wave that indiscriminately engulf a growing portion of the capital stock.

The key to Rustow's theory is the enormous productivity differentials between older and newer capital goods. Rustow's data suggest that newer capital goods are commonly four to five times more productive than many of the older capital goods (Rustow 1978, p. 413; Rustow 1967).

Normal competitive processes can become so powerful that they force industry to lower prices. Some less efficient factories cannot continue at that price level. As these firms exit their industries, they make competition become even more intense, creating a cumulative downward spiral of prices leading toward an economic collapse.

As firms scrap their weakest operations, they lay off workers. By reducing their payrolls, business also reduces demand for its products. Consequently, the underlying crisis intensifies as the domestic market narrows, creating more pressure for further de-industrialization. The least productive remaining operations now become vulnerable and eventually fall out of use, leaving another layer of unproductive plants ready to suffer the same fate.

Once this process begins, markets have no inherent force to reverse its course, striking efficient as well as inefficient firms. Rustow's model suggests that this pattern of de-industrialization might be a normal outcome in a market economy.

The Big Question

We have seen strong competitive pressures can produce two different outcomes. In a healthy economy, competition can lead to capital deepening. In a fragile economy, it can result in a cumulative de-industrialization.

Economists typically make confident pronouncements about the inevitability of one outcome or the other. In truth, we lack any scientific method for determining whether or not a particular economy is destined to collapse.

We can say that we have few examples of a thriving laissez-faire economy. When we review the course of British history, we find that from the seventeenth century on, a series of imperial conquests supported British development. Certainly, the leaders of the American Revolution believed so, as did Irish and Indian nationalists.

Once the United States freed itself from its bonds with England, it refused to trust its future to market forces. Instead, the government developed a system of tariffs, bounties, subsidies, and grants of monopolies to foster economic development. More importantly, the economic strength of the society rested on the products of slaves rather than a system of free markets.

The election of Andrew Jackson in 1828 represented a challenge to this system of government market controls. Much of the success of his administration came from his policy of expelling native Americans from their land to make way for more cotton production. Once his vice-president, Andrew Van Buren, succeeded him, the economy suffered a severe depression.

With a couple of decades, the Republic party was formed with the intent of protecting domestic industries and artificially promoting development. The Civil War created strong demand for domestic products. With this stimulus, as well as the generous federal grants to the railroads, the economy flourished. Giant industrial developments emerged, employing the most modern technologies.

The productive capacity of these new industries overwhelmed the purchasing capacity of the United States market by the 1870s. As cut-throat competition became common place. The resulting depression was as severe as the Great Depression of the 1930s.

Industry banded together to protect itself. Companies formed trusts, cartels and monopolies. Government leaders as well as most economists applauded their efforts. In fact, the American Economic Association was founded in order to provide a platform for anti-laissez faire ideas (Perelman 1991).

This mistrust of the market lasted until World War I broke out. After the war, the United States elected Calvin Coolidge, its most laissez faire president since Andrew Jackson. Soon thereafter, the Great Depression swept across the economic landscape.

This brief survey of the history of market economies does not offer much hope that competitive forces will automatically restore economic health. We do know that these forces can and do ravage the economy from time to time. What reason do we have to be confident that this pattern will not repeat itself?

6 Finance, the Falling Rate of Profit and Economic Devastation

Finance and the Momentum of the Decline

In this chapter, we shall investigate the contribution of financial forces to the economic decline. Although most economists hold that financial institutions are designed to channel resources into productive activities, they do not necessarily do so. Indeed, the financial pressures associated with a decline can lead investors to withhold their funds from productive activities while they dissipate their funds in investments of the most wasteful sort.

The ease of discovering opportunities for producing useful goods and services fluctuates with the state of the economy. While an economy prospers, opportunities for productive behaviour may abound, but over time some capitalists, seeing how others have prospered, overreach themselves, getting caught up in their own overconfidence.

Generally, after a boom has persisted for a while, more and more capitalists become swept up with this general feeling of optimism. Lacking strong competitive pressures, managers become profligate with the resources of their firms. They also foolishly sink money into losing projects. The cumulative effect of their eventual disappointments finally reverses the economic momentum, leading to a recession or even a depression.

In short, a boom provides some incentives to invest in productive activities. Over time, the same conditions that led to productive investment become perverted and lure people into wasteful economic practices.

A depression also leads capitalists in two different directions. Depressions create forces that can lead to renewed prosperity. For example, as an economy sinks lower and lower, capitalists' expectations eventually recede. Moreover, as bankruptcies wipe out old debts, business may have an easier time turning a profit. In addition, many capitalists require less profit to make them feel successful after a prolonged recession.

As a result, many economists conclude that recessions naturally contain the seeds of their own recovery. Consequently, they should not last very long or become very severe. Some little accident, say a good harvest or a new invention, can swiftly turn their pessimism to optimism, sending the economy on an upward course once again.

Most people reject the economists' easy confidence about the self-correcting nature of a recession. The popular belief that war is necessary to shake an economy out of a depression reflects an intuitive understanding of the difficulty of reversing the downward momentum of an economic decline. Is this popular view something more than a common economic superstition or is it grounded in reality?

Keynes demonstrated long ago that popular opinion may be closer to the truth than conventional economic dogma. With a particular mix of conditions, an economy can easily become stuck in a stagnant position rather than responding with a round of capital renewal. We can take Keynes' argument one step further, arguing that the existing financial incentives may not just be insufficient to take the economy back to prosperity; they may actually reinforce the decline.

Once an economy begins a downward spiral, factories fall into disrepair, while firms try to cut costs in ways that impair their long-term efficiency. Workers suffering long-term unemployment lose some of their job skills (see Cross 1987). This deterioration of both the capital stock and the workforce contributes to a further decline in the rate of profit. Consequently, once the economy falls into one of these perverse patterns of stagnation, then indeed only a dramatic event, such as a war, may be capable of moving the economy onto a different course.

Now we shall discuss why an initial fall in the profit rate, which normally accompanies a recession, can contribute to a further decline in the rate of profit.

Falling Profits and Rising Interest Rates

Profits are the most important incentive in a market economy. A combination of forces responsible for the economic decline, including the prolonged absence of strong domestic competition, the ageing of the capital stock, recent pressure of strong international competition, as well as the poor treatment of labour, have resulted in a fall in the rate of profit. As the rate of profit falls, most capitalist agents must make adjustments. Unfortunately, these adjustments have exacerbated the decline.

To begin with, the fall in the profit rate gives more power to financial interests. In any economy, some investors will be highly leveraged. In this section, we will include both individuals and firms as investors, even if these firms are industrial operations.

In general, just before the end of a boom the proportion of investors who are highly leveraged will be at a peak. These investors need a certain cash flow in order to stay afloat because they have substantial outstanding credit obligations. A temporary reduction in profits threatens to push the highly leveraged investors into bankruptcy. The difference between their needed cash flow and their profits is not that great, even in good times. Such is the nature of leverage. Consequently, a small swing in profit margins suffices to cause these investors to suffer irreparable losses.

Since profits in general fall during recessions, most investments will earn less during recessions than they did when the economy was more prosperous. For these investors, the failure to earn as much profit as they expected triggers a desperate search for funds no matter how much interest they have to pay. These investors reason that, if only they can weather the storm, the return of good times will allow them to salvage at least some of their positions.

Typical firms will also feel financial pressure from a falling rate of profit since they ordinarily use some of their profits to finance investments. As the average rate of profit falls, many firms lack the financial resources to cover much of their investment needs. Recall that competitive forces will tend to pressures firms to renew their capital stocks at such times to remain competitive.

In short, firms are likely to become dependent on borrowed money when the rate of profit falls. To make matters worse, with the fall in the rate of profits, a major source of investment funds shrinks. This rise in the demand for funds coinciding with a drop in the supply of available funds can put upward pressure on real interest rates.

All these forces taken together contribute to a perverse situation: as profits fall, investors can demand a higher rate of profit on their money. Because the cost of money is escalating, firms become disinclined to commit their funds to any project that fails to promise a high rate of return. All these forces combine to reinforce the conditions that made the rate of profit decline in the first place.

Profits are falling, yet investors are looking for a rate of profit that is so high that it precludes all but a very few capital investment projects. This situation parallels our earlier discussion of the paradox of the Chinese Wall.

The Falling Rate of Profit and Increasing Risk

While the economy is prospering, many investors can find what seem to be relatively safe investment opportunities that promise to return what they consider to be a reasonable rate of profit. When the economy sinks into a recession and average profits fall, the majority of investors typically will become less optimistic. They will respond to the deteriorating economic conditions by cutting back on their investment and just holding on until the economy improves.

The highly leveraged investors, whom we discussed earlier, will behave differently. We can compare these investors to a gambler at a race track. All but one race has been already run. Imagine that the gambler has run up substantial debts. The gambler needs to win a certain amount of money to pay off the bookie.

Suppose that the gambler feels relatively confident that a particular horse stands a good chance of winning. The gambler expects that placing money on that horse can provide the required amount of money if the horse wins the race. As the time of the race approaches, more and more people come to agree with the gambler. As the odds on the horse become more unfavourable, betting on it will no longer pay enough money to satisfy the gambler's need. The only way the gambler can win enough money will be to bet on a horse that seems to have a lesser chance of winning.

In this example, the gambler shifts to a more risky investment in order to meet the objective of a fixed reward objective. A minority of investors behaves similarly. These investors shift to more and more risky investments in order to maintain the possibility of obtaining the same level of rewards. Because of the greater level of risk these investors take on, a higher share of them will fail, intensifying a sense of economic desperation and fueling the decline.

The proportion of investors who behave like the gambler will depend upon a complex set of circumstances. The greater the level of debt, the more investors will feel compelled to opt for more risky investments. In addition, investors who feel that other investors are unduly pessimistic will also be more likely to increase the risk.

If this tendency to increase risk becomes common enough, it can compound the economic decline. In this case, the quest for profits will not keep the economy on a steady path of economic growth. It can just as likely lead the economy into stagnation, or even worse – a downward spiral.

The tendency toward increasing risk is associated with a parallel tendency toward increasingly speculative investments. After all, successful speculation can bring rates of return many times more than what a firm can earn from building a new factory. Moreover, the investor can earn these speculative profits quickly rather than waiting for years as would be the case in building a factory. Consequently, an increasing share of the national resources have been devoted to speculation rather than productive activities. The revolution in finance has reinforced the increasingly speculative nature of the U.S. economy.

What Banks Ideally Do

Now let us take a moment and consider the role of banks. Most people think of banks as money lenders, but they do not exactly lend money. At least, they do not generally lend their own money in the way a pure money lender would. Instead banks lend other people's money, but they do not just lend other people's money. They also lend money that they create by giving credit to the banks' borrowers.

People give banks their money to let them lend it out because they believe that banks can place this money more effectively than they could do themselves. Although the banks charge a higher rate than they give their depositors, banks promise depositors a fixed return and the right to withdraw funds almost at will. Banks then lend these funds to borrowers for long periods of time, for years or even decades.

If some adversity should make the borrower unable to repay the loan, the bank still has to obligation to honor its debt to the depositor. In effect, the bank shields the depositor against uncertainty. John Maynard Keynes summed up this arrangement, explaining that 'the banking system . . . interposes its guarantee between its depositors who lend it money, and its borrowing customers to whom it loans money wherewith to finance the purchase of real assets' (Keynes 1931a, p. 151).

Ideally, banks can lower the risk of lending money out for the long-term while borrowing for the short-term because of bankers' superior efficiency in making loans. In part, bankers can be efficient because they enjoy economies of scale. They can pool large amounts of money together, simplifying the business of borrowing money. Instead of a giant borrower having to go to the trouble of soliciting a few dollars here and a few dollars there, it can go to a bank and borrow significant amounts of money on the spot.

Bankers' supposedly superior knowledge of the business of lending money represents a much more important source of potential efficiency in lending money. You or I might have difficulty in evaluating the creditworthiness of a corporate borrower. We might not understand the intricacies of its business or the soundness of its books. Bankers specialize in ferreting out crucial information about such subjects. Armed with this specialized knowledge, banks are willing to accept the risk of borrowing short and lending long.

Given the advantages that a bank enjoys in the business of lending funds, depositors are willing to deposit their money into the bank rather than lending money directly. The banks repay them a portion of the money that they earn from lending it out. The rest of the banks' earnings, over and above their operating expenses, goes to the bank as profits.

In reality, the banking system is not quite as neat and tidy as this idealized version. To begin with, individual depositors have no guarantee that the bank is a safe place for their funds. If depositors lack the wherewithal to evaluate the creditworthiness of the typical corporation, how can depositors judge the creditworthiness of banks that lend money to such borrowers.

Bankers traditionally attempted to reassure their depositors by exuding a sense of trust. They would do their business in solid looking buildings. They would dress conservatively. Still, the individual depositor would have no way of penetrating that facade until it was too late.

Once people come to doubt the efficiency of any particular banker, they will rush to withdraw their deposits. This reaction is dangerous for the bankers, because they have most of the money tied up in loans, which will not be repaid until sometime in the future. Relatively few depositors can quickly strip the bank of all of its cash.

If a run hits a single bank, it can borrow from other banks to tide it over until confidence returns. When people become skeptical about the health of banks in general, such temporary borrowing becomes impossible. The history of the nineteenth and early twentieth century is replete with frequent runs on the banking system.

Even the Federal Reserve System, which was supposedly capable of supplying banks with sufficient funds to stop banking panics, was unable to stem the tide when it faced its first serious panic during the Great Depression. The government had to close the banking system to keep depositors from withdrawing all their funds.

On the Regulation of the Financial System

Once the Great Depression set off a wave of bank runs, the government saw no alternative to insuring the deposits of small investors as part of the Glass-Steagall Banking Act of 1933. In addition, the Federal Reserve Code contained a provision, known as Regulation Q, which prohibited banks from offering interest on checking accounts and limited the rate of interest paid on savings deposits. Savings and loans could pay a slight premium over what banks could offer under Regulation Q. Typically, economists regarded Regulation Q as an unnecessary intrusion into the banking system, although it made sound sense.

Even Adam Smith, the patron saint of laissez faire – certainly an economist who was not known to favour active intervention in economic affairs – observed more than two centuries ago, that putting a ceiling on interest rates can benefit society. He explained:

> If the legal rate of interest . . . was fixed so high as eight or ten per cent., the greater part of the money which was to be lent, would be lent to prodigals or projectors, who alone would be willing to give this high interest. Sober people, who will give for the use of money no more than a part of what they are likely to make by the use of it, would not venture into the competition. A great part of the capital of the country would thus be kept out of the hands which were most likely to make a profitable and advantageous use of it, and thrown into those which were most likely to waste and destroy it. When the legal rate of interest . . . is fixed but a very little above the market rate, sober people are universally preferred, as borrowers, to prodigals and projectors. (Smith 1776, II.iv.15, p. 357)

In other words, when interest rates are high, the people who borrow are likely to be those who are speculating on risky projects.

More recently, Joseph Stiglitz and Andrew Weiss added a valuable institutional insight to Smith's observation. They noted that selling credit differs from selling other goods. When merchants sell shoes, they expect to be paid in full. In contrast, banks do not receive their payments until a later time once the debt becomes due. As a result, they face a risk of default. Lacking full information about the credit worthiness of their potential customers, banks fall back on a variety of screening devices, including the interest rate that consumers are willing to pay.

The logic of insight of Stiglitz and Weiss flows from the realization that the borrower who is willing to pay an extremely high interest rate typically has a greater than average chance of being a poor interest risk (Stiglitz and Weiss 1981). Stiglitz has also observed that a higher interest rate can actually encourage a borrower to take more risks (Stiglitz 1987, p. 18).

In light of this situation, Stiglitz and Weiss, writing during the dawn of financial deregulation when interest rate regulations were still more or less in effect, assumed that banks would not necessarily lend to those who offered to pay the highest return. Instead, they would ration credit to the most creditworthy customers, thereby protecting the integrity of the banking system.

Dr Smith was correct in his analysis, but Regulation Q was incapable of maintaining the soundness of the banking system since banks soon found a way to circumvent it. After all, from the banker's perspective, Regulation Q limited the growth potential of the banks, especially because other borrowers, especially the government, generally paid higher rates of interest.

Indeed, large depositors could usually earn more interest buying Treasury bills than they could by depositing their money in banks. Unfortunately, as competition in the banking sector heated up, forcing banks to pay more for their money, banks ceased to behave in line with the theories of Stiglitz and Weiss. Instead, they actively sought out those who would pay the highest rates. The results were disastrous.

The Circumvention of Bank Regulation

During the 1960 recession, as the rate on Treasury bills fell, the banks saw an opening. Since the rewards from purchasing government securities were no longer so much higher than placing money in banks, the large banks tried to entice major corporations and other large depositors to place their money in the banks. Toward this end, First National City Bank invented the Certificate of Deposit. The bank offered to pay between a quarter and a half a percent above the going Treasury bill rate. Moreover, it created a market in which corporations could buy and sell their CDs if they needed cash in a hurry (Mayer 1974, p. 200).

Soon, CDs were everywhere. During the early 1960s, California thrifts attempted to attract as much money as possible to meet the demands of the California building boom by offering interest rates that were a tad higher than the going rate. They even advertised these rates in East Coast newspapers.

These banks and thrifts did not seem to realize that these moves, which were profitable in the short-run, eventually would make them more vulnerable. Under an effective Regulation Q, banks would mostly serve depositors who were satisfied with low rates of return. These depositors would not quickly shift their funds around in search of the highest interest rate. Such depositors would offer banks a stable base.

Remember that this stable base was important. Banks have to commit funds for a long period of time. If depositors remove a relatively small portion of their funds from a bank, they can drive it to insolvency. Once banks come to depend upon interest-sensitive depositors, they have to continue to offer a high rate of return to keep their depositor.

This need to pay a high interest rate requires the banks to earn a high rate of profit, in effect transforming them from conservative institutions into something resembling Adam Smith's prodigals and projectors. The evidence of this vulnerability was not long coming.

Remember that the CDs were attractive, only because the Treasury bill rate was depressed in 1960. As Treasury bill rates rose between 1962 and 1966, the Fed systematically raised the maximum interest rates that banks could pay under Regulation Q so that the CD rates remained under the maximum that Regulation Q permitted. By 1966, when the Vietnam War had begun to fuel inflation, which raised the rate of interest on Treasury bills well over rates permitted and above (Mayer 1990, pp. 34–5).

California savings and loan banks soon learned about the danger of depending on hot money. In 1966, Franklin National Bank, began advertising CDs of $1,000 denominations, carrying an interest rate higher than the legal maximum on savings accounts. Within a month, Franklin had sold $420 million worth of CDs. So much of this money came from the California thrifts, that these withdrawals nearly ruined these thrifts (ibid., p. 204). Once the crisis passed, the industry forgot any lessons that it might have learned from the experience.

Franklin National Bank, however, soon returned to the vortex of financial instability (see Wolfson 1988). In 1972, Fasco International purchased 21.6 per cent of Franklin, bringing the bank into the vast and complex international empire of Michele Sindona, a shadowy figure with ties to the Vatican, International intelligence agencies and right-wing extremists. Sindona had looted about $15 million from Franklin, according to a criminal indictment (ibid., p. 96).

Under Sindona's direction, Franklin suffered significant losses speculating in bonds and foreign currencies in 1973 (ibid., pp. 76–8). By May 1974, national bank examiners criticized the soundness of loans equivalent to 62 per cent of its total capital (Spero 1980, pp. 71–2). Soon thereafter, Franklin, once the twentieth largest bank in the United States, became insolvent.

The regulators of the financial system failed to learn the lesson of the failure of Franklin National Bank. To begin with, Franklin could appear to be sound, even after it had experienced crippling losses, because it posted fictitious profits on transactions with some of Sindona's European banks (Spero 1980, pp. 81–2). In addition, because of Franklin's dependence on volatile, interest-sensitive accounts, it had an inducement to invest in speculative transactions that could turn a quick profit.

The dealings of the Franklin National Bank were atypical. Nonetheless, the rest of the banking system was coming to resemble Franklin National Bank more and more. For example, at the end of the World War II, banks in the United States were extraordinarily healthy. Banks primarily held relatively riskless Treasury bills. By 1984, the commercial banks held only 13.0 per cent in government financial assets and an additional 30.0 per cent in the assets of other U.S. government agencies (Minsky 1986, pp. 71 and 74).

The dangers of increased risk were even more extreme for the savings and loan industry. Although Franklin disappeared, the savings and loan problems did not. Depositors continued to search for the highest possible returns. Withdrawals threatened savings and loan banks because they had frequently committed themselves to 30 year mortgage loans. Many competed by offering higher and higher interest rates on CDs of their own. This strategy was self-defeating since they could not increase the rates on their existing home loans.

The government responded by allowing the thrifts to engage in the same sort of speculative practices that bankrupted Franklin, reasoning that only the higher profits from risky behaviour could save the industry. The lifting of regulatory oversight opened the door to a torrent of fraud and financial abuses. With the collapse of the markets for junk bonds and commercial real estate, the thrift industry approached bankruptcy.

Today, estimates of the ultimate cost of the savings and loan bailout range from one hundred to five hundred billion dollars, but the estimates keep escalating over time. In addition, because of the vast sums of money that the bailout consumes, the government must curtail spending on health, education, and infrastructure.

The savings and loan crisis burdened society in other ways. For example, so-called zombie thrifts which were on the verge of bankruptcy offered incredibly high rates for CDs to stave off their inevitable fate. This practice significantly raised interest rates. For example, one study estimated in 1990 the federal government had to spend an extra $73 to $266 billion just to compete for funds with the zombies (Shoven, Smart, and Waldfogel 1992).

New Dimensions to Speculation

The speculative investments of banks suggest a further dimension to undermining of the regulatory structure of the banks. The Federal Reserve requires that banks keep a specified portion of their loans in reserves, either as cash or as deposits with the Federal Reserve Bank. For the banks, these reserves partially represent a loss of earning potential. Yes, they know that they need to set aside some money to take care of a few unusual withdrawals, but not nearly as much money as the Federal Reserve requires.

When banks get access to money through CDs, they do not have to set aside reserves the way they do with ordinary deposits. They have developed other, even more elaborate, ways of raising money without any reserve requirements. These manœuvres make the banking system more vulnerable.

Even more dangerously, banks can take on speculative risks without the need to have immediate access to cash by taking on commitments that do not appear on their balance sheets. Many banks do not have to hold reserves to tide them over if this sort of speculation turns sour.

For example, Franklin speculated on the fall of the British pound, the French franc and other foreign currencies relative to the dollar. When the dollar fell instead during the first quarter of 1974, Franklin lost $33 million (Spero 1980, p. 86).

Today, Franklin's dealings are small potatoes. Consider the example of Citicorp. At the end of 1990, it held $1.2 trillion worth of outstanding contracts in futures, forwards, swaps and options on interest rates and foreign exchange alone, up from $980 billion the previous year, and six times its assets. Its credit risk exposure on these contracts was $24.5 billion, up from $14.1 billion the year before (Anon. 1991a). Citicorp was already strained by its holdings of bad loans. Should the company experience a run of bad luck in these speculative holdings, its net worth could quickly turn negative.

When banks speculate in risky investments with volatile money, the financial system becomes fragile. Small events can push a couple of banks into insolvency, weakening confidence in the others, leading ultimately to a panic of the first order.

Finance and the Decline of U.S. Manufacturing

These financial excesses did not arise spontaneously. The fall in the rate of profit was the driving force in the financial revolution, which, in turn, reinforced the effect of the falling rate of profit by reinforcing the insidious process of de-industrialization.

Let us begin our discussion of this subject by putting the financial system into perspective. During the Golden Age, most individual investors favoured blue chip stocks, which they held for long-term appreciation. Similarly, institutional investors behaved conservatively, perhaps because of the lingering memories of the aftermath of the excess that preceded the Great Depression. As late as 1952, commercial banks, mutual savings banks and insurance companies held over 69 per cent of all outstanding

U.S. corporate bonds. Life insurance companies alone held 58 per cent of all outstanding U.S. bonds, but only 1.5 per cent of U.S. corporate stocks (Lazonick 1989; citing Goldsmith 1958, pp. 224–5).

Over time, institutional investors became the dominant traders in the U.S. stock exchange. They began to hold an increasing share of nation's equities. As profits from industrial activity declined, institutional investors attempted gain an edge by quickly shifting their funds around in terms of short-term profits. Since they turned their holdings over so quickly, institutional investors accounted for a disproportional amount of stock purchases and sales.

In 1960, institutional investors owned 17.2 per cent of the value of the shares and accounted for 24.3 per cent of the volume of trading on the New York Stock Exchange. After 1960, these powerful financial institutions became more aggressive. Mutual funds led the search for higher yields. Rather than hold their funds with a stock that promised significant long-term growth, the mutual funds tried to shift their funds about rapidly in anticipation of short-term movements in the market. Their success led pension funds to follow a similar strategy.

By 1982, institutional investors owned 24.3 per cent of the value of all shares and accounted for 83.8 per cent of the volume of trading. The turnover of shares on the New York Stock Exchange rose from 12 per cent in 1960 to 54 per cent in 1985. Trades of over 10,000 shares increased from 3 per cent in 1965 to 52 per cent in 1985 (Lazonick 1989; citing Light and Perold 1987, p. 108).

As a result, money managers have been exercising increasing control over corporate policy. This new breed of institutional investor is too impatient to wait for long-lived capital investments to turn a profit. If, at any time, management fails to show a healthy rate of return, these money managers can threaten to organize a corporate takeover to oust management. Corporate executives, fearful of this threat, must struggle to keep profits high.

Even when managers realize that longer-term investment projects were in the best interest of the company, they understood that the stock market would only reward those who made the next quarterly earnings report as favourable as possible. Managers who invested for the long-term could cause a decline in their company's stock and even perhaps their own dismissal.

Andrew Sigler, Chief Executive Officer of Champion International and chair of the Business Roundtable's Corporate-Responsibility Task Force, dramatically explained how this change in the investment climate affected corporate investment strategy. He declared:

The problem is deciding who the hell the corporation is responsible to. I can't ask my shareholders what they want. 75 per cent of Champion is owned by institutions, and my shareholders change so fast I don't even know who they are. We're owned by a bunch of index funds. Who votes for an index fund? Some damn mathematical formula votes your stock. (cited in Sloan 1985)

Within this environment, managers cannot invest in the sort of long-run project that could improve the economic health. As a result, profits suffer, intensifying the pressure for short-term financial gains.

The Falling Rate of Profit and Capital Renewal

Earlier, we saw that strong competitive pressures are instrumental in inducing firms to renew their capital. Falling profits inevitably accompany increased competition, yet, we are making the case here that falling profits have undermined competitiveness.

We should not be surprised at this apparent paradox. Throughout this book we have seen how economic categories such as competition and depression have a contradictory nature. The notion of profits is also fraught with contradictions, preventing us from making any simplistic pronouncements about the influence of the falling rate of profits.

Some whole industries will indeed wither under the strain of intense competition and financial pressure. Some firms will rise to the challenge, developing improved competitive practices.

Generalizations about how firms will respond to the decline are difficult, but we do see the broad outlines of one change in the financial structure, which makes optimistic outcomes less likely. During the Great Depression, many banks viewed their relations with their clients as long-term affairs. Doing what they could to help their clients through the hard times would ensure profitable future business relation once the depression had past.

Within the current financial structure, the relationship between firms and their creditors is decidedly short-term. Banks no longer have any reason to give special treatment to individual businesses. Even if the current managers would feel a sense of gratitude, management changes so fast that this good will can become worthless in short order.

As a result, banks now aim for the highest possible short-run return. Consequently, they are less likely to finance renewal of the capital stock. In addition, many firms are too saddled with debt to be able to consider investing for the long-term.

Corporate management, stymied from investing in their firm's future, often joined with the institutional investors in actively seeking quick financial returns. They found that they could acquire assets cheaper by buying other firms than by investing in their own productive capacity.

The government also promoted the process of de-industrialization by abandoning all pretense of an effective anti-trust policy as part of its fanatical pursuit of deregulation. As a result, firms became virtually free to speculate in the takeovers of other firms rather than making their own lines of business more efficient. In this sense, industry began to resemble a division of the financial sector.

The Inefficiency of Corporate Takeovers and Leveraged Buyouts

During the 1980s, a wave of corporate takeovers swept across Wall Street. Of the 100 largest mergers and acquisitions on record prior to 1984, 65 occurred between 1981 and 1983 compared to only 11 before 1979. During 1981–4, 45 takeovers involved more than $1 billion (Varian 1988, p. 3).

A small group of takeover specialists accumulated fabulous fortunes through leveraged buy outs. The takeover artist would offer stock holders much more money than their stock was worth on the open market. This offer would be contingent on the firm selling high-yield junk bonds to finance the purchase. After the completion of the deal, the typical firm would be left with a huge debt (see Bruck 1989).

For a while some of the largest firms were immune from such pressures. Lacking confidence to invest in productive projects, they would sit on large accumulations of cash, waiting for the right opportunity. For example, the editors of *Business Week*, in commenting on a 1985 story about Exxon's massive cash surplus, worried, 'The sight of so many companies sitting on bags of cash they cannot find profitable use for raises some distressing questions about the vitality of the U.S. economy' (cited in Magdoff and Sweezy 1985, p. 11).

Business Week was justified in its concerns. Why, with so many unmet needs in society, could the major corporations not find anything useful to do with their cash hoards?

Eventually, the takeover movement reached such proportions that even managers of the largest corporations took measures to restructure their corporation in much the same way that the takeover would have done by buying back stock and taking on debt.

Michael Jensen proposed that this accumulation of debt was in the public interest. According to his argument, the paid managers who normally run large corporations do not have their stockholders interest at heart. They use the corporate resources for their own personal aggrandizement. Given their comfortable situation, they fail to take measures that would make the firm efficient. For Jensen, 'the debt created in a hostile takeover (or takeover defence)' means 'that it cannot continue to exist in its old form' because it 'creates the crisis to motivate cuts' (Jensen 1988, p. 30).

In other words, the takeover would push the firm to the edge. The firm would have to struggle to earn enough cash to cover its debt payments. Should it fail to do so, creditors would compel the firm to declare bankruptcy. Given this necessity to be efficient, managers would rise to the challenge, making the firm competitive.

Jensen's theory has some merit. Certainly, corporate management in the United States had a poor record on many counts. Managers often used corporate resources to finance corporate jets, boats and limousines, elegant offices, and corporate retreats that did little to contribute to corporate efficiency. In this respect, Jensen is correct.

The question remains, did the corporate restructuring make management more efficient? To begin with, consider Jensen's notion that the creation of a crisis atmosphere will be conducive to greater productivity. As Amitai Etzioni noted, 'A large body of research shows that under stress people's decision-making becomes less rational' (Etzioni 1988, p. 73).

Consider the case of Exxon again. After all, Jensen often used the petroleum industry as a prime example of the benefits of restructuring, might have difficulty reconciling his theory with the actual outcome (Jensen 1988, p. 33). According to a writer for the *Wall Street Journal*, Exxon's workers were stretched thin, but not necessarily in a manner that was conducive to efficiency. Several fires broke out in the company's largest refinery in Baytown, Texas because Exxon was too tight fisted when it came to winterizing pipes against freezing, even though they were warned beforehand (Sullivan 1990).

In fairness, we should note that some of Exxon's negligence predated its restructuring. In New York City, where a pipeline ruptured, local and federal officials charged that Exxon was negligent and irresponsible in ignoring a faulty leak detection system for 12 years (Welles 1990).

Many observers do believe that restructuring was ultimately responsible for Exxon's most famous mishap, the tragic oil spill of the Exxon Valdez. Alaskan officials allege that Exxon's systems for training and monitoring employees were ineffectual. The company's own tanker captains complained of heavy crew cutbacks and other unsafe operating procedures. Numerous former Exxon executives claim that Rawl's cost cutting system, as one put it, 'created an accident prone system' (Welles 1990, p. 75).

Financial Capital versus Industrial Capital

Even where financial restructuring was not an issue, the need to raise profits enough to satisfy money managers proved to be another important factor in promoting de-industrialization. In this environment, when U.S. firms attempted to turn their cash to a profitable use, more often than not they neglected productive investment, thereby reinforcing the decline.

Rather than attempting to make plants more productive, managers often took the easy road of shutting them down. Indeed, a good deal of anecdotal evidence suggests that a number of plant closings were related to what seems to be a sharp increase in the expected rate of return on existing plant and equipment, rather than a competitive crisis. For example, during a pre-negotiation meeting between General Electric and the representatives of workers at its Fort Edward capacitor facility in 1982, 'local management announced that while heretofore 9 percent profit had been considered satisfactory, GE nationally was then insisting that all of its facilities show at least a 12 percent profit margin in the future' (Bloch 1983, p. 30).

David Broderick, Chairman of the Board of United States Steel, told a Pittsburgh audience that the huge Dorothy Six operation would not be worth saving unless it were able to earn 18 to 20 per cent profit each year (Morse 1985, p. 175). Bluestone and Harrison cite a similar example:

> The Herkimer [New York] plant, producing library furniture, had been acquired by Sperry Rand in 1955. The plant had made a profit every year except one through the next two decades, and yet Sperry Rand decided to close the plant [in part because it] was not yielding a 22 percent profit on invested capital. That was the standard used by this conglomerate management in determining an acceptable rate of return on its investments. (Bluestone and Harrison 1982, p. 151)

The 1977 annual report of Genesco, Inc. provides further evidence of increased corporate profit requirements: 'In all cases, the ultimate consideration was: 'Does this operation have the potential to produce a 25 percent pre-tax return on assets employed'' (cited in Bluestone and Harrison 1982, p. 151).

The behaviour of Genesco and Sperry Rand might increase measured profits and even productivity. By eliminating all but the most profitable operations, the average performance of the residual divisions may be higher. Indeed, de-industrialization has raised measured productivity. In fact, the 10 per cent decline in manufacturing employment accounted for an estimated 36 per cent in the recorded improvement in labour productivity in the United States between 1979 and 1986 (Dertouzos *et al.* 1989, p. 31).

Like the quick pay-back rule, de-industrialization might raise the profit rate while depressing total profits if the process were confined to a single country. Because firms such as General Electric can shift their operations from one economy to another, they need not experience any adverse effects from de-industrialization. For the multi-national sector, profits as well as profit rates can increase.

No wonder de-industrialization seems to be a fact of life in the midst of the economic decline! The long-run consequences of this pattern of cutting back investment altogether in the face of stepped up competitive pressures rather than investing in capital deepening presents a frightful prospect for the U.S. economy. If too many firms begin to follow the same strategy, they can create a cumulative down-turn, which can hurt just about every business.

A third factor also increases the momentum of de-industrialization. Many firms threaten to shut down in an effort to coerce labour into accepting lower wages or reductions in employee benefits (as we saw before). Such threats are effective only to the extent that they are credible. Occasionally, firms must actually follow through with their threatened shut-downs in order to make workers comply with the demands that the firms make.

Business Week denounced this tendency to increase productivity by shutting down plant and equipment, instead of making it more efficient. It called such behaviour, 'slash-and-burn cost-cutting.' It cited Stephen S. Roach of Morgan Stanley and Co., who warned that it is a 'really dangerous . . . recipe for total capitulation of market share' (Pennar 1991).

This pattern of de-industrialization reverberates throughout the economy. The United States is now importing more and more of its manufactured goods, such as automobiles and consumer electronics. On an aggregate level, the U.S. share of world manufacturing exports fell from 17.1 per cent in 1966 to 11.7 per cent in 1986, a drop of more than ⅔ (Epstein 1990–91, p. 33).

In this manner, we foolishly trudge along the road to ruin.

The Unproductive Labour Dissipated in Corporate Takeovers

This wave of corporate takeovers did not come cheap. For example, in 1984, the three investment banking houses involved in the Gulf-Socal merger earned a total of $63 million for their efforts (see DuBoff and Herman 1989, p. 123). The *Wall Street Journal* predicted that, if Texaco's

$9.89 bid for Getty Oil would be successful, four investment banking firms would be expected to share a record $47.1 million in fees. The largest single fee was expected to go to Kidder, Peabody, and Co., which was slated to receive $15 million for advising the Sarah C. Getty Trust. Salomon Brothers, which declined to confirm it, was slated to receive a reported $4 million. First Boston was Texaco's advisor. For 79 hours work, it was to receive $10 million or $126,582 an hour (Anon. 1983).

As time went on, the merger fees grew apace. By 1988, Campeau's $6.6 billion bid for Federated Department Stores produced $200 million in fees. "It's called the Wall Street Fair Employment Act of 1988,' said a lawyer involved in the deal (DuBoff and Herman 1983, p. 123; citing Labaton 1988).

Lawyers have also fared quite well from the boom in corporate takeovers. The *Wall Street Journal* recently reported that one in nine U.S. lawyers was a millionaire in 1986 (see Gray 1986). Of course, not all these lawyers owed their wealth to takeovers, but a good number did. For example, the firm of Wachtell Lipton earned $20 million in just two weeks advising Kraft on its $12.9 billion attempt to take over Philip Morris Cos. This works out to about $5000 an hour assuming virtual round-the-clock work by a couple of dozen lawyers (Adler and Cohen 1988).

Individuals who handed the finances of takeovers also prospered. In 1987, over and above his normal salary and the millions and millions of dollars that he earned using inside information for trading on his own account, Michael Milken received a bonus from Drexel Burnham Lambert amounting to an astounding $550 million (Stewart 1991, p. 208). Some commentators noted that this bonus exceeded the profits that McDonald's, the 65th largest corporation in the United States, earned at the time (Abelson 1989). Such huge merger fees naturally induced financial agents to go to great lengths to construct mergers and takeovers.

Young people understood that even lesser figures in the financial world still earned astronomical amounts. For example, a well-placed Wall Street employee could make several hundred thousand dollars within a couple of years after graduating from college. In light of the enormous amounts of money changing hands, highly-educated, young people directed their energies and ambitions to participating in speculative activities rather than productive activities. For example, 40 per cent of the 1986 graduating class of Yale applied for a job at First Boston Co. (Lewis 1989, p. 24)!

Of course, we need to give our youth more constructive incentives. Countries with a high share of engineering college majors grew faster than those who train their youth as lawyers and financial experts (Murphy, Shleifer and Vishny 1991).

Unproductive Labour and the Hobbling of the Corporate Sector

Although the takeover movement proved to be a bonanza for the financial and legal sector, the herculean efforts to change the structure of corporate ownership did nothing to enhance the productive capacity of our economy. Instead they dissipated much of the remaining vitality of the productive sectors of the economy.

Certainly, excessive amounts of money went to financial transactions or legal manœuvring rather than productive investment. Texaco's failed takeover of Getty Oil, mentioned above, is a case in point. Penzoil sued Texaco, claiming it had a prior agreement with Getty. Between 1984 and 1988, Texaco and Penzoil waged an intense legal battle. Penzoil eventually won. The court initially awarded it a judgement that was worth more than $10 billion, but the ultimate settlement was a paltry $3 billion. Even so, an enormous amount of resources was dissipated in the process.

Not unexpectedly, the value of Penzoil's stock rose and Texaco's fell, since Texaco had to give so much money to Pennzoil. What is noteworthy was the imbalance in the movements of the respective stocks. The fall in Texaco's value exceeded the rise in Penzoil's. The combined value of the stocks in the two firms fell by about $21 billion.

Could the legal fees consumed in this struggle explain this loss? Probably not. Texaco's legal fees accounted for about $250 million, but the after-tax cost would be only $165 million (Cutler and Summers 1988). The combined productive capacity of these two firms shrunk so much because management squandered time and energy in legal manœuvres rather than devoting their resources to make their firms more efficient.

The direct financial costs and the dissipation of talent associated with the assembling of these financial deals were but a small part of the damage created by the wave of mergers, takeovers, and leveraged buyouts. This speculative frenzy left many corporations saddled with so much debt that they could no longer function effectively.

Perhaps nothing typifies the perverse association between the financial sector and the decline in manufacturing than the relationship between Burlington Industries and the great investment banking house, Morgan Stanley. Asher Edelman, a famous corporate raider, was threatening to take over Burlington, the largest textile company in the United States. Morgan offered to rescue Burlington, which it then purchased for $2.2 billion (Anders 1990).

Morgan itself put up only $46 million of the total cost. Bank loans and later junk bond offerings provided the rest. In return, Morgan got all of the Class A voting stock and control of the company. In the first 50 days of owning the company, Morgan collected $87 million in fees, almost double what it paid to gain control.

Morgan charged $29 million for 'advising' Burlington on how to be bought by Morgan. Morgan received $8.24 million for underwriting $12.5 million of junk bonds in Burlington. Its fees equaled 4 per cent of the value of the acquisition, well above the 3.02 per cent that was the average charged for floating junk bonds. Of course, Burlington could not complain. After all, Morgan controlled the board of directors.

For the first two years after the buy-out, Burlington laid off 900 headquarters workers and sold 20 businesses to help repay its debt. The divestitures generated $1 billion in cash, which Burlington used to pay down debt. The work force ultimately shrunk from 44,000 in 1986 to 27,000. Consequently, the company ceased to be the leader in the textile industry.

Faced with dissatisfaction from Burlington's management, Morgan devised an Employee Stock Ownership Plan (ESOP) to put stock into workers' hands. The plan required that Burlington pay $175.3 million in dividends to its equity holders, chiefly Morgan. Morgan's dividend of $56 million equalled more than half of the bank's entire 1989 third quarter dividend. Although Morgan profited from this transaction, it added another $212.5 million junk bond debt on the textile company, making Burlington's total debt reach $1.6 billion.

The ESOP plan purchased 2.9 million worth of total outstanding Class A voting stock, 36 per cent of the total outstanding. Wilson Ellis, an Atlanta Banker who helped create the ESOP, said that Morgan Stanley insisted that the ESOP pay $50 per share, five times what Morgan had paid for the stock only two years earlier. After a month of 'aggressive negotiation' the plan agreed to purchase the stock at $37.80 a share.

Morgan relied on the appraisal firm, Houlthan, Lokey, Howard and Zukin, to help it determine a fair value for the stock. This same firm had aided Morgan in appraising Burlington in 1987 when it purchased the company at $10 per share. Presumably, the appraisers felt that Morgan had added substantial value to the firm. Soon after the formation of the ESOP, the same appraisal firm valued the employee's stock at $14.62, less than half the price the employees paid 14 months earlier. Again, Morgan's association was so valuable, once it distanced itself from the firm, the value of the stock plummeted.

The Morgan affair left Burlington in shambles, but Morgan, Stanley profited handsomely. All in all, Morgan, Stanley collected $176 million from the captive textile company, including more than $120 in investment-banking fees and another $56 million in a special dividend. In addition, the company collected a windfall on its sale of its stock. Quite a return on its initial investment of $46 million!

Financial Services and Unproductive Labour

Even though everybody hates paperwork, we keep doing more and more of it. Most of us consider paperwork to be unavoidable. In contrast, he corporate sector enthusiastically concentrates its attention on profiting by unproductive paperwork, while shutting down its factories. These financial manipulations consume an enormous amount of time and energy. Just consider the quantity of paper that has to be shuffled to complete one of the epidemic of giant corporate takeovers which swept over the United States during the 1970s and 1980s.

In the case of Dupont's $7.5 billion takeover over Conoco, First New Jersey National Bank had the responsibility of overseeing the deal. W. E. Buchsbaum, DuPont's vice-president for finance said that First Jersey was beset with 'great, great volumes of paperwork' and 'a lot of mismatches between what people said they would tender and the stock certificates that have arrived'.

The result: the bank worked from 9 a.m. till midnight. The work overflowed into the bank cafeteria. On weekends, 16 branch managers and some people from DuPont had to work on the paperwork for this transaction (Anders 1981).

Had some government regulation required the same quantity of paperwork, statements of outrage would pepper the business press. Political candidates would campaign with anecdotes about the imposition of excessive paperwork. Instead, such transactions were held up as examples of capitalist efficiency.

The upsurge in this sort of financial transactions was a consequence, as well as a cause, of the economic decline of the U.S. economy. As the decline took hold, we saw that people, as well as firms, turned to speculation rather than producing useful goods and services because they saw relatively little promise from productive activities.

The wave of corporate takeovers that occurred during the 1970s and 1980s caused only part of the explosion of financial transactions. Much of the unproductive financial work is unrelated to corporate restructuring. Increasingly fewer people in the United States perform work that results in useful goods and services. Just look at the Yellow Pages of your phone book under the headings of real estate. Compare the number of firms on these pages with the number of places that are employing people who are engaged in the production of useful goods and services.

Fred Moseley lays the bulk of the blame for the falling rate of profit on the escalation of unproductive labour and unproductive investment (Moseley 1991). He estimates that a little more than one half of the workers in the U.S. economy in 1980 were doing productive labour (Moseley 1988; see also Wolff 1987). This estimate is conservative on two counts. First, all evidence suggests that the share of unproductive labour has been increasing over time (see Dawson and Foster 1981).

Moseley himself estimates that the ratio of productive to unproductive labour rose by about 70 per cent between 1950 and 1980 (Moseley 1988; see also Moseley 1991, p. 113). The increasing pace of de-industrialization of the 1980s obviously accelerated the trend. By 1987, Moseley calculates that the ratio had almost doubled its 1950 level (Moseley 1991, p. 121). I know of no indication that this trend toward an increasing share of unproductive labour is tapering off.

Second, much of the productive labour is actually used to produce goods and services that are used for activities that are unproductive. For example, even though paper workers are productive, their work is dissipated unproductively when paper is consumed up in the course of corporate takeovers. A goodly number of paper workers or people assembling computers, through no fault of their own, end up producing more paper work rather than contributing to our standard of living.

Christopher Niggle illustrates the growing importance by analyzing the growth of financial services in the U.S. economy. He notes that the ratio of the book value of financial institutions to the Gross National Product of the United States was 78.4 in 1960. In 1970, it was only still 82.9. By 1984, it reached 107.4 (Niggle 1988, p. 585).

Niggle suggests a second ratio to demonstrate the enormous growth of the financial sector: the ratio of financial institutions' assets to the assets of non-financial institutions. In 1960, this ratio was 0.957, meaning that the financial and the non-financial sectors were about equal. By 1970, the financial sector had overtaken the non-financial sector, boosting the ratio grew to 1.094. By 1983, the dominance of the non-financial sector had driven the ratio to 1.202 (ibid.).

Finally, Niggle reports the growing size of the part of the economy known by the acronym, FIRE, which stands for Finance, Insurance, and Real Estate. In 1960, the FIRE sector represented 14.3 per cent of the Gross Domestic Product of the United States; in 1980, 15.1 per cent. The 1983 share of the FIRE sector was 16.4 per cent, meaning that within these mere three years the relative importance of the FIRE sector grew by more than it had in the previous 20 years (ibid.).

Just consider the explosion in transactions in the stock market. In 1960,

766 million shares were traded on the New York Stock Exchange. In 1987, 900 million shares changed hands in the average week. More shares were traded on the lowest volume day in 1987 than in any month in 1960. More shares were traded in the first 15 minutes of 19 and 20 October 1987 than in any week in 1960 (Summers and Summers 1989).

The stock market represents a relatively small share of all financial speculation. Speculators trade many different types of assets. For example, they buy and sell derivative securities, such as stock futures, which provide the rights to buy or sell stocks at a set price a specified time in the future. Organized markets in such derivative securities did not even exist in 1970. Today, the value of trades in stock futures exceeds that of the trades in stocks themselves. Trade in the New York Stock Exchange averages less than $10 billion per day; government bonds, $25 billion; daily trade in foreign exchange averages more than $25 billion. Trade in index options equals that of stock futures (ibid.).

How much do all these transactions cost? The combined receipts of firms on the New York Stock Exchange was $53 billion in 1987 – an enormous sum considering that the total income for the entire corporate sector in the United States was only $310.4 billion. Beside these direct costs, corporations whose stock is traded in organized markets devote much time and energy to efforts to influence the markets. For example, chief executive officers of major corporations commonly spend a week or more each quarter just telling their corporate story to security analysts. In addition, both individuals and firms spend a great number of resources monitoring their portfolios, acquiring information about securities or making investment decisions. If these supplementary costs are one-half as much as direct payments to security firms, then the cost of operating the securities markets was greater than $75 billion (ibid.).

Notice how the various symptoms of the decline reinforce each other. The falling rate of profit produce the pressure for deregulation and lax government regulation as well as a scramble for higher and quicker returns from investments. These factors perversely combine to create an environment in which corporations put more energy into shuffling paper than producing useful goods and services.

The commitment of an increasing portion of our economic energies into unproductive channels makes the decline more severe, putting more downward pressure on the rate of profit. Here again we see a problem (excessive paperwork) resulting from another problems, such as deregulation, which itself is response to still another problem – the falling rate of profit.

Tracking the Elusive Profit Rate

We have already alluded to the fall in the rate of profit, but it is more serious than Table 1.2 in Chapter 1 indicates. However, despite the pervasive importance of profits, economists have no precise method for measuring them. Even worse, economists cannot measure either of the two numbers – total profits and total capital – the ratio of which determines the rate of profit.

Let us begin with total profits. We get our estimate of profits from reports from accountants (see Fisher and McGowan 1983). Unfortunately, accounting is not an exact science. Accountants can adopt a number of different procedures for calculating profits. Obviously, they will choose the method that is most beneficial to the firm.

In an economy where taxes depend on profits, firms profit by keeping the books in a way that makes their earnings appear to be as small as possible. For example, accountants can choose different ways to depreciate their capital goods. Large firms, perhaps because they can afford more sophisticated accounting personnel, typically adopt accounting methods that make their profits appear smaller than they would be if these large firms used the same accounting methods that smaller firms do (Salamon 1985, p. 497). Accountants also have to keep in mind how the books will appear to investors and lenders.

All these considerations will distort accounting measures of profit. These complications pale beside a more serious complication: time. Accounting profits indicate merely how much the firm earned in the most recent period. In general, a firm's profits today depend on actions, which it took in the past. In the case of long-lived capital goods, investments made many years ago may influence profits today. In this sense, profits are backward-looking, but backward-looking profit rates give us only part of the picture.

In particular, policies which maximize immediate profits might be detrimental to the long-run health of the firm. For example, no firm would engage in research and development if it were trying to increase its accounting profit; that is, its profit today. Research and development might not pay off for years and years.

As a result, economists use a conception of profits that is forward-looking. They argue that, to be successful, a firm must try to earn a stream of profits over an extended period of time into the future (Jordon 1989; Fisher and McGowan 1983). Economists think in terms of what they call, 'the discounted present value of profits.' These profits are forward-looking.

Economists calculate the discounted present value of profits by adding up this year's profits plus a fraction of next year's expected profits plus a smaller fraction of the following years expected profits, etc. The decreasing fractions reflect the fact that money tomorrow is worth less than money today.

Of course, these expected future profits are impossible to measure. To begin with, they depend on what will happen in the future. In addition, we have no scientific method for choosing the appropriate fractions by which we discount these future profits. As a result, when we talk about profits, we are stuck with the data that we have despite its glaring inadequacies.

We have similar problems to face in coming to grips with the measurement of the capital invested, the second number used in the calculation of the profit rate. Even if we knew exactly how much every firm has spent for its capital – and we don't – we would have to add together old and new buildings and equipment of all kinds. Over time some of this stuff wears out and becomes obsolete. Some depreciates quickly. Some does not. We have no adequate method to take account of that depreciation process.

Consider what has been happening with computer prices over the last decades. The original purchase price of a typical ten-year-old micro-computer is many times what a comparable system would cost today. So economists develop formulae to tell them how much of its original value a three-year-old computer retains today. These formulae are very crude and very rigid. For example, they assume that all office machinery (not just computers) will depreciate at some pre-ordained rate.

To make matters worse, accurate calculation of depreciation must take into account what will happen in the future. Notice that these formulae are predetermined based on past accounting practices. They ignore the fact that changing economic conditions or a shift in technology can dramatically alter the value of capital in unexpected ways.

Consider a company that began making slide rules just before pocket calculators first became inexpensive. The market values of the capital owned by the slide rule firm would probably depreciate relatively slowly – perhaps in line with the formula – until people began to realize that the factory's product would be obsolete. Suddenly much of its capital stock would be worthless, except for what it could bring in scrap. Nonetheless, according to the depreciation formula, this capital still would retain considerable value.

All economists recognize the inadequacies of this method of handling the data, but it is all we have to work with so far. Hopefully, the innumerable errors will average out, but we have no reason to believe that they will. The data may be reasonably good in stable economic conditions, but they will be of substantially less value in turbulent periods. For this reason, we have to be wary of relying on our usual economic measures during times of rapid transition.

I am convinced that the strong competitive pressures that are sweeping across the U.S. economy are wiping out a good part of the existing capital values. This destruction of capital values is more substantial than what the fall in the estimated rate of profit indicates.

The Dual Nature of the Profit Rate

The lure of future profits help to determine economic conditions by serving as an incentive to guide business behaviour. Both investors and managers know that, to the extent that capitalists succeed in taking advantage of economic opportunities, they will earn profits. Conversely, the profits that firms collect today are, at least in part, a consequence of general economic conditions, which as Keynes understood, are determined to a large extent by the previous profit-seeking actions of all other capitalists taken together.

This particular dualism often causes markets to move along destructive paths. An ideal economic system would include a feed-back mechanism capable of signalling economic agents that their actions are either socially beneficial or socially harmful. Markets contain no such feed-back mechanism.

Individual capitalists only take their own profits into account when they make an economic decision. They have no reason to consider the indirect effects of their actions on overall economic conditions, nor whether these effects will be socially beneficial or not.

Of course, our subjective feelings will influence some of what we consider to be socially beneficial. Products, which provide enjoyment for one party, often inconvenience another. We can think of any number of examples. Another person's smoking, loud music or fast cars can make life less pleasant for many of us.

Still, as a rough approximation we can say that, to the extent that capitalists do pursue socially useful activities, the market leads to desirable outcomes. To the extent that capitalists direct their energy into channels that are socially wasteful or even destructive, society is the loser.

We can identify some economic activity that leads to no social gains. For example, speculation is a wasteful activity. For the most part, my speculative gains are only possible if you or somebody else experiences a corresponding speculative loss (although some economists make the questionable assumption that speculators perform an useful service by absorbing risk for those who wish to avoid it).

Although we cannot all agree on which particular firms are behaving in a positive or a negative manner, we can conclude that if firms predominately are acting productively then our lives are more likely to be better off than if they are making wasteful decisions. The nature of economic decline does suggest that non-productive activity is becoming the rule rather than the exception.

Our earlier discussion of the forward-looking and backward-looking nature of profits suggests one aspect of the contradictory nature of profits. This discussion reminds us that profits are both a cause and an effect of economic conditions.

7 De-industrialization and the Rise of the Service Economy

Post-industrial Vision

Should we be concerned about the elimination of manufacturing jobs and the rise of service employment in the United States? In the past, economists as far apart as Karl Marx and Adam Smith regarded services as decidedly unproductive. Recently, the attitude toward services has shifted. Despite the prevalence of low-wage service employment, some modern economists welcome the replacement of manufacturing employment as a positive development.

We take care in referring to the growth of the service sector with a grain of salt. The category of services, as such, has no fixed meaning. In fact, the service industry is not really an industry at all. Instead, it is a catch-all category that includes all businesses that do not fall within the established industrial categories (see Hill 1977).

Even if we knew what services were, we would still have difficulty identifying service workers. In general, we could count workers as service workers if they work for a company that supplies a service. For example, a person writing an owner's manual in an automobile factory is an industrial worker. A person writing a program for a computer software company is a service worker. Since the program is recorded on a floppy disk or a tape, both the automobile manual and the program take on a physical form. Both the manual and the program can help the purchaser make better use of a piece of hardware, yet we count only one of these workers as a service worker.

This approach to counting service workers becomes more problematical when jobs are shifted from one sort of business to another. For example, manufacturing firms can make arrangements to contract for services that their own employees would otherwise perform. Still, by any measure, the service sector has indeed expanded by replacing manufacturing in the United States.

We can identify three different classes of writers who find the replace-

ment of manufacturing by services to be benign. The first group wel-
comes de-industrialization because it supposedly heralds the dawn of
a new post-industrial, service-oriented stage of economic development.
The second group says that the previous examples of de-industrialization
constitute nothing more than a collection of isolated incidents; that de-
industrialization is not occurring or, if it is, it only represents a normal
rearrangement of economic world-wide activity. In either case, we have
no reason to worry. The third group contends that de-industrialization may
be a normal, but long overdue cyclical correction, which is clearing away
obsolete and inefficient capital stock.

First, we will turn to the theory of a post-industrial economy, which
has permeated popular culture (Bell 1976; Toffler 1990; see also Frankel
1987). This theory holds that the United States will inevitably retire from
manufacturing and specialize in the creation of intellectual property and the
performance of sophisticated services, while the less developed economies
do the less rewarding work of building the material goods that we enjoy.

These writers are correct in so far as they point out the obvious fact that
service work has been displacing manufacturing. With rates of profit in
domestic manufacturing operations sagging, firms in the United States have
been expanding their investment in service industries, rather than investing
in manufacturing.

Although the meaning of the service sector as a whole is fuzzy at best,
these theorists of post-industrial society write as if service employment
were synonymous with highly skilled professional work. In this sense, the
post-industrial visionaries correctly grasp that we cannot build a successful
economy on a strategy of low wages. Their mistake is to delude themselves
into proceeding as if the majority of the new service jobs were professional
service jobs, rather than low-wage, dead-end service jobs, which neither
draw upon nor develop workers' skills.

The Hollow Economy and the Dangers of Post-industrial Utopianism

Given the ever greater reliance on low-wage service employment, we
can dismiss out of hand the unrealistic, utopian vision of post-industrial
society. The U.S. economy will not prosper simply by moving beyond
manufacturing, yet a number of major businesses are behaving as if the
United States can build a future on a service economy. According to
Business Week

In industry after industry, manufacturers are closing up shop or curtailing

their operations and becoming marketing organizations for other producers, mostly foreign . . . . The result is the evolution of a new
kind of company: manufacturers that do little or no manufacturing are
increasingly becoming service oriented . . . . In contrast to traditional
manufacturers, they are hollow corporations. Unchecked, this trend will
ultimately hurt the U.S. economy. (Anon. 1986a, p. 57)

For example, Lewis Galoob Toys, Inc., a corporation listed on the New
York Stock Exchange, has only 115 employees. Everything depends on
contracts with other corporations. Nike is depicted in similar terms.
Business Week cited Raymond E. Miles, Dean of the School of Business
Administration at the University of California, Berkeley, 'What you'll
have is a switchboard instead of a corporation' (ibid., p. 64). *Business
Week* concluded:

By shifting production overseas or shopping abroad for parts and
components, U.S. companies are whittling away at the critical mass
essential to a strong industrial base. (Ibid., p. 60)

Business Week also cited a warning by Jack D. Kuehler, senior vice-
president of International Business Corp., who warned that U.S. companies
will gradually become less adept at understanding how new technology
can be exploited and eventually 'lose the ability to design' (Anon., 1986,
p. 61).

We cannot afford to be complacent about this trend. The concentration of unskilled service jobs promises to accelerate the process of
de-industrialization. Professional service jobs are not a substitute for
manufacturing. If anything, professional service jobs are the result of
successful manufacturing activities.

For example, when Britain was a major industrial power, British banks
were pre-eminent. Similarly, U.S. banks were world leaders during the
ascendancy of U.S. industry. Today, seven of the ten largest banks are
Japanese. Only one U.S. bank, the wounded Citibank, ranks among the
ten largest banks world-wide (Glasgall 1988).

Because few U.S. banks have the size to compete in the global market
for financial services, they have closed about 100 foreign branches since
1985 (Mandel and Bernstein 1990, p. 62). Within the U.S. economy,
foreign-owned banks are gaining more and more market share. Many of
the more skilled management positions in these banks will remain in the
home office outside of the United States.

Over and above the loss of high-skilled jobs to foreign competitors within the banking sector, the decline of the banking sector presents an ominous specter for manufacturing. For example, Stephen S. Cohen, director of the Berkeley Roundtable on the International Economy, says, 'We are witnessing a big decline in financial services and what might be the beginning of a steep decline in computers' (Mandel and Bernstein 1990, p. 70).

Let us put Mr Cohen's warning into perspective. Financial services are not actually in decline in the United States. The opposite is true, as we have seen. However, the United States might be losing its dominance in the financial service industry as the off-shore banks and other foreign owned financial services come to play a more important role.

Suppose that Japanese banks continue to displace U.S. banks and that they centralize their operations in Tokyo. The main offices may purchase their computers in Tokyo. After all, these mainframe computers by themselves are of little value to most large businesses without specialized software. Purchasers of computers want close support from suppliers. As a result, the U.S. computer industry could well lose a major market, depriving it of the economies of scale necessary to remain competitive, thereby reinforcing the dependence on low-wage service employment.

The example of decline of the U.S. banking industry illustrates the fallacy of the notion that the United States will ride the service industry to a prosperous future. The erosion of manufacturing undermines the demand for skilled service sector jobs – in this case, banking – and the subsequent diminution in the banking sector threatens future markets for manufacturing – in this case, computers.

As the demand for computer services in the United States fails to keep pace with the world-wide rate of growth, U.S. computer manufacturers, lacking the close contact with the needs of its customers, will find themselves at a competitive disadvantage. This reciprocal action is a perfect example of the downward spiral of the economic decline.

The Electronics Industry in the Age of Post-industrialism

The direction of the semi-conductor industry represents an even more ominous threat to the U.S. economy. Many new innovative semi-conductor companies avoid any involvement in fabricating their products. Instead, these so-called 'fabless' companies farm their production out to mostly foreign producers, which they refer to as foundries.

In effect, these companies are beginning to transform the semi-conductor industry from a manufacturing industry to a service industry, just as the post-industrial utopians would have them do it. According to one industry insider, James Koford of LSI Logic, 'Silicon Valley and Route 128 are worlds of intellectual property, not capital equipment and production. Most of the employees of U.S. high technology live in southeast Asia' (cited in Kenney and Florida 1990b, p. 237). Some like George Gilder applaud this arrangement, arguing that these companies will maximize their profits by specializing in the design of computer chips (Gilder 1989).

The move toward fabless corporations poses a serious danger for the U.S. semi-conductor industry. In the process of manufacturing for U.S. firms, these foreign foundries gain a great deal of expertise. Before they can begin production for the U.S. contractors, these firms must develop the expertise in transferring the technology from blueprints to the production equipment. They must also develop an understanding of product specification, machinery and the engineering required to assist with manufacturing setup and quality control (Florida and Kenney 1990a, p. 135). These tasks require considerable sophistication.

After years of subcontracting-out their manufacturing, the U.S. semi-conductor industry has been losing touch with the manufacturing process. As a result, the industry has had to establish manufacturing partnerships to gain access to state of the art Japanese production technologies. For example, Intel, the giant semi-conductor firm, is unusual because it manufactures its own chips, although many of its operations are abroad. Even Intel is not immune from the symptoms of a lack of hands-on experience. *Business Week* reported that:

> Intel had to call in Malaysian experts from its Penang factory to help set up the chip assembly line at an automated chipmaking factory it started building in Arizona three years ago. None of its U.S. employees had that expertise any longer. (Anon. 1986a, p. 62)

The semi-conductor industry is famous for groups of employees with strategic information defecting to begin their own firms. Fortunately for Intel, the Malaysian experts were still in its employ at the time. Had these Malaysian experts followed the example of the U.S. counterparts, the lack of manufacturing experience might have wounded Intel.

More recently, even Intel had to look outside of its own circle of employees for assistance in manufacturing. Not long ago, Intel established a joint venture with NMB Semiconductor to market the Japanese company's memory chips and to acquire NMB's production technology for use in Intel's manufacturing. A top Intel executive said, 'One big thing we get out of this is to have them help us with automated factories' (Florida and Kenney 1990a, p. 135).

Similarly, Advanced Micro Devices recently sold one of its Texas factories to Sony for $55 million. As part of the deal, Sony will upgrade the plant and use it as a base to teach AMD executives and engineers about Japanese production technology (ibid.).

Can the semi-conductor industry ensure that this form of de-industrialization stops with the transfer of manufacturing abroad? The off-shore companies that now produce these semi-conductors can easily learn to reverse engineer and clone these products. The Japanese already followed this route. Other economies are intent on emulating the Japanese in this respect. For example, Hyundai now actively seeks semi-conductor subcontracting business (ibid.).

The long-term prognosis for the U.S. semi-conductor industry is not optimistic. As people elsewhere learn to manufacture semi-conductors, they will also learn to design them. In general, in the words of a *Harvard Business Review* article:

> [B]usiness cannot design in a vacuum. It cannot exploit new technol-ogies if it has no chance to apply them . . . . The fact is, design and manufacturing are linked. A company that subcontracts its manufactur-ing to foreigners will soon lose the expertise in design and the ability to innovate because it won't get the feedback it needs. (Markides and Berg 1988; cited in Kenney and Florida 1990a, p. 134)

Perhaps more than any other industry, the semi-conductor producers attempted to follow that post-industrial path. It seems to be a dead end. Instead of concentrating on the desirable, service-related aspects of the industry, the semi-conductor producers seem to be on their way to ceding the entire field to foreign competition.

To make matters worse, offshore competitors are beginning to apply the same techniques to some service jobs that made their manufactur-ing so efficient. The software industry is a case in point. Presently, Japanese programmers produce 50 to 70 per cent more code than U.S. programmers with one-third to one-half as many errors based on a sam-ple of 40 large U.S. and Japanese computer systems (Cusumano 1991, p. 53).

In the not too distant future, the seemingly invincible U.S. software industry may suffer the same fate as the U.S. automobile industry. (ibid., p. 5). According to Michael Cusumano, Toyota had 50 per cent more efficiency [than the U.S.] in 1965, but the cars were terrible.' He predicts that the same will occur in software (Schlesinger 1990).

So much for the vision of a post-industrial utopia!

Services and High Technology

While we may accept that manufacturing is an essential part of a successful economy, we should not conclude that the service industry is inherently bad, any more than it is inherently unproductive. Instead, we must avoid generalizations about services in general. The fate of an economy will depend more upon the precise mix of spillovers and linkages associated with the industries that it retains rather than the proportions of manufacturing and services.

If we want to analyze the impact of the growth of the service economy, we must take account of the specific services that are performed as well as the context in which they are performed. For example, we have already suggested that service productivity growth has been more rapid in countries such as Germany, Japan and France, where services are paid more relative to manufacturing than they are in the United States. We pointed to the possibility that a higher remuneration of European and Japanese labour is responsible for a significant amount of the superior growth of labour productivity in services in those economies.

Historically, concern about services was not based on the low productivity of service jobs. Instead, economists singled out manufacturing jobs because of the nature of the effects of manufacturing employment on the rest of the economy. They believed that manufacturing was more desirable than services because manufacturing jobs appeared to promote the further growth of manufacturing jobs as well as service employment, while services did not appear to induce manufacturing jobs to grow to the same degree.

For example, the bicycle industry, which was centered in the Detroit area, created a pool of skilled workers and suppliers that gave this region a head start in developing the automobile industry. As the automobile industry evolved, it stimulated the spawning of a multitude of suppliers, including suppliers of services. Few service industries created such 'agglomeration economies' (Malecki 1991, p. 84), since services tend to be so labour-intensive.

To make matters worse, along with the increasing size of the service sector, the U.S. economy has been devoting more and more of its capital stock to services rather than industry. True, some services are indeed very capital-intensive, but they are the exceptions rather than the rule. True, the growth of the aggregate capital stock in the service sector has outpaced the expansion of employment in services, making the service sector more capital-intensive over time. However, manufacturing has become even more capital-intensive.

At the end of 1948, over 80 per cent of the net stock of private non-residential structures and equipment was used in agriculture, mining, construction, manufacturing, transportation and public utilities – what we now call, the 'primary sector' (Magdoff and Sweezy 1990, p. 5). Harry Magdoff and Paul Sweezy observe that, between 1978 and 1988, the net stock of manufacturing capital rose 21 per cent. The net stock of capital used in finance rose by an astounding 80 per cent (Magdoff and Sweezy 1990, p. 8; see also Magdoff and Sweezy 1985).

By the end of 1988, the net stock of private non-residential capital found in the primary sector represented less than 50 per cent of the total net stock of private non-residential equipment and structures. Not unexpectedly, the relative position of each of these primary industries declined steadily throughout the past few decades, in part, because the capital investment, which could have made these industries more productive, went to the service sector (Magdoff and Sweezy 1990, p. 5).

Figure 7.1 compares the change in capital per worker in the manufacturing sector with that of the service sector between 1960 and 1985. We see that the relative intensity of capital in manufacturing compared to that of services was only half as great in 1985 as it was in 1960. In conclusion, although some service jobs are capital-intensive, high-technology jobs, most service jobs are found in the stagnant low-skill, low-wage economic backwaters.

Besides generating the demand for auxiliary suppliers, investment in manufacturing seems to be particularly advantageous, because it creates spillovers of knowledge, such as we described before. The companies that benefit from this new knowledge need not be in the same industry. For example, large Japanese companies use microelectronic innovations to develop cutting-edge consumer electronic goods. They then apply these same innovations from consumer goods to high-technology products. For example, they used the technology for Watchman televisions to improve the displays for laptop computer displays (Florida and Kenney 1990a, p. 145).

The Demand for Services and the Proximity to Manufacturing

In making the case that manufacturing jobs are more advantageous than service jobs, we are implicitly introducing proximity into the argument. Proximity is relevant because services generally use less specific tools than manufacturing does. For example, typewriters may not differ much from office to office, but manufacturing frequently requires quite specialized equipment. The more specialized the equipment, the more valuable close

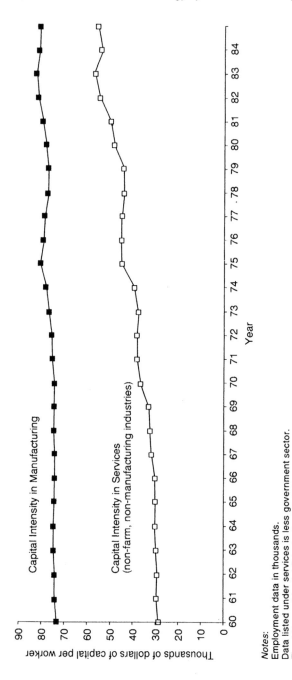

Capital Intensity in Manufacturing

Capital Intensity in Services
(non-farm, non-manufacturing industries)

Year

Thousands of dollars of capital per worker

Notes:
Employment data in thousands.
Data listed under services is less government sector.
Fixed Nonresidential Private Capital: Millions of 1982 dollars.

Sources:
U.S. Department of Labor. 1989. Employment and Earnings. Vol. 36, No. 9 (September), p. 43, Table B-1 'Employees on Nonagricultural Payrolls by Major Industry, 1937 to Date.'

U.S. Department of Commerce, Bureau of Economic Analysis.1987. Fixed Reproducible Tangible Wealth in the United States, 1982 – 1985 (Washington, D.C.: U.S. Government Printing Office), pp. 166 – 7.

Figure 7.1   Capital intensity in services and manufacturing

contact with suppliers will be. For this reason, manufacturing is more likely to spawn new employment than services.

I suspect that even service industries using high technology generally require more generic manufactured inputs than manufacturing industries do. For example, companies that produce fiber-optic cable may not have to tailor them closely to the particular needs of the firms that purchase them. If this is the case, for the producer of fiber-optic cable that intends to sell to one of the great communications companies of today, the cost of maintaining close connections with this handful of giant communications companies would not be great, so long as these companies could provide unambiguous specifications for the fiber-optic cable that they purchase.

Unlike the example of the early Detroit automobile industry, an expansion of services in one city may be less likely to create many new jobs in the vicinity, especially now that the economy is more global in scope. Consequently, spillovers from services are not necessarily contained within a specific region.

If the potential benefits from spillovers from manufacturing accrue to all firms in an industry, regardless of their location, we should be indifferent about whether a particular manufacturing process occurs in Detroit or Dakar. While Japanese firms produce the Watchman, U.S. firms could apply this same knowledge to the production of laptop displays if proximity did not matter.

Unfortunately, the current Japanese dominance in laptop displays suggests that proximity is indeed important. The fact that the same firm produces both the laptop display and the Watchman is not an issue here as we saw earlier in our discussion of the semi-conductor industry. The linkage could just as easily connect separate firms in a given locale rather than two divisions within the same firm.

Theoretically, services as well as industry can create spillovers of information, as well as other linkages. For example, the growth of communications services necessitates a corresponding growth in the production of goods, such as fiber optic cables or satellites. In addition, the growth of modern communications services allows for a greater delocalization of economic activity.

In this sense, manufacturing jobs still might have an advantage over services in terms of stimulating a particular region, since manufacturing typically requires a wider array of complementary inputs than services do. Nonetheless, any generalization about this relationship should be taken skeptically.

In the case of other service industries that are more typical than fiber-optic communications, suppliers that are in close proximity to their potential customers may very well have a competitive edge. Even so, the growth of such an industry is unlikely to provide the same degree of beneficial spillovers that manufacturing has traditionally provided.

While the previous examples suggest the importance of manufacturing, they should also remind us of the pitfalls in generalizing about the nature of services. At the very least, we should be careful about blindly asserting that service jobs are more or less productive than other types of employment. Some services can be highly productive. Other service work is unproductive, or at least, not particularly productive.

Even to the extent that the post-industrial utopians are correct that we shall see an ever greater demand for highly trained, professional service work, the future would not likely be as rosy as they have predicted it to be. We should not be concerned with the growth of services as such, given that services can be both capital-intensive and highly productive. People in the United States, however, do have good reason to be worried about the sort of services that are becoming dominant in the U.S. economy. As the conditions of temporary workers suggest, productivity will continue to suffer so long as workers have reason to be resentful about the baneful conditions of their employment.

Does De-industrialization Exist?

At last, we are ready address the other two theories that dismiss concerns about de-industrialization as alarmist. We can begin with the theories of those economists who dismiss the reality of de-industrialization altogether. They insist that manufacturing is not decreasing at all. They take heart in the fact that U.S. business still employs about the same number of people in manufacturing as it did in the late 1960s, although substantial changes have occurred during this period (Lawrence 1983).

In part, this controversy revolves around semantics. The term 'de-industrialization' unfortunately conjures up a misleading image of an economy without any manufacturing whatsoever. Obviously, manufacturing has not disappeared from the United States.

Although, we must be careful not to overstate the extent of de-industrialization, nobody can deny that the cumulative impact of plant closings throughout the nation has been devastating. Today, the region that once represented the core of this manufacturing prosperity is now popularly known as the Rust Belt.

Still, those who are skeptical about the existence of de-industrialization are partially correct. Manufacturing employment has indeed remained relatively steady, but at the same time the relative importance of manufacturing employment has fallen considerably, because total employment in the country has expanded by about 50 per cent since the late 1960s (United States President 1989, p. 357). Indicative of the declining importance of production workers, the Bureau of Labor Statistics of the United States Department of Commerce found that by 1983, the U.S. had one sales worker for about every production worker (Bils 1990).

Similarly, those skeptics, who question the existence of de-industrializat-ion, are correct that government data actually did show that manufacturing as a share of total domestic output remained relatively steady between 1973 to 1985, but we must put this fact in perspective. The share of manufacturing has remained steady even though the amount of labour involved has steadily declined because the average manufacturing worker is so much more productive than the typical service worker.

However, these same skeptics fail to take account of the fact that the government data are misleading because they overstate the share of manufacturing in the aggregate economy for they fail to account for the imports used in production. Instead, the government merely tallies the final output of the manufacturing sector (see Mishel 1988).

This procedure is unwarranted because manufacturing in the United States is relying more and more on imported inputs. Consider the example of the automobile industry. Suppose we want to use the government's measure to test for de-industrialization in that industry. During the 1960s, an automobile produced in the United States consisted largely of domes-tically built parts. Today, an automobile assembled in the United States contains a enormous number of imported parts.

If the number of cars produced remained constant, we would find no evidence of de-industrialization because the government data would just count the value of final product, the car, as a measure of manufactur-ing activity in the economy. In reality, the car represents considerably less domestic manufacturing than it did when the parts were produced domestically.

Other data indicate also indicate a decline in the domestic content of U.S. manufacturing – meaning the value of work performed in the United States as share of the total value of a typical manufactured item. For example, finished goods are an increasing share of United States imports while their share of exports has remained virtually unchanged in recent years (Hickok 1991, p. 27).

The failure to account for the falling domestic content of manufacturing in the United States masks the process of de-industrialization. As a result, the government data may not show that manufacturing activity has been shrinking even though, in reality, it has been declining.

Now let us discuss a position that some economists have taken, that de-industrialization may well exist, but it does not necessarily represent the failure of American corporations. Recall how the Vietnam War paved the way for an exodus of business from the shores of the United States. First to leave were labour-intensive industries, such as textiles and footwear. Based on the success of these pioneers, heavier industry followed suit. Business no longer had to respond to higher wages with better technology; it would suffice just to leave in search of cheaper wages.

While manufacturing in the United States receded, U.S. multinational firms lost no ground whatsoever. Instead, they maintained their share of world markets. In fact, foreign affiliates of U.S. multinationals actually *increased* their share from 8.0 per cent to 9.8 per cent between 1966 and 1986 (Epstein 1990–91, p. 33; see also Kravis and Lipsey 1989).

U.S. exports are declining to those countries that are experiencing increases in U.S. multinational production. This pattern suggests that, what appears as de-industrialization is part of a larger strategy in which multinationals reduce their investment at home, while they increase their investment abroad (Epstein 1990–91, p. 36; see also Kravis and Lipsey 1988).

Robert Reich notes 'Overall, the evidence suggests that the U.S. companies have not lost their competitive edge over the last 20 years – they've just moved their base of operations' (Reich 1990, p. 55). For example, today 40 per cent of IBM's employees are foreign and the percentage is increasing (ibid., p. 54).

In addition, Reich might have observed that corporate ownership is becoming diffused. In the process, U.S. multinational corporations become truly multinational, losing their identity as U.S. firms and becoming stateless entities whose influence rivals that of many existing nation states.

Once again, we should mention that our current adherence to the Haitian path will not prevent further de-industrialization from the denationalization of the corporate sector. Originally, a prime purpose of this denationalization was to take advantage of cheap labour, but this process has evolved since then. Today, corporate refugees from the United States do not just seek out low-wage economies. Many of the advanced corporations locate their affiliates to take advantage of superior training that students get in other countries.

The example of IBM reminds us of the fallacy of a low-wage strategy. For example, IBM-Japan has 18,000 employees, enjoys annual sales of $6 billion and is one of Japan's largest exporters of computers. Texas

Instruments employs over 5000 people in Japan to make advanced semi-conductors, almost half of which are eventually exported to the United States (Reich 1990, p. 54).

Is De-industrialization the Rule in Market Economies?

Finally, we turn to a different approach to de-industrialization: specifically, we will ask if can we take comfort in the idea that the current wave of de-industrialization simply represents the elimination of a backlog of phantom capacity? Alternatively, might de-industrialization be nothing more than the normal response of an economy to a sharp increase in competitive pressures?

Common sense, as well as our previous analysis, tells us that any healthy economy certainly would need a mechanism to shed outmoded and obsolete productive capacity. Now ask yourself, what incentive do individual firms have to engage in this process?

Ideally, normal competitive pressures should induce firms to modernize. Unfortunately, modernization is easier said than done. To scrap a piece of equipment that could still be put to work constitutes a capital loss for its owner. As a result, in the absence of strong competitive pressures, firms will have insufficient reason to pare away inefficient plant and equipment. Under normal conditions, firms will just attempt to keep their plant and equipment in operation as long as possible, so long as their business is expanding.

For this reason, as we have seen, a market economy requires periodic down-turns in order to generate enough competitive pressure to rid itself of old and outmoded plant and equipment. This purgative process should be part of the normal life-cycle of capitalism; otherwise, an excessive build-up of phantom capacity will accumulate, eventually undermining the health of the economy.

Despite the necessity of competition for a healthy economy, competition does not occur without substantial costs. Markets impose great hardships on innocent bystanders. Plant closings are a case in point.

Political leaders often attempt to protect business from the harsh consequences of competitive processes. Although such policies may turn out to be counterproductive, the political leaders do not do so out of sheer stupidity. Instead, they want to shield firms and individuals from the disruptive actions of markets.

In the United States, military Keynesian was not so much designed to protect markets from communism; its more basic goal was to shield firms and people from markets. True, in the process, military Keynesianism weakened the U.S. economy in the long-run because, without the competitive pressures that military Keynesian suppressed, firms had little incentive to invest in capital deepening in the form of more efficient productive capacity. Economists should have foreseen the eventual economic atrophy, which we are calling de-industrialization, but they did not.

Economists might have been slow to come to grips with de-industrialization because of the complexity of the competitive process. Competitive pressures are not constant over time. When they become intense, manufacturing capacity shrinks, causing the economy to experience something like de-industrialization, in the sense that a typical down-turn will annihilate both efficient and inefficient production units.

Although de-industrialization and the ideal business down-turn both rid the economy of old and obsolete plant and equipment, we should take care to distinguish between the two phenomena. Although sharp increases in competitive pressures might cause the economy to recede temporarily, economists' ideal of a business down-turn does not lead into an outright collapse. Instead, the ideal business cycle produces short set-backs embedded within a long-run process of economic growth. In contrast, de-industrialization, as we have been using the term, is a long-run trend, rather than a normal phase in the business cycle.

In both the ideal economic down-turn and de-industrialization, firms do not attempt to renew their industrial capacity. Instead, they attempt to increase productivity merely by eliminating less profitable plant and equipment. In the context of an ideal economic down-turn, this paring of industrial capacity is a temporary phenomenon, which soon corrects itself.

This on-going reduction of a manufacturing presence during de-industrialization differs significantly from the virtuous cycle in which competitive pressures coerce firms to renew their capital stock. In contrast to an ideal economic down-turn, the vicious downward spiral of de-industrialization turns pathological.

The corrosive process of de-industrialization stubbornly eats away at the very foundations of the economy for an extended period of time. Such a force might even turn out to be irreversible. In this sense, we can say that a healthy economy does not de-industrialize, unless we accept vision of the post industrial utopia.

As we saw during our discussion of military Keynesianism, once an economic down-turn threatens to become serious, governments typically intervene rather than letting the economy take its course. For this reason, we have no way of knowing if the business cycles conform to economists' vision of an ideal business cycle.

In this sense, while waves of competitive pressure have promoted economic modernization in the past, we cannot be sure whether the economies in question avoided collapse because of built-in economic forces or if administrative or institutional processes might be responsible for avoiding immediate catastrophe. In other words, we do not know if market economies are inherently healthy or if they are saddled with a congenital tendency toward convulsive de-industrialization.

If economic down-turns are such that the downward momentum naturally continues unabated in the absence of some outside intervention, then the distinction that I have been making between de-industrialization and the healthy response to competitive pressures is inappropriate. Although most economists take it for granted that they are justified in presuming that a market economy is naturally healthy, they neglect to examine the grounds for their belief.

Rustow's analysis suggests that, in the normal economic structure in which great disparities of productivity exist between the most and the least efficient plants in an industry, then economic down-turns will naturally evolve into collapses. We might note that the behaviour of political leaders when a market economy experiences a crisis, suggests that they believed that the market would be incapable of recovering on its own. After all, why should the government act to cushion the blow if the problem is temporary? As a result, we do not have much opportunity to learn about the ability of a market economy to recuperate from a serious depression without government intervention.

If economic down-turns naturally give way to long-term de-industrialization, then we can disregard our concerns about the need for competitive pressures, which was grounded on the assumption that the economy could correct itself in the long-run. If, in fact, markets tend to self-destruct, then we have good reason to worry about our future as a market economy.

Debates over De-industrialization

Relatively few economists have addressed the question of whether down-turns are necessary for the economic health of a market economy or if they tend to self-destruct. Most of our knowledge of the nature of slumps comes from scholars who have analyzed the historical conditions of specific economic crises.

For example, the experience of the Great Depression does not offer a great deal of hope for believers in the free market. The downturn began in 1929. Despite energetic actions by the U.S. government, the depression did not end until World War II commenced, after more than a decade of economic hardship. In this respect, military Keynesianism seemed at the time to be necessary to the long-term survival of capitalism in the United States.

Mainstream economists often disregard the history of economic crises. Instead, they generally build theoretical models, which either assume that down-turns need not occur at all or purport to prove that they could not occur in the absence of some non-market force. More often than not, members of this school of thought lay the blame for crises entirely at the foot of government for naively interfering with natural economic forces.

These free-market ideologues argue that once some non-market force makes an economy experience a down-turn, then market forces alone suffice to bring the economy back to health; that government intervention, which they believe had originally caused the problem, can only make things worse. Economists build their models of the robustness of the market on unrealistic assumptions that bear little relationship to the real world. These economists tend to ground their theory more on faith instead of realistic observations of actual economic events.

Among those heretical schools of thought, which do attempt to study the nature of economic slumps, we find widely divergent views. Although Keynes devoted much energy to devising a theoretical analysis of slumps, he was relatively uninterested in studying how economies would go into a depression. His concern was that an economy would remain in a depressed state for an extended period of time, not that the depression could set off a continuing downward spiral. In contrast, Marx believed that economics crises would eventually spell the end for capitalism. Although this part of his work remained sketchy, it was very advanced for its time (see Perelman 1987).

Still, we cannot know with certainty which side is correct until we are willing to experiment by standing aside and allowing the economy to go into a free fall during some future recession. We do know that competitive pressures seem to have a built-in tendency to drive down both prices and profit rates. Firms will attempt to protect themselves by cutting wages by a greater extent than the reduction in the prices of the goods that they sell.

Investment and Taxes

As the decline became more pervasive, a growing number of economists and public officials came to accept the reality of de-industrialization, without using that specific term. They recognized that, given the floundering state of the U.S. economy, saddled with an ageing and increasingly uncompetitive capital stock, something had to be done.

The Reagan administration thought that it had the answer: a program of massive tax cuts, bolstered by a strong commitment to deregulation. The administration convinced the American public that tax cuts would unleash the enormous potential of the entrepreneurial spirit of American business.

According to this scenario, reducing taxes would create a stronger economy, which would help everybody, even the tax collectors. Supposedly, with a larger tax base, total taxes would rise despite falling tax rates. In the long-run, we would have more money to spend on infrastructure, education and government services by enacting tax limitations.

In reality, taxes are a horribly inefficient instrument for stimulating basic industry. Despite its long-standing claim that excessive taxes remove much of the incentive to invest in plant and equipment, business is surprisingly insensitive to the generous tax provisions that are designed to promote investment (see Neild 1964). For example, the U.S. government has to give business an estimated $2 of immediate tax benefits to induce it to increase its investment by a single dollar (Eisner and Chirinko 1983).

To make matters worse, because U.S. business fears risking its money by investing in long-lived capital goods, much investment will be used for making money through finance rather than providing useful goods and services. For example, the Wall Street manager for Sun Microsystems expected to sell $70 million worth of computer workstations in 1991, triple the level of two years ago (Anders 1991). These systems are especially attractive to traders who want to devise new programs for extracting profits from the financial markets.

Nonetheless, the Reagan administration passed the 1981 Economic Recovery Tax Act, which dramatically cut business taxes, ostensibly to encourage investment. Indeed, business seemed to respond to the tax cut just as the Reagan administration had predicted. It increased investment in producers durable equipment by 42 per cent between the second quarter of 1982 and the fourth quarter of 1984 (Bosworth 1985, p. 1).

Upon further reflection, this investment record turned out to be less impressive than it appeared to be at first sight. In 1982, the economy was emerging from the worst recession of the post-war period. Indeed, a study by the Federal Reserve Bank of New York found that modifications of the business tax code accounted for only about one-fifth of the 1983–4 increases (Sahling and Akhtar 1984–5).

Consideration of the actual composition of the investment goods leads to even more skepticism about the effectiveness of the tax incentives. Harry Magdoff and Paul Sweezy noted that investment in manufacturing capacity accounts for barely 10 per cent of the total of what the government counts as capital investment (Magdoff and Sweezy 1985, p. 3). In fact, between

1979 and 1985, an astounding 93 per cent of all of the growth in investment was confined to only two categories of goods: office equipment (such as computers) and transportation equipment (largely automobiles leased by business) (Bosworth 1985, p. 4).

In fact, the new tax law did not deserve much credit for the investment in office equipment. The 1981 tax law actually made investment in computers less attractive (ibid., p. 4). In addition, the category of office equipment includes personal home computers, some of which should be classified as consumer goods.

Even if we assume that the new tax code spurred the investment in office equipment, it did little to make the economy healthier. To begin with, much of the office equipment was used to take advantage of the new opportunities made possible by the deregulation of the financial sector. In other words, a considerable portion of this office equipment helped to erect junk bond empires and to steer the Savings and Loan system toward disaster.

In addition, productive businesses often installed office equipment to eliminate jobs rather than to expand production. Theoretically, this office equipment could have made business more productive. The resulting gains in efficiency could have stimulated general economic activity. Unfortunately, the massive infusion of office equipment did little or nothing to make management more efficient.

Much of the investment in transportation equipment did little to help the economy since it merely reflected the growing practice of leasing automobiles to take advantage of the tax laws. Leasing becomes attractive when the tax break to the automobile-leasing company is generous enough to allow it to make a profit, after passing some of the savings on to its customers.

When an individual purchases a car, the government counts the car as a consumption expenditure. In contrast, the government includes leased automobiles as investments, regardless of whether they are leased for private or business uses (Sahling and Akhtar 1984–5). Although the tax laws affected the profitability of leasing, this practice did not contribute much to economic efficiency.

Of course, debating whether or not the tax laws stimulated investment suggests that the key to economic progress is investment. Yes, new investment can benefit future economic activity, but investment is not the be-all and end-all of economics.

Economists understandably tend to think of progress in terms of investment. After all, training in economics infuses students with a spirit of thorough-going Calvinism. It indoctrinates students to believe that economic growth comes entirely from sacrifice, hard work, and saving. In truth, economic growth springs from two other far more important sources: the natural wealth of the planet and the creativity of the people who inhabit the planet.

Creativity Again

The Reagan administration expressed no doubts that the mix of tax cuts and deregulation would create an environment in which the creativity of the American people would flourish, thereby assuring that the U.S. economy would regain its competitiveness. No one noticed a problem with the deteriorating public capital stock. No one seemed concerned about the dangers of curtailing spending on education. The magic of the marketplace would solve all existing problems.

In one sense, the Reagan administration was not far off the mark. True, the tax cut never sparked the burst of investment that was supposed to revitalize the U.S. economy. Yes, the erosion of the public capital stock crippled the economy and public schools failed to prepare our children for the future. Still, the Reaganauts were correct in pointing to the spirit and creativity of the people as the hope for the economy.

The mistake of the Reaganauts was to accept that greed, and greed alone, could rouse the spirit and creativity of the people. Yes, self-interest plays a role in motivating people to act, but a sense of a broader social purpose is more effective than greed in spurring creativity.

8 High Wages, Enlightened Management, and Economic Productivity

High Wages as a Defence against De-industrialization

This book has tried to make the case that government policy-makers are caught on the horns of a dilemma. Market economies have an inherent tendency to create strong pulses of competitive pressures, which can drive the economy into crises. Governments have a range of policy options to counteract the threat of economic collapse under competitive pressures. First, they can attempt to prevent competitive pressures from gaining strength. Military Keynesianism represents an excellent example of this strategy. Governments can also change the legal structure, allowing firms to collude to inhibit competition. All such measures, as we have seen, will eventually weaken the economy, although perhaps not as much as unbridled competition will.

When many firms attempt to maximize profits by cutting wages, markets will contract, making firms fearful about making investments. This process combines with the phenomenon, which Rustow described: strong competitive pressure leads to the on-going elimination of the weakest firms without a corresponding creation of a comparable quantity of new and more efficient firms. Other firms may attempt to reduce wage costs by shifting their operations abroad to low wage economies.

This combination of forces drives the economy toward de-industrialization. For example the recent experience of the U.S. economy with its falling real wages and runaway shops certainly conforms to the pattern of de-industrialization that Rustow's theory suggests.

Unless we can identify some sufficiently strong offsetting influence, we may have no alternative to concluding that, market economies have an inherent tendency toward de-industrialization. When the financial pressures of highly leveraged firms reinforce this tendency toward falling wages and de-industrialization, the economy will have a tendency to go into violent convulsions.

One avenue does exist that allows strong competitive pressures to co-exist with an expanding market: gradually raising the level of real wages. Bhaduri and Marglin provide a suggestive model that shows how increasing wages can fuel economic growth (Bhaduri and Marglin 1990).

Although wage growth may be an effective countermeasure to prevent the tendency toward de-industrialization, protecting wages is no easy matter. Unfortunately, market economies have no inherent tendency to make real wages expand, especially when competition is strong. For example, we shall see how the U.S. government ultimately failed in its attempt to persuade corporations to resist the temptation to cut wages during the Great Depression.

Although higher wages may benefit business in general, an individual firm will profit – especially in the short-run – from a reduction in its own labour costs, providing all other employers continue to pay higher wages. Instead, business has a powerful incentive to curtail wage growth. If government wants to make sure that firms do not cut wages when competitive pressures intensify, it must somehow impose regulations (such as minimum wage laws) or change the legal structure (for example, to foster the growth of unions).

Admittedly, devising effective legislation to ensure growth in wages is no easy matter, even in a closed economy without any international trade. In an open economy in which exports and imports are significant, protecting the wage level may be all but impossible without international co-ordination or protectionism.

As things stand today, we see firm after firm attempting to circumvent the high wage levels in the United States by moving their manufacturing operations abroad. If U.S. economy is to be able to perform well, it needs some mechanism to protect itself from the natural tendency to depress wages when the economy is in retreat.

The Two Faces of Management-Labour Relations

Most economists are ill prepared to come to grips with this tendency to depress wages because they habitually fall into the trap of oversimplifying the multi-faceted nature of the labour-management relationship. This failing has been no less dangerous than the disregard for the two-sided nature of competition and depressions.

As a first step in addressing the complexity of the labour-management relationship, we shall highlight one important dualism in this relationship: on the one side, we have what we may call the financial perspective; on the other, the production perspective.

The financial perspective presumes that labour is a passive participant in the production process, indistinguishable from the other inert, raw materials that businesses purchase. Within this perspective, when employers buy labour as a commodity, the workers need only contribute their physical presence and superficial obedience.

This interpretation of the labour-management relationship is consistent with the world as seen from the firm's account books. Indeed, business has the object of shoring up its financial health, in part, by purchasing all inputs as cheaply as possible. In this respect, business justifiably treats labour as a commodity like any other – to be purchased as advantageously as possible.

In terms of the process of actually producing goods and services, labour takes on an entirely different appearance. On the shop floor and in the office, business must pay close attention to the specific details of labour's activities. In this respect, employers expect more than just the bodily presence and superficial obedience of their workers. Herein lies the essence of this other face of management-labour relations.

In evaluating the production process, some employers recognize that they will profit when workers feel obligated to exert themselves and perhaps even to bring creativity and ingenuity to their work. Some employers even call upon their workers to excel, but nobody exerts himself or herself to the utmost without a strong desire to do so – certainly not people who feel that their employer regards them as nothing more than a mere commodity to be bought as cheaply as possible.

How then should employers cajole or entice their workers into performing their tasks as well as possible relative to the wages that they earn? Employers have a wide range of options for managing labour at their disposal. At one extreme, business can resort to the threat of punishment for unsatisfactory work. Workers under this sort of regime soon realize that, if they fail to perform adequately, they will be rendered unable to feed themselves and their families. Under a regime based on strict discipline, business practices are consistent with the financial perspective.

This method has several drawbacks. First, in a prosperous economy, workers have the option of finding alternative employment if they lose their jobs. Second, while a heightened anxiety can admittedly increase work effort, it also impairs the performance of skilled tasks (Fenoaltea 1984).

In short, this system of threats can only be effective for tasks that are easy to monitor and that require a minimum of care (see Fenoaltea 1984). Resentful workers will always find ways to withhold effort or even to sabotage the business where they work. As Genovese has shown, not even slave owners were able to achieve absolute dominance over the workplace even though the technical complexity of the slave's responsibilities was relatively limited (Genovese 1976).

At the other extreme, employers can attempt to instil a spirit of cooperation, in which workers identify with the interest of their employer. Employers have various options for eliciting this cooperation. They can reward workers financially for good work or they can appeal to the workers by offering them an exciting challenge. For example, in his award-winning book, *The Soul of a New Machine*, Tracy Kidder depicted the zeal with which engineers for Data General competed to develop a new computer (Kidder 1982).

Most of all, if employers want to use the carrot to elicit effort rather than to rely on the proverbial stick, they will have to treat workers with respect. We should not be surprised that sticks are more popular than carrots in management circles in the contemporary United States. After all, the allure of treating labour as a commodity is self-evident. Using punishment to control the labour process is devilishly simple to administer, even though it is relatively ineffective for anything but the crudest sort of labour. In contrast, the use of incentives can be extremely effective, but incentives are exceedingly difficult to administer.

Of course, no firm relies exclusively either on threats or on positive incentives. In effect, employers choose a mix of these two seemingly contradictory sets of incentives. The employer promises to reward workers to make them perform their jobs well or even take pride in their work. They appeal to the workers' ambition and self-respect.

Because employers have no assurance that the bargain will create the desired attitude in their labour force, employers also tell the workers that they are entirely dispensable. Employers convey the message – perhaps even intentionally – that no individual worker is anything special. Should any employee fail to satisfy the employer or ask for too much money, then the employer stands ready to fire that worker and hire another, who presumably will do a better job.

In this sense, the employer's message is essentially antagonistic. Yet, in appealing to the workers to put a great deal of themselves into their work, the employers' message conveys co-operation and a mutuality of interests.

The Internal Politics of Management-Labour Relations

Finding the proper mix of threat and incentive is no simple task, but the employer must somehow make these two essentially contradictory messages coherent. Coherence is all the more elusive because of the subtlety of the labour-management relationship.

Workers evaluate the specific combination of signals within any employment relationship in terms of an unstated norm of 'fairness'. When workers perceive employers as fair – when they feel that they are treated with respect – they respond accordingly.

Both labour and management attempt to control the labour process. From this perspective, we see workers as active agents, with goals of their own and the with ingenuity and creativity to accomplish these goals, at least in part. If an employer violates workers' norm of fairness, the employees will seek redress by withholding their cooperation.

These disgruntled workers often go to great lengths to exercise some control over the labour process, even when they have no expectation of wringing any concessions from management, often with dire consequences for the firm. Michael Burawoy attempted to come to grips with the depth of the tensions between labour and management by interpreting the workplace as an 'internal state' (Burawoy 1979, p. 11). Within this state, each party, labour and management, has certain unspecified powers.

Indeed, the idea of exercising some control over their activity, even when that control is nothing more than the disruption of the labour process, can be a source of utility and even delight to workers. In fact, workers, who might not be inclined to work harder for monetary rewards, sometimes go to great lengths just to assert their independence *vis-à-vis* management.

For example, Burawoy described a piecework machine shop that produced parts for truck engines, where workers transformed the incentive system into a game to relieve their boredom. Within this game, these workers developed a complex equilibrium with inspectors. If an inspector challenged them by rejecting articles with marginal tolerance, workers would retaliate by turning out scrap after the first piece was rejected, making the inspector look bad. Underlying their game was a need to relieve boredom rather than any economic motives (Burawoy 1979, p. 89). Workers sometimes attempted to produce as much as 140 per cent of the norm. They resisted producing any more than 140 per cent only because they feared an upward revision of the norm.

These workers could have turned their creativity to making the plant more productive, but to do so would not have done much for their self-respect. When this cynical creativity becomes general, the economy as a whole will become less competitive within the world economy.

Because management typically adheres to the financial perspective of labour-management relations, it is unable to comprehend how much it loses by failing to tap workers creativity. Academic authorities – especially economists – do not offer much guidance in this regard. Burawoy rightfully charged that, 'Political economy has conspired in a separation of economics and politics, never attempting to theorize a politics of production. Production has both ideological and political effects' (ibid., p. 7).

In many cases, management attacks labour in order to wring economic concessions from the workers. In many other cases, the financial perspective leads management to display an insensitivity that can push workers to turn their creativity to disruptive ends. Harley Shaiken writes of an incident that illustrates the importance of according adequate respect to the workers:

> A familiar sight in most shops is an engineer walking in with a stack of blueprints to ask the worker if a particular job is feasible. The machinist carefully studies the prints, looks at the engineer, and says, 'Well, it can be tried like this but it will never work.' Grabbing a pencil, the machinist marks up the print and, in effect, redesigns the job based on years of experience . . .
>
> [In one shop, when] management initiated a campaign to strictly enforce lunch periods and wash-up time, the judgment of some machinists began to fade. About this time a foreman dashed up to the shop with a 'hot' job . . . . Anxious to get the job done quickly, the foreman insisted that the machinist run the lathe at a high speed and plunge the drill through the part. Under normal circumstances the machinist would have tried to talk the foreman out of this approach but now he was only too happy to oblige what were, after all, direct orders. The part not only turned out to be scrap, but part of the lathe turned blue from the friction generated by the high speed. The disciplinary campaign was short-lived. (Shaiken 1985, pp. 19–20)

Shaiken's vignette illustrates business's dependence on labour's co-operation. Once labour withdraws this co-operative spirit, business is in trouble. Observing a similar situation, Shoshana Zuboff captured the subtle ambivalence of the management labour-relationship, noting 'obedience fed by cynicism became a form of revenge' (Zuboff 1988, p. 273).

We hear much about employers imploring their workers to excellence, but this excellence is of a particular kind. Management expects workers to perform to their utmost according to the directives that it gives them. Workers are unlikely to display such unthinking, excellence. Even if they were, it would be impossible unless the employer were able to anticipate all contingencies in advance. Shaiken's vignette suggests how difficult it would be to 'pre-program' workers for their tasks. Instead, an efficient workforce must be able to find some satisfaction in the work it performs.

The Advantage of a Co-operative Policy toward Labour

The need to tap workers' creativity is especially crucial in highly advanced technological systems, where management depends on labour in developing the best possible methods of production (see Glyn, Hughes, Lipietz, and Singh 1990, p. 89). Unfortunately, relatively few employers adequately acknowledge the degree of skill involved on the job.

Instead, employers prefer to attempt to coerce labour into absolute obedience with the threat of unemployment. By compelling obedience through coercion, management stifles the creativity which is central to the successful functioning of modern industry. This approach does serious harm to the economy. As Richard Walton, an expert on progressive pay schemes, has observed:

> Especially in a high-wage country like the United States, market success depends on a superior level of performance, a level that, in return requires the deep commitment, not merely the obedience – if you could obtain it – of workers. And as painful experience shows, this commitment cannot flourish in a workplace dominated by the familiar model of control. (Walton 1985, pp. 77–78; cited in Glyn, Hughes, Lipietz, and Singh 1990, p. 89)

In contrast to the United States, Japanese firms have been extremely successful tapping the knowledge of their workers. For example, the average worker in a Toyota plant gave 31.8 suggestions in 1983. Of these, 96 per cent were accepted (Kaplinsky 1988, p. 460).

The Japanese approach is not novel. In fact, during the late nineteenth century foreign observers associated this approach with the United States. For example, British industrialists visiting the United States realized that worker involvement was an integral part of the success of the U.S. economy. An industrialist, A. Mosely, head of one of the many delegations of British industrialists that visited the United States at the beginning of this century, reported:

> One point that has struck me with enormous force, as I believe it has all the delegates, is the close touch and sympathy between master and man, which is carried a step further in the enlistment of the men's good offices to improve factory methods. Suggestions are welcomed, the more so because the American manufacturer has realized that it is not the man sitting in the counting-house or private office who is best able to judge

where improvements can be made in machine or method, but he who attends that machine from morning to night . . . . In short, the man feels that the work of his brains will handsomely benefit himself. Is it any wonder, therefore, that American machinery is continually changing and improving, that the evolution of methods is ever and rapidly going on? . . . . As a rule the British employer hardly knows his men, seldom leaves his office for the workshop. (Offer 1989, p. 124)

A co-operative labor policy can and will make an economy healthier. If the United States is going to regain its previous position, it will have to win the respect and the loyalty of labour.

Nonetheless, treating labour with respect and rewarding workers to encourage productivity is not a panacea, which can permanently rid the economy of crises. Moreover, the inevitable extended bouts of unemployment, typical of a market economy, will work to embitter workers. Still, within the bounds of a market economy, a co-operative labour policy is about the best rule to follow. The alternative is the Haitian road to development.

The Economy of High Wages

We often hear that high wages are the root of many of the ills of the U.S. economy today. Presumably, our economy could prosper if only we could maintain low enough wages. Such reasoning is absolute nonsense.

Low wages ensure *low*, not high productivity. In fact, the United States historically enjoyed a high rate of productivity growth just because U.S. wages exceeded those of the rest of the world.

Economists usually turn this analysis around. From the very beginning of their introductory economics classes, most students learn that high productivity causes high wages rather than the other way around. The conventional theory is correct insofar as a group of workers with an especially valuable skill can command a high wage rate, but it explains only part of the wage-productivity relationship. This section analyzes the other side of the coin: that higher wages can result in greater productivity.

Because the expression, 'the economy of high wages,' has a long and distinguished lineage, dating from the late nineteenth century, we will continue to refer to high wages. Moreover, we will not often be led astray in this discussion by thinking of high wages in terms of our common sense understanding of what high wages means, although we will see that what constitutes high wages has a subjective component.

Now let us explore several means by which high wages can benefit an economy. To begin with, high wages stimulate demand.

Second, the increasing demand associated with high wages helps to create what economists call, 'economies of scale,' a term that refers to the savings that high-volume producers enjoy. As these economies of scale develop, firms can afford to pay higher wages, augmenting demand still more. Here again we have an example of cumulative causation.

Third, high wages encourage employers to develop improved technologies to save labour.

Fourth, high wages stimulate workers to be more productive. A number of studies show that workers respond to higher wages by contributing more effort to the jobs (Akerlof and Yellen 1986).

Finally, to the extent that high wages promote investment in new technologies, workers often respond to the challenge of working with new techniques by developing their own skills and abilities. Shoshana Zuboff's work offers dramatic examples of this response by workers in a variety of environments (Zuboff 1988).

Despite the numerous economies of high wages, we must be careful not to treat the subject dogmatically. For example, high wages will not necessarily create economies of scale in all economies at all times. Imagine a small country in a crowded region of the world with cheap transportation and relatively free trade, say Luxembourg. If wages rise there, employers could conceivably move to a neighbouring country to take advantage of cheaper labour costs – although in this particular example such an exodus has not occurred.

In addition, much of the extension of demand is likely to be dissipated in imports. In a massive nation, such as the United States, which was geographically isolated from much of the rest of the industrialized world and which was largely protected from foreign competition by high tariffs and duties on imported goods, high wages have worked magnificently. To the extent that improvements in transportation and communication make the economy more open, the benefits of high wages are less assured.

In addition, the benefits of high wages partially depend on the ability of business to discover new labour-saving technologies, which will ultimately promote competitiveness. We have no guarantee that the new methods of production that business develops will be so efficient that firms will be able to more than compensate for a higher level of wages.

Despite such qualifications to the theory of high wages, maintaining a healthy rate of wage growth offers a far more promising outcome than attempting to compete by depressing wages.

Efficiency Wages

Let us explore in more detail the notion that high wages can improve the human element in the production process. We can not do much better in this respect than to cite Alfred Marshall, the author of the leading text book on economics during the first quarter of this century. Marshall wisely observed:

> [I]t was only in the last generation that a careful study was begun to be made on the effects that high wages have in increasing the efficiency not only of those who receive them, but also of their children and grandchildren. In this the lead have been taken by Walker and other American economists; and the application of the comparative method of study to the industrial problems of different countries of the old and new worlds is forcing constantly more and more attention to the fact that highly paid labour is generally efficient and therefore not dear labour. (Marshall 1920, p. 510)

This statement is interesting in several respects. First Marshall's reference to children and grandchildren – to which we will return later – indicates how high wages can changes workers' character so profoundly that the benefits of high wages will carry over to their children and grandchildren. This is relevant to our earlier discussion of the contemporary crisis in education in the United States.

Secondly, Marshall's uses of the term 'forcing' reminds us that most business people and economists still resisted the notion that 'highly paid labour is generally efficient and therefore, not dear labor', although, as we shall see, larger firms were more aware of the benefits of high wages.

Finally, Marshall knew that the United States paid higher wages than anywhere else and that its economy was the most powerful in the world. As a result, he could mention without any need for further comment that the American economists were the pioneers in discovering the beneficial influence of high wages.

Marshall's words suggest that the technical competency that accompanies high wages becomes contagious. In the first place, high wages allow other family members and even friends to become acquainted with modern technologies. Just as children acquire computer skills through video games today, during the Golden Age, many children developed mechanical abilities by fixing up old cars.

The transmission of skills does not depend only on learning through consumer goods. Workers who take pride in their work will share their experiences with other workers, on and off the job. In this way, expertise will permeate society.

Given these important pathways through which high wages induce workers to develop their abilities, individual employers will reap only part of the spillovers from the high wages that they pay. They will be willing to pay only for the direct benefits they receive from their expenditures on wages. They will not take the indirect benefits into account. In terms of economic theory, this situation creates an insufficient incentive to pay high enough wages.

To make matters worse, many employers fail to realize that high wages can improve the quality of their workers' output. In this sense they will not even take into account all the direct benefits that they can reap from paying their workers more.

Of course, some employers had understood the benefits of high wages, even long before the writers that Marshall cited. For example, in 1835 a British writer, Andrew Ure, posed a question about the subject to a number of authorities. He asked 'how with . . . surplus hands the wages of fine spinners can be maintained at their present high pitch?' Ure reported:

> One of the best informed manufacturers made me this reply: 'We find a moderate saving in the wages to be of little consequence in comparison of contentment and we therefore keep them as high as we can possibly afford, in order to be entitled to the best quality of work. A spinner reckons the charge of a pair of mules in our factory a fortune for life, he will therefore do his utmost to retain his situation, and to uphold the high character of our yarn.' (Ure 1835, p. 336; cited in Marglin 1990, p. 15)

Lamentably, we have forgotten much since the days of Ure.

The Tradition of the United States as a High-Wage Economy

The historical record of the U.S. economy does suggest that business did indeed manage to create new technologies fast enough to make prices fall, even in the face of rising wages.

Certainly the rapidity of technical change struck most observers of the early United States. For example, the renowned French visitor, Alexis de Tocqueville, reported:

> I accost an American sailor, and I inquire why the ships of his country are built so as to last for a short time; he answers without hesitation that

the art of navigation is every day making such a rapid progress that the finest vessel would become almost useless if it lasted beyond a certain number of years. (de Tocqueville 1848, II, p. 420)

H. J. Habakkuk wrote an entire book about the positive effect of high wages on technical change in the United States during the nineteenth century. According to Habakkuk:

The Secretary of the Treasury reported in 1832, that the garrets and outhouses of most textile mills were crowded with discarded machinery. One Rhode Island mill built in 1813 had by 1827 scrapped and replaced every original machine. (Habakkuk 1962, p. 57; and the numerous references he cites)

The anticipation of early retirement of plant and equipment in the United States was so pervasive that manufacturers in the United States built their machinery from wood rather than more durable materials, such as iron (Strassman 1959, p. 88).

Throughout the nineteenth century, commentators continued to echo de Tocqueville's observation that technology in the United States was designed to be short-lived (Schoenhof 1893). For example, in the late nineteenth century, the U.S. States Secretary of State commissioned Joseph Schoenhof to inquire into the effects of high wages on the competitiveness of business in the United States. Schoenhof concluded:

The employer of labor is . . . benefitted by the inevitable results of a high rate of wages . . . . [T]he first object of the employer is to economize its employment.

Manufacturers introducing a change in manufactures have a machine built to accomplish what in other countries would be left to hand labor to bring about. Machinery, used to the limit of its life in Europe, is cast aside in America if only partially worn. (Schoenhof 1893, pp. 33–4)

The Cornell economist, Jeremiah Jenks asserted:

No sooner has the capitalist fairly adopted one improved machine, than it must be thrown away for a still later and better invention, which must be purchased at a dear cost, if the manufacturer would not see himself eclipsed by his rival. (Jenks 1890, p. 254; cited in Livingston 1986, p. 39)

This pattern of rapid capital renewal made the manufacturing capacity in United States the envy of the world. By the turn of the century, exports from the United States were inundating Europe, much the same as Japanese exports are displacing U.S. production today. Just as people in the United States today try to discover the secret of Japanese ascendancy in popular books, English readers pored over alarmist books with titles, such as *The American Invaders* (1901), *The Americanization of the World* (1901), or *The American Invasion* (1902) (Wright 1990, p. 652).

By the late nineteenth century, rapid technical change had brought productivity in the United States to such a high level that the rationale for high wages shifted from the first reason to the second and third.

High Wages and Protectionism

By the late Nineteenth Century, rapid technical change had brought productivity in the United States to such a high level that the rationale for high wages shifted. The early case for high wages rested on the notion that high wages (together with protectionism) would stimulate the demand for new industries, helping them grow and mature, and eventually to benefit from economies of scale. The new emphasis stressed greater substitution of capital for labour and the promotion of a more productive labour force.

In fact, leading protectionists, such as David Wells, became so confident about the competitive position of the U.S. economy that they abandoned their previous advocacy of protective tariffs and called for free trade (Wells 1885). Wells and his school were certain that the highly-paid U.S. labour force could out-compete what they regarded as pauper labour in the rest of the world.

Where Ure's previously cited informant made the case for high wages in terms of 'the high character of our yarn', writers in the United States were more likely to discuss the association of high wages with a high character of the worker. For example, Wells observed:

> High wages, then, are the normal result of low cost, and low cost is the normal result in turn of intelligence, conjoined with good machinery, applied to great resources for production. (Wells 1885, p. 138)

Wells's insight has been lost on most business people in recent decades. Today, they seem to be infatuated with the financial perspective on the complex relationship between labour and capital.

Wells noted that wages in England's cotton industry were from 30 to 50 per cent higher than in France, Belgium and Germany. He observed that an English cotton operative received more wages in a week than a Russian in a month. Yet the continent demanded protection against English labour (Wells 1885, p. 137).

Gregory Clark published an extensive survey of this relationship between high wages and British competitiveness in an article entitled, 'Why Isn't the Whole World Developed? Lessons from the Cotton Mills' (Clark 1987). Although British wages were less than those earned in the United States, they were high relative to the rest of the world. According to Clark, compared with Manchester, hourly wages on the Continent ranged from less than 25 per cent as high in Prussia to 47 per cent in Rouen (ibid., p. 142).

In 1911, 140 years after the first cotton mills and despite an enormous wage cost disadvantage, 40 per cent of all factory spindles were in England. Another 22 per cent were in the United States and Canada. Low-wage countries had only 39 per cent of all spindles worldwide (ibid., p. 143).

Clark reported that in 1910, one New England cotton textile worker was equivalent to 1.5 British or 2.3 German workers. Compared to lower wage economies, the difference was phenomenal. New England textile operatives tended six times as much machinery per shift as workers in the Greek, Japanese, Indian or Chinese textile industries (ibid, p. 150).

A Test of the Theory of High Falling Wages during the Great Depression

During the period following World War I, Well's vision was widely shared. At the time, business, especially small business, took great pains to crush unions and root out 'subversives,' suggesting that this willingness to pay high wages was not driven by some humanitarian instinct. Business understood the wisdom of the notion that high wages could augment profits. For example, Herbert Hoover told an audience on 12 May 1926:

> The very essence of great production is high wages and low prices . . . . the acceptance of these ideas is obviously not universal. Not all employers . . . nor has every union abandoned the fallacy of restricted effort . . . . But . . . for both employer and employee to think in terms of the mutual interest of increased production has gained in strength. It is a long cry from the conception of the old economics. (cited in Barber 1985, p. 30)

Hoover's reasoning was that sufficiently high wages would eliminate the appeal of unions; that high wages would make labour feel that its interests were at one with those of business. The key to the high-wage policy of the 1920s was the restriction of immigration – although the restrictions drew upon xenophobic emotions as well as economic realism. Thomas Nixon Carver, a famous Harvard economist exclaimed:

> To be alive today, in this country, and to remember the years from 1870 to 1920 is to awake from a nightmare. Those were the years when our ideas were all but obscured by floods of cheap laborers upon whose cheap labor great fortunes were made, and by floods of abuse because we were not instantaneously solving all the social and economic problems these newcomers were inflicting upon us. Those were the years of slums and socialist agitators, of blatant demagogues and social legislation. (Carver 1925, pp. 261–2; cited in Barber 1985, p. 30)

For both Hoover and Carver, the degree of the appeal of the socialist agitator was an excellent indicator of the level of intelligence of the worker. Limiting immigration and raising wages would expand the intelligence of the American worker, which, in turn, would increase productivity. Stripped of their racial and political biases, Carver and Hoover were correct about the outcome of cutting back on the supply of low-wage workers.

The average number of immigrants fell dramatically, from 856,000 in 1910–15 to 356,000 in 1915–30. The decrease in male immigrants was even more extreme, falling from 584,000 to 217,000. This decline in this major source of unskilled labour coincided with a rise in the demand for manufactured goods (Oshima 1984, p. 163).

Standard economic theory suggests that curtailing immigration will create a shortage of unskilled workers relative to skilled workers. We should expect that the wages of unskilled workers would rise relative to the wages of skilled workers.

Nothing of the kind occurred. Instead, employers invested in an enormous quantity of machines, so much so that the wages of unskilled labour fell 8 per cent compared with 3 per cent for skilled workers between 1920 and 1929 (ibid., p. 164). In the process, output per hour of work increased by 48 per cent during this same period (Jerome 1934, p. 5; see also Dumenil, Glick and Rangel 1987). Given this increase in productivity, personal consumption expenditures for manufactured goods climbed from $11 billion in 1912–1921, measured in 1929 dollars, to $17 billion, 1922–31, again measured in 1929 dollars (Oshima 1984, p. 163).

Falling Wages during the Great Depression

Even with the onset of the Great Depression, a substantial portion of big business refrained from cutting wages. In the words of Jacob Viner:

> the Hoover Administration became apostles of the . . . doctrine that high wages are a guarantee and an essential of prosperity. At the beginning of the depression, Hoover pledged industry not to cut wages, and for a long time large-scale industry adhered to this pledge. (Viner 1933, p. 12; cited in O'Brien 1989, pp. 724–5)

Many firms, especially large firms, were in agreement with President Hoover, convinced that cutting wages would only intensify the crisis. As a result, during the early years of the Depression, wages remained surprisingly steady. In fact, hourly wages in manufacturing declined only about 2 per cent by January 1931, 17 months into the downturn (O'Brien 1989, p. 720). Since prices were falling during the first years of the Depression, the buying power of the hourly wage was rising.

Rather than cutting wages, firms employed their workers for fewer hours (Bernanke 1986; Sherman 1981). In some industries, the total number of hours worked dropped by more than 50 per cent, far more than the drop in the numbers of workers employed. Bernanke estimates that changes in the average number of hours worked per week contributed nearly much as changes in employment to variations in the earnings of labour over the course of the Depression (Bernanke 1986, p. 82).

Large firms' initial reluctance to cut wages substantially dampened the intensity of the initial contraction in the United States. Large employers, committed to maintaining a steady level of wages, would be likely to turn to capital renewal as the obvious strategy to make their operations more efficient. Such investment helped to buffer the shock of the Depression.

This capital renewal was far from insignificant. Think back to Staehle's estimates about the extent to which firms renewed their capital stock during the Depression. His estimates underestimate the extent of capital renewal since they only begin in 1933, after the wage collapse was underway.

The pattern of intensity of research and development offers more evidence of emphasis on modernization during the depression. Although we might expect to find a curtailment of research and development during a depression, such was not the case. Many large firms also responded to the crisis by intensifying their research and development. In fact, the value of research and development expenditures, adjusted for inflation, actually increased during the Great Depression and fell during the war (U.S. Department of Labor 1989).

Large corporations' willingness to refrain from cutting wages for a long time after the onset of the depression was remarkable, but it was not enough to stave off the contractionary forces that eventually overwhelmed the economy. We can best understand the inevitability of the collapse in light of the interplay between the differing situations of large and small business operations.

Large firms had a number of advantages over small firms. Let us concern ourselves with only two. To begin with, many large firms enjoyed economies of scale. Second, during the Great Depression, banks tended to ration credit to their most valued customers, which tend to be the large firms rather than their smaller counterparts (Hunter 1982). As a result, small firms were less able to invest than large firms were (see Calomaris and Hubbard 1990; Fazzari, Hubbard and Peterson 1988). Presumably, this lack of access to credit precluded many small firms from competing through modernization. Given their circumstances, many small firms had little choice but to lower wages.

The large manufacturing firms tend to achieve their economies of scale by creating relatively inflexible, capital-intensive production structures that can only operate efficiently at high levels of output. In contrast, although small manufacturing firms have higher costs, they are more agile and are better able to absorb fluctuations in demand. In general, the output of small firms tends to be more unstable that of large firms (Mills and Schumann 1985; and Carlson 1989).

Now consider the differential impact of a depression on large and small firms. Under depression conditions, the output of small firms will fall to a much greater extent than their larger counterparts. Since small-scale firms are more labour-intensive, they will experience more pressure to cut wage costs, especially since the depression will hit them harder than the large manufacturing firm.

Wages began to collapse only by October of 1931. The result bore out big business's initial fear of the impact of wage cutting, since soon thereafter the depression moved into a far more serious phase (O'Brien 1989, p. 720).

At this point, with firms laying off workers and shutting down factories, the inclination towards capital deepening would be likely to be far weaker than it would have been during the initial phase of the Depression. We can allude to Richards's observation that the short-payback rule became common after 1932 as anecdotal evidence of this weakening of the intensity of capital renewal at the time (Richards 1933). Unfortunately, I know of no data base capable of confirming or refuting my hypothesis about the pattern of capital renewal.

Mitigating Factors

The Great Depression wreaked havoc on society, especially after wages began to collapse, but depression was not as destructive as it might have been. Fortunately, many large corporations did not altogether abandon their longer term perspective all at once. Having superior access to credit, many large corporations took advantage of the situation to make some use of their excess capacity by redirecting production into new industries.

The dean of U.S. business historians, Alfred Chandler, offered numerous examples of firms that responded to the crisis brought on by the Depression by expanding the scope of their operations. In an early work on the subject, he wrote:

> It took the economic pressure created by the slowing down of the economy in the 1920s and its miserable performance in the 1930s to turn these technically sophisticated enterprises to the new strategy of expansion. Precisely because these firms had accumulated vast resources in skilled manpower, facilities, and equipment, their executives were under even greater pressure than those of the smaller firms to find new markets as the old one's ceased to grow . . . . During the Depression General Motors moved into diesels, appliances, tractors, and airplanes. Some makers of primary materials, particular aluminum and copper, turned to consumer products like kitchen ware and household fittings, while rubber firms developed the possibilities of rubber chemistry to compensate for declining tire sales. In the same period food companies employed their existing distribution organizations to market an increasing variety of products. (Chandler 1969, p. 275)

Later, Chandler wrote:

> In the 1930s, as the depression in farming contracted the agricultural equipment market, International Harvester began to produce construction equipment, trucks, and other commercial vehicles. (Chandler 1990, p. 603)

Although such diversification might occur at any time, Michael Gort found statistical evidence that, among the large firms that he studied, it was more frequent during the Depression than at other times (Gort 1962). Gort's data may even understate the importance of the impetus that the Depression gave to diversification.

The Dissipation of the Residual Momentum of High Wages

As wages began to decline, the wisdom of an economy of high wages fell into oblivion. Nonetheless, high wages continued to work to the benefit of the U.S. economy throughout the first half of the twentieth century and into the Golden Age even though economic and political leaders ceased to believe in the economy of high wages.

Consider the relative prices of labour and capital. For example, from 1939 to 1947, average hourly wages of industrial workers in the United States increased by 95 per cent, compared with only 39 per cent for the prices of machine tools. In fact, some authors have singled out high wages as the key to the success of the Golden Age (see Glyn *et al.* 1990, p. 57).

The era of high wages did not continue indefinitely. It came to an end in the mid-to-late 1960s, just as the first signs of the economic decline began to appear. Seymour Melman uses the relative growth of wages and the average prices of metal working tools to track this phenomenon. During the Golden Age, wages rose much faster than the prices of metalworking tools, sparking a great deal of investment. Then, from 1965 to 1977, when the productivity collapse first became apparent, the average prices of metalworking tools rose by almost the same amount as wages. During the latter part of that period, the ratio became even more unfavorable to labour. Between 1971 and 1978, wages increased 72 per cent. In comparison, the prices of machine tools rose 85 per cent (Melman 1983, pp. 3–5).

In fact, each year after 1975, the index of capital costs grew more than the index of unit labour costs (Melman 1983, pp. 3–5 and 168). In the case of the agricultural sector, the ratio of farm labour costs to machinery costs explained a substantial portion of the rise in the investment in tractors (Kislev and Peterson 1982).

As real wages fell in the advanced capitalist countries during the late 1960s and 1970s, business reduced the real value of the equipment with which it supplied the average worker, just as we would expect (Schmid 1981). From 1950 to 1965, business expanded its capital stock by two percentage points more than the growth in total hours. After 1965, the capital stock rate exceeded the rate of growth in hours by only 1 per cent (Kopcke 1980, p. 26).

Today, the business and political leaders of the United States are unanimous in calling for an economy of low wages – a certain recipe for economic disaster. The disastrous results of falling wages seem to convince them to become even more resolute in their advocacy of the Haitian road to development.

High Wages in an International Context

High wages can benefit developing countries as well as advanced countries. For example, Arghiri Emmanuel even went so far as to identify imperialism as a process that unfairly kept wages high in the developed countries (Emmanuel 1972). Here is his capsule summary of British relations with India:

> Britain exchanged her cotton goods for Indian cotton and gained from this exchange the means of paying high wages to her workers. The day when India took up weaving . . . . Britain changed her approach. She began to exchange her cotton yarn for Indian cotton and Indian fabrics. Then India started to produce her own yarn. So now Britain exchanges her looms and spindles for Indian fabrics, still obtaining the wherewithal to pay her workers high wages. (Ibid., p. 146)

According to Emmanuel, 'there is not a single example where high wages have not led to economic development' (ibid., p. 124). Although Emmanuel is prone to overstate his case, there was more than an element of truth in his analysis. Certainly, he is far closer to the truth than those who advocate low wages. Of course, if real wages rise too quickly, profits can collapse, but a steady rise in wages is probably an essential element of a competitive economy.

In reality, an economy can enjoy the benefits of high wages even when it pays wages considerably below the norm for other parts of the world. The recently developing, low-wage nations of South East Asia constitute a case in point. In countries, such as these, which begin with a poor agricultural population, industrial workers may consider themselves to be earning high wages during the initial stages of development, even when their wages are a pittance by our own standards. Industrial wages have continued to grow in these nations, in part, due to economies of high wages. This pattern of rising wages serves these economies well.

Even though we are told that we must lower wages in the United States in order to compete with the low wages paid in these nations, workers themselves may consider their wages to be high so long as they base their norm on the level of agricultural wages. In this sense, we may consider these economies to be high-wage countries.

Over time, these workers will revise their notion of high wages. As a result, wages must continue to increase at a relatively brisk rate. If they do not, workers may turn to political activism to bring their wages in line with their evolving norms of fairness.

For example, the Korean government long used savage repression to keep wages in check. Once the Korean government suddenly reduced the level of repression in 1988, wages soared. For example, at Lucky-Goldstar, wages doubled from 1988 to 1990 (Nakarmi 1991). Not surprisingly, profits fell considerably, but given a bit of time to adjust to these higher wages, advances in technology could more than compensate firms for their higher wage costs.

Should wages in this region continue to rise, within a few decades, these poor, but perhaps subjectively high-wage countries will evolve into what we might objectively consider to be a high-wage countries.

Surprise! Unions Can Promote Productivity

Now that the theory of efficiency wages has fallen from view, the popular press has conditioned us to associate high wages with the scourge of unionization. This ominous force that has supposedly sabotaged the health and welfare of the U.S. economy in more ways than we can count.

In fact, unions play, at worst, an ambiguous role in the economy. True, to protect the welfare of their members, unions have created numerous work rules that impede productivity. Of course, many of these work rule serve valuable purposes, often protecting workers' health and safety.

Conversely, unions have promoted productivity in important ways. To begin with, by raising wages, unions have prodded employers to devise new and improved, labour-saving methods of production, just as the theory of efficiency wages suggests. The precise impact of this effect will not be obvious, since many non-union firms will also eventually adopt these new techniques. Consequently, the spread of these techniques will appear to be part of the general pattern of industrial progress.

Even so, economists consistently find that workers in unionized firms are more productive than workers in comparable non-union companies, despite the impact of union work-rules. For example, Freeman and Medoff conclude that effects of union work rules on efficiency tends to be very small (Freeman and Medoff 1984, p. 12). They provide 'striking new evidence on what unions do to productivity' (ibid., p. 163). They call their results 'striking' because they conclude, 'In sum, most studies of productivity find that unionized establishments are more productive than otherwise comparable nonunion establishments' (ibid., p. 169).

Freeman and Medoff are not alone in regarding unionization to be consistent with high productivity. For example, Steven Allen estimates that union work rules increase typical office building costs by about 2 per cent (Allen 1986a). Allen found that union productivity, measured in square feet of floor space completed per hour worked, was at least 30 per cent higher than non-union productivity.

In the construction of school projects, union productivity was equal to non-union productivity measured by the number of workers required to build a project. Measured in terms of value-added, union productivity was 20 per cent higher then non-union productivity (Allen 1986b). Allen also found that union projects produce 51 per cent more square footage per hour than non-union projects (Allen 1988a). After reviewing the literature concerning the relationship between unions and productivity, Allen concluded that most studies find that union workers are more productive than non-union workers in comparable establishments (Allen 1988b).

Unions even make teachers more productive. For example, students from schools with a unionized environment score about 4.7 per cent higher on their college entrance exams than their counterparts from a non-union environment (Register and Grimes, 1991).

In fairness, we cannot conclude that unions necessarily cause this increase in productivity. In part, unions may be an effect, rather than a cause of high productivity. In other words, firms that are highly productive may be forcing workers to exert themselves beyond what the employees consider to be fair. Indeed, as Tibor Scitovsky noted, in the West in general, workers who felt exploited and resentful frequently turned to unionization in an attempt to create a defensive force to match the force of their employers (Scitovsky 1990, p. 144).

Several authors have built on generalizations, such as Scitovsky's, to reach the conclusion that workers tend to join unions in situations where the work demands are high (FitzRoy and Kraft 1987; and Duncan and Stafford 1980; 1982). According to this line of reasoning, workers are not more productive because they belong to unions. Instead, they belong to unions because their work environment forces them to be more productive.

Freeman and Medoff also lend support to the notion that unions may be the effect, in part, rather than just the cause of high productivity. They concluded that unionized workers in the United States express less satisfaction with their jobs than non-union workers, but are less willing to quit, presumably because of their superior wages (Freeman and Medoff 1984).

Although we cannot prove the extent to which unions are the cause or the effect of higher productivity, the superior efficiency of unionized teachers lends support to the notion that unions do indeed promote productivity. A school administration might treat teachers poorly or deny them adequate resources, but such policies would not be likely to make students learn better. We would have to stretch our imaginations to see how policies that improve students' test scores would drive teachers to join unions.

In any case, unions, however, can be advantageous to employers for several reasons. To begin with, unions can be a boon to employers, especially large-scale employers, who would otherwise have difficulty in recruiting employees to work on weekend and overtime shifts (Allen 1987, p. 352).

Besides raising wages and helping with the mobilization of the labour force, unions can benefit employers by changing workers' feelings about their situation. Freeman and Medoff build on Albert Hirshmann's notion of the importance of voice within an organization. According to Freeman and Medoff, without unions, many workers would lack a voice in the large, faceless corporation.

With a voice, workers can take more satisfaction in knowing that they can make management know how they feel. Without a voice, workers would be reduced to making their negative feelings felt by exit, causing employers to bear the expense of costly employee turnover.

Japan offers some suggestive material regarding the role of unions in giving workers a voice. Japanese unions are company unions. Japanese employers only turned to unionization after a period of intense labour militancy. Workers might be reluctant to cast their lot with company unions, which do not take a particularly adversarial position toward business. In order to make these unions more credible, Japanese firms first offered lifetime employment (Kenney and Florida 1988, p. 128). In the process, Japanese firms soon realized that offering the workers more respect and better working conditions induces better performance (Scitovsky 1990, p. 144).

Although Freeman and Medoff found that unions generally promoted efficiency, they do not always do so to the same extent. At times, unions can even become counterproductive. Freeman and Medoff blame these periods of a negative association between unions and productivity on shifts in labour-management relations, but they do not elaborate on this hypothesis (Freeman and Medoff 1984, p. 168). Presumably, Freeman and Medoff mean that when labour-management relationships deteriorate, unions can assist workers in resisting capital.

Although many students of labour-management relations recognize the benefits of unions, business has been slow in coming around to this position. Instead, it comforts itself by blaming problems on others – on the government, on foreigners, and whenever possible on unions. All the while, we allow our economy the progressively weaken.

How Good Management Can Prod Labour to Work Hard

To the extent that unions can force improvements in labour-management relations, they will make workers more productive. Of course, enlightened management on its own without the intervention of unions can and sometimes does take actions, which improve the relations between labour and capital.

For example, Tom DeMarco and Timothy Lister, report on what they called the Coding Games War, a test that they organized for programmers between 1984 and 1986. They included 600 program developers from 92 companies. Each employee was measured on the ability to design, code and test a medium-size program. The investigators found that pleasantness of the office work environment closely correlated with performance. Developers in top quartile were 30 to 50 per cent more likely to say that their work spaces were acceptably quiet, private and spacious compared with those in lowest quartile (DeMarco and Lister 1987, p. 49). The best programmers seemed to work in an atmosphere of independence. Instead of attributing good programming to stringent monitoring, DeMarco and Lister suggest that the best programmers migrate to those companies that provide the best work environment (ibid., p. 48).

In general, recent experience has shown that workers, who are given detailed rules and are more closely monitored, experience less job satisfaction and are less motivated and place more importance on external rewards, such as compensation (Deci, Connell and Ryan 1985; cited in Akerlof and Yellen 1987). The famous Hawthorne experiments also seemed to indicate that workplace democracy can increase job satisfaction and work effort although some recent work has questioned these results (see Drago 1986).

Harvey Leibenstein suggests that Japanese employers have turned this principle to good effect. He recalled:

Recently I spent six months in Japan and visited some large firms. In all cases I inquired about the way in which employees were monitored. The managers were extremely sensitive to the idea and convinced me . . . that no monitoring by superiors was attempted. Promotions, by and large were a consequence of age and duration of employment. Here we have examples of some highly . . . efficient firms who did everything possible to avoid monitoring. The managers were aware that such practices were carried out in the United States, but these were practices that they assiduously chose not to use, despite the fact that at some earlier period they were tried by some Japanese firms and dropped. (Leibenstein 1983, p. 838)

Unfortunately, the attitude that Leibenstein found in Japan is exceedingly rare in the United States.

Low Wages and the Structure of De-industrialization

Rustow's model highlights what conventional economics obscures: the importance of the structure of the capital stock. If an economy were somehow to develop without severe disruptions, we would expect the amount of new investment to exceed the amount of disinvestment. We would not expect to see many but the very least efficient plants scrapped or turned to more appropriate ends.

Unfortunately, we know very little about the specifics of disinvestment, to a large extent, because economists have an almost pathological aversion to analyzing this subject. A. Lamfalussy, head of the Bank for International Settlements, has observed in this respect, 'Disinvestment is a necessary corollary to growth.' He continued:

> Theoretical economists over the last fifteen years have been so busy analyzing growth that they seem to have forgotten that, even assuming fairly rapid expansion, growth in one industry may occur at the expense of another, so that growth in one field may be associated, indeed is likely to be so, with decline in others. This neglect is based on the implicit assumption that there is little to be said about declining industries. (Lamfalussy 1961, p. xiv)

Even Lamfalussy confined his remarks to disinvestment within the context of declining industries, whereas Rustow reminds us that disinvestment is also an important part of growing industries as well because economic growth itself is a source of disruption.

Unlike Rustow, most economists build models in which the rate of growth is a smooth and regular process. The motivation of their models is a desire for mathematical simplicity rather than realism.

Why should market forces cause an economy to shed a constant percentage of its capital stock each year? Whey should the excess of the rate of new investment relative to the rate of disinvestment constitute another fixed percentage?

Now let us look at Rustow's model again and ask ourselves: why should the economic process proceed tranquilly? Rustow's model calls for us to ask another, more difficult question: if disinvestment does occur irregularly, what market forces stand in the way of disinvestment accumulating so much momentum that it destroys an economy?

Rustow's model warns us of the danger of a disinflationary disinvestment process getting out of hand. In other words, normal competitive processes can become so powerful that they force industry to lower prices. Some firms cannot continue at that price level. As these firms exit their industries, they make competition become even more intense, creating a cumulative downward spiral leading toward a Haitian road to economic development.

Because conventional economic models either treat capital goods as a whole or assume that each good depreciates away at a regular rate, they are ill equipped to address the important questions which Rustow's model poses. As a result, economists regularly conclude that the dangers of a competition-induced disinflation are non-existent. Unfortunately, they arrive at this conclusion without even seriously considering the question.

In this book, I have been arguing that the ignorance of the conventional economists put them in a frame of mind that led them to promote policies that blocked the process of reinvestment. In this respect, they compounded the danger of an economic collapse, but the possibility of a collapse exists irrespective of their policies.

We have observed an alternative route to disinvestment: augmenting wages. High wage pressures can cause less efficient firms to depart, but the increased purchasing power of higher wages can create a wide enough market to accommodate new firms with even more efficient production methods. Consequently, labour can increase wages to capture some of the benefits of this new technology. In the process, some other plants will fall by the wayside, but other new and more efficient plants will take their place.

In the beginning of this book, I argued that I knew of no single economic panacea. We have seen the failure of both regulation and deregulation, of both Keynesian and anti-Keynesian policies. Still a policy of high wages does have some promise. Wage growth is consistent with expanding profits, so long as wages do not accelerate too rapidly, although I know of no measure that could ensure that wages would remain within the necessary bounds.

We can say that a low-wage economy has proven to be a disaster. A high-wage economy certainly could do no worse than what we are witnessing today.

Creativity and Economics

Although economic models assume some sort of efficiency or optimality, economies, like people, rarely work to their full potential. We catch a glimpse of this potential during periods of emergencies when people respond to broader social purposes than just greed. For example, consider how the economy behaves during war time. Robert Lucas estimated the average level of economic efficiency by calculating the trend of the ratio of output per unit of capital in the United States between 1890 and 1954. He found that, at times, for instance during depressions, the actual output per unit of capital fell below his trend line. At other times, the actual output per unit of capital exceeded the trend line.

Lucas discovered that during the war years, 1944 through 1946, the output per unit of capital surpassed the trend line by more than 20 per cent. At no time, before or after, did the U.S. economy match this remarkable performance (Lucas 1970, p. 154).

This achievement is extraordinary because, during this period, many of the most qualified workers were in the military rather than on the shop floor. The workers who replaced them had considerably less work experience. Because of decades of discrimination, the black workers who came from the South to work in Northern factories had much less education than the workers that they replaced. Similarly, many women without much experience working for wages effectively 'manned' the assembly lines.

Conventional economic theory suggests that industrial efficiency should have suffered dire consequences from this reliance on supposedly less qualified labour force, yet Lucas shows that nothing of the sort happened. Instead, productivity soared.

Of course, we are accustomed to expecting productivity to increase during war time. In part, the military Keynesians were correct that war stimulates demand. Lucas himself attributes some of the marvelous performance of the war time economy to the use of overtime in industry.

While increased demand and overtime might have been a factor in stimulating the economy, another important force was at work: war makes people pull together. War creates a sense of urgency. As a result, powerful ideals motivated the people who laboured in the factories in the United States during the war to do their best to help in the struggle against fascism. Such ideals were more compelling than greed for most workers.

Eventually, the consensus frayed around the edges. Workers became frustrated seeing their sacrifices unmatched by their employers who were enjoying unparalleled profits. As a result, toward the end of the war, strike activity began to pick up. Still, the spirit of community was sufficiently strong to produce high levels of productivity.

The war-time experience of Japan and Germany offer an even more powerful illustration of the ability of people to overcome adversity. Jack Hirschleifer reports that ten days of bombing raids during July and August 1943 destroyed half the buildings in Hamburg. Yet, within five months the city had regained up to 80 per cent of its productive capacity (Hirschleifer 1987, pp. 32–3).

On 6 August 1945, the United States Air Force dropped an atomic bomb on Hiroshima. The next day, electric power service was restored to surviving areas. One week later, telephone service restarted (ibid., p. 34).

No doubt the Germans and the Japanese worked also overtime to rebuild their economic capacity, but even trebling the average work day would not have sufficed to accomplish what they did. Their success in reconstructing their economy required enormous creativity and ingenuity.

We also see a more intensive development of new technologies during periods of crisis. Ordinarily, the typical large corporation is timid about exploring new ideas, yet the same people, who typically display little creativity within the confines of the large corporations, make great scientific breakthroughs under the urgency of war.

The development of the computer is a case in point. The U.S. scientific community developed the computer in relatively short order. True, the scientists who participated in this project had no idea of the ultimate potential of the computer. Recall Howard Aitken's firm dismissal of the commercial potential of the computer. Their intention was merely to create a tool to calculate the path of artillery shells more quickly.

Nonetheless, this limited goal spurred them on to important discoveries that revolutionized modern technology. In contrast, even after the microcomputer technology had proven itself, IBM saw no reason to consider changing its reliance on mainframe computers.

Under intense pressure from a few engineers who were more far-sighted than upper management, the company finally agreed to produce a few microcomputers. Nonetheless, the company officially predicted that it would sell only about 250,000 microcomputers over the five-year life cycle of the product (LaPlante and Scannell 1989).

On some level, the company must have realized the potential of the microcomputer. For example, developers of the original PC line chose the 8088 chip rather than the more powerful 8086 because the corporate headquarters would never allow the computer to be built with the 8086, which might threaten the existing IBM line of computers (see Chposky and Leonisis, 1988, pp. 23–4).

The contrast between the innovative spirit of the pioneers of the computer industry and the marketing mentality of modern-day multinational corporations could not be more striking. No wonder so many political leaders become bored by peace and enamoured with war!

Creative Destruction and Destructive Creativity

Joseph Schumpeter, one of the greatest economists of the twentieth century, proposed that large corporations are ideally suited to leading the way in innovations. For Schumpeter, the giant corporations clear the way for progress by developing new products and processes that make huge swaths of the economy obsolete. Schumpeter described this process as 'creative destruction' (Schumpeter 1950).

Some giant corporations in the United States may indeed have grown large by virtue of creative destruction, but, in general, once these organizations have reaped their initial rewards they become lethargic dinosaurs that are destructive of creativity. Recall IBM's attitude toward the micro-computer.

War can sometimes energize these beasts for a while. This destructive creativity gives the illusion that military spending promotes innovation. It does not. Instead, the urgency of the war effort changes people's mind set. The people who contribute their creativity to the war effort see themselves as serving a higher purpose, however misguided they might be.

Our challenge should be to develop creative channels through which people can contribute to more noble goals than the slaughter of their fellow humans. We need to find a way to make people feel the same sense of urgency when a child goes to bed hungry as they do when a flag suffers a supposed indignity. We need to feel as much pride in our smart students as our smart bombs.

Conclusion

In this book, I have tried to demonstrate the fallaciousness of the commonly held conviction that the logic of competition somehow compels U.S. workers to lower their standard of living in order to compete. This Haitian road to development cannot not succeed. If lower wages would give the United States an edge, other countries, including Haiti, would lower their wage levels as well until wages world-wide would fall to a bare subsistence level. The austerity of the Haitian road only promises a greater emphasis on low-wage service jobs and more self-defeating cut-backs in education and infrastructure, further crippling productive capacity.

The Keynesian road points in another direction. It protects the economy from the ravages of competition. In doing so, it also undermines productive capacity by freeing business from the compulsion to renew capital goods. Military Keynesian is doubly destructive since it combines all the disadvantages of Keynesianism with the waste and laxity of the military.

An economy of high wages can provide the competitive pressure required to keep an economy strong without destroying demand. In such an environment, finance will no longer dominate production.

I have repeatedly warned that an economy of high wages by itself is no panacea. A high-wage economy demands a commitment to providing an adequate infrastructure, both physical and intellectual, in the form of an improved educational system. It also requires finding a method to keep corporations from moving their operations abroad to economies that do follow the Haitian road. It requires developing a method that keeps wages high and growing, without letting the wages explode so much that they collapse profit rates.

Still, so long as we adhere to the rules of a market economy, an economy of high wages is the best that we can expect.

Bibliography

Aaron, Henry J. 1990. 'Comments on Aschauer.' In Alicia H. Munnell (ed.), *Is There a Shortfall in Public Capital Investment?* Proceedings of a Conference Held in June 1990, Conference Series No. 34 (Boston: Federal Reserve Bank of Boston): pp. 51–63.

Abelson, Alan. 1989. 'The Rise and Fall of the King of Junk.' *Barrons* (3 April): p. 1.

Abken, Peter A. 1992. 'Corporate Pensions and Government Insurance: Deja Vu All Over Again.' *Economic Review of the Federal Reserve Bank of Atlanta*, Vol. 77, No. 2 (March/April): pp. 1–16.

Adams, Gordon and David Gold. 1987. *Defense Spending and the Economy: Does the Defense Dollar Make a Difference?*, Defense Budget Project at the Center on Budget and Policy Priorities (Washington, D.C.).

Adams, Larry T. 1985. 'Changing Employment Patterns of Organized Workers.' *Monthly Labor Review*, Vol. 108, No. 2 (February): pp. 25–31.

Adams, Walter and Mueller, Hans. 1982. 'The Steel Industry.' in Walter Adams (ed.) *The Structure of American Industry* (New York: Macmillan): pp. 73–135.

Adler, Stephen J. and Laurie P. Cohen. 1988. 'Even Lawyers Gasp Over the Stiff Fees of Wachtell Lipton: Firm's $20 Million Bill to Kraft for Two Weeks of Work Sets New Legal Standard.' *Wall Street Journal* (2 November): pp. A1 and A5.

Akerlof, George A. and Yellen, Janet L. 1986. *Efficiency Wage Models of the Labor Market* (Cambridge University Press).

——. 1987. 'Rational Models of Irrational Behavior.' *American Economic Review*, Vol. 77, No. 2 (May): pp. 137–42.

Alesina, A. and G. Tabellini. 1986. 'A Positive Theory of Fiscal Deficits and Government Debt in a Democracy.' NBER working paper No. 2308 (July).

Allen, Steven G. 1986a. 'Union Work Rules and Efficiency in the Building Trades.' *Journal of Labor Economics*, Vol. 4, No. 2 (April): pp. 212–42.

——. 1986b. 'Unionization and Productivity in Office Building and School Construction.' *Industrial and Labor Relations Review*, Vol. 9, No. 2 (January): pp. 187–202.

——. 1987. 'Can Union Labor Ever Cost Less?' *Quarterly Journal of Economics*, Vol. 52, No. 2 (May): pp. 347–73.

——. 1988a. 'Further Evidence on Union Efficiency in Construction.' *Industrial Relations*, Vol. 27, No. 2 (Spring): pp. 232–40.

——. 1988b. 'Productivity Levels and Productivity Change Under Unionism.' *Industrial Relations*, Vol. 27, No. 1 (Winter): pp. 94–113.

Anders, George. 1981. 'DuPont Deal Puts a Strain on Agent Bank.' *Wall*

Street Journal (25 August): p. 25.

——. 1990. 'Captive Client: Morgan Stanley Found A Gold Mine of Fees by Buying Burlington.' *Wall Street Journal* (14 December): pp. A1 and A6.

——. 1991. 'Computers Bypass Wall Street Middlemen and Stir Controversy.' *Wall Street Journal* (28 August): pp. A1 and A4.

Anon. 1949. 'From Cold War to Cold Peace?' *Business Week* (12 February): pp. 19–20.

Anon. 1950. 'The Treaty of Detroit.' *Fortune*, Vol. 62, No. 1 (July): pp. 53–55.

Anon. 1974. 'Did Controls Flunk Their First Peacetime Test.' *Business Week* (27 April): pp. 106–117.

Anon. 1981. 'State and Local Government in Trouble: Special Report' *Business Week* (26 October).

Anon. 1983. 'For 4 Days' Work, $126,582 an Hour.' *Wall Street Journal* (17 January): p. 33.

Anon. 1984. 'The Worldwide Steel Industry: Struggling to Survive.' *Business Week* (20 August).

Anon. 1986a. The Hollow Corporation: The Decline of Manufacturing Threatens the Entire U.S. Economy.' *Business Week* (3 March).

Anon. 1986b. 'No Comment.' *Monthly Review*, Vol. 38, No. 2 (June): p. 19.

Anon. 1991a. 'American Investment Banking: Beyond the Balance Sheet.' *The Economist* (11 May): pp. 74–8.

Anon. 1991b. 'Swimming on Line One . . . ' *Sports Illustrated* (28 January): p. 28.

Anon. 1991c. 'American Pensions: Gray Peril.' *The Economist* (11 May): pp. 78–9.

Anon. 1992. 'Public School Problems: 1940 vs. 1980.' *CO Researcher* (11 September): p. 797.

Arrow, Kenneth J. 1973. 'Higher Education as a Filter.' *Journal of Public Economics*, Vol. 2 (July): 193–216.

Arthur, W. Brian. 1989. 'Competing Technologies, Increasing Returns, and Lock-in by Historical Events.' *The Economic Journal*, Vol. 99 (March): pp. 116–31.

Aschauer, David Alan. 1988a. 'Is Public Expenditure Productive?' *Journal of Monetary Economics*, Vol. 23, No. 2 (March): pp. 177–200.

——. 1988b. 'Government Spending and the 'Falling Rate of Profit'.' *Chicago Economic Perspectives: A Review From the Federal Reserve Bank of Chicago*, Vol. 13, No. 3 (May/June): pp. 11–17.

——. 1989a. 'Public Investment and Productivity Growth in the Group of Seven.' *Chicago Economic Perspectives: A Review form the Federal Reserve Bank of Chicago*, Vol. 13, No. 5 (September/October): pp. 17–25.

——. 1989b. 'Does Public Capital Crowd Out Private Capital?' *Journal of Monetary Economics*, Vol. 24, No. 2 (September): pp. 171–89.

——. 1990a. ' *Public Investment and Private Sector Growth: The Economic Benefits of Reducing America's 'Third Deficit'* (Washington: D.C. Economic Policy Institute).

——. 1990b. 'Why is Infrastructure Important?' in Alicia H. Munnell, ed. *Is There a Shortfall in Public Capital Investment? Proceedings of a Conference Held in June 1990* Conference Series No. 34 (Boston: Federal Reserve Bank of Boston): pp. 21–50.

——. 1990c. 'Public Spending for Private Profit.' *Wall Street Journal* (14 March): p. A16.

——. 1990. 'Is Government Spending Stimulative?' *Contemporary Policy Issues*, Vol. 8, No. 4 (October): pp. 30–46.

Bahl, Roy. 1984. *Financing State and Local Government in the 1980s* (New York: Oxford University Press).

Bailey, Stephen Kemp. 1950. *Congress Makes a Law: The Story Behind the Employment Act of 1946* (New York: Columbia University Press).

Baily, Martin Neil. 1978. 'The Effectiveness of Anticipated Policy.' *Brookings Papers on Economic Activity*, No. 1: pp. 11–60.

——. 1981a. 'Productivity and the Services of Capital and Labor.' *Brookings Papers on Economic Activity*, No. 1, pp. 1–50.

——. 1981b. 'The Productivity Growth Slowdown and Capital Accumulation.' *American Economic Review*, Vol. 71, No. 2 (May): pp. 326–31.

Balke, Nathan S. and Robert J. Gordon. 1989. 'The Estimation of Prewar Gross National Product: Methodology and New Evidence.' *Journal of Political Economy*, Vol. 97, No. 1 (February): pp. 38–92.

Baran, Paul A. and Sweezy, Paul M. 1966. *Monopoly Capital: An Essay on the American Economic and Social Order* (New York: Monthly Review Press).

Barber, William J. 1985. *From New Era to New Deal: Herbert Hoover, the Economists, and American Economic Policy, 1921–1933* (Cambridge: Cambridge University Press).

Barnett, Donald F. and Schorsch, Louis. 1983. *Steel: Upheaval in a Basic Industry* (Cambridge, Massachusetts: Ballinger).

Bassie, V. L. 1946. 'Consumers' Expenditures in War and Transition.' *Review of Economic Statistics*, Vol. 28, No. 3 (August): pp. 121–9.

Baumgarner, Mary, Jorge Martinez-Vazquez and David L. Sjoquist. 1991. 'Municipal Capital Maintenance and Fiscal Distress.' *Review of Economics and Statistics*, Vol. 73, No. 1 (February): pp. 33–39.

Beck, E. M. and Stewart E. Tolnay. 1990. 'The Killing Fields of the Deep South: The Market for Cotton and the Lynching of Blacks, 1882–1930.' *American Sociological Review*, Vol. 55 (August): pp. 526–38.

Bedwell, Donald E. and Gary W. Tapp. 1982. 'Supply-Side Economics Conference in Atlanta.' *Economic Review of the Federal Reserve Bank of Atlanta*, Vol. 57, No. 5 (May): pp. 25–35.

Bell, Daniel. 1976. *The Coming of Post-Industrial Society* (New York: Basic Books).

Belous, Richard S. 1989. 'How Human Resource Systems Adjust to the Shift toward Contingent Workers.' *Monthly Labor Review*, Vol. 112, No. 3 (March): pp. 7–12.

Bernanke, Ben S. 1986. 'Employment, Hours, and Earnings in the Depression: An Analysis of 8 Manufacturing Industries.' *American Economic Review*, Vol. 76, No. 1 (March): pp. 83–109.

Berndt, Ernst R. 1980. 'Energy Price Increases and the Productivity Slowdown in United States Manufacturing.' in Federal Reserve Bank of Boston, *The Decline in Productivity Growth* (Boston: Federal Reserve Bank of Boston): pp. 60–89.

Bernstein, Aaron. 1988. 'Where the Jobs are is where the Skills Aren't.' *Business Week* (19 September): pp. 104–8.

——. 1990. 'In Search of the Vanishing Nest Egg.' *Business Week* (30 July): p. 46.

Bernstein, Peter L. 1983. 'Capital Stock and Management Decisions.' *Journal of Post Keynesian Economics*, Vol 6, No. 1 (Fall): pp. 20–38.

Bhaduri, Amit and Stephen Marglin. 1990. 'Unemployment and the Real Wage: The Economic Basis for Contesting Political Ideologies.' *Cambridge Journal of Economics*, Vol. 14, No. 4 (December): pp. 378–93.

Bils, Mark. 1909. 'Selling versus Producing in Market Fluctuations.' *Carnegie-Rochester Conference Series on Public Policy* (Autumn).

Bishop, John H. 1989. 'Is the Test Score Decline Responsible for the Productivity Growth Decline?' *American Economic Review*, Vol. 79, No. 1 (March): pp. 178–94.

——. 1991a. 'Docility and Apathy: Its Cause and Cure.' *Educational Reform: Social Change or Political Rhetoric*, Saumel Bacharach, ed. (New York: Allyn Bacon): pp. 234–58.

——. 1991b. 'The Productivity Consequences of What is Learned in High School.' *Journal of Curriculum Studies*, Vol. 22, No. 2: pp. 101–26.

Blank, Rebecca and Alan Blinder. 1986. 'Macroeconomics, Income Distribution and Poverty.' in Sheldon Danziger and Daniel Weinberg, eds. *Fighting Poverty: What Works, What Doesn't* (Harvard: Harvard University Press): pp. 180–208.

Blank, Rebecca and Emma Rothschild. 1985. 'The Effect of United States Defense Spending on Employment and Output.' *International Labour Review*, Vol. 124, No. 6 (November/December): pp. 677–97.

Blinder, Alan. 1981. *Economic Policy and the Great Stagflation* (New York: Academic Press).

Bloch, Ed. 1983. 'Trade and Unemployment: Global Bread-and-Butter Issues.' *Monthly Review*, Vol. 35, No. 5 (October): pp. 28–34.

Block, Fred L. 1977. *The Origins of International Economic Disorder: A Study of United States International Monetary Policy from World War II to the Present* (Berkeley: University of California Press).

Bloom, David E. and Richard B. Freeman. 1992. 'The Fall in Private Pension Coverage in the United States.' *American Economic Review*, Vol. 82, No. 2 (May): pp. 539–45.

Bluestone, Barry and Harrison, Bennett. 1982. *The Deindustrialization of America: Plant Closings, Community Abandonment, and the Dismantling of Basic Industry* (New York: Basic Books).

Bluestone, Barry. 1988. 'Deindustrialization and Unemployment in America.' *Review of Black Political Economy*, Vol. 17, No. 2 (Fall): pp. 29–44.

Bosworth, Barry P. 1985. 'Taxes and the Investment Recovery.' *Brookings Papers on Economic Activity*, No. 1: pp. 1–45.

Bowles, Samuel, David M. Gordon, and Thomas E. Weisskopf. 1983. *Beyond the Wasteland: The Democratic Alternative to Economic Decline* (Garden City, New York: Doubleday).

——. 1989. 'Business Ascendancy and Economic Impasse: A Structural Retrospective on Conservative Economics, 1979–87.' *Journal of Economic Perspectives*, Vol. 3, No. 1 (Winter): pp. 107–34.

Brauer, David. 1991. 'The Effect of Imports on U.S. Manufacturing Wages.' *Federal Reserve Bank of New York Quarterly Review*, Vol. 16, No. 1 (Spring): pp. 14–26.

Bronfenbrenner, Martin, (ed.) 1969a. *Is the Business Cycle Obsolete? Based on a Conference of the Social Science Council Committee on Economic Stability* (New York: Wiley-Interscience).

——. 1969b. 'Summary of the Discussion.' in Bronfenbrenner (ed.) 1969a, pp. 505–59.

Bruck, Connie. 1989. *The Predators' Ball: The Inside Story of Drexel Burnham and the Rise of the Junk Bond Traders* (New York: Penguin).

Buckley, William F., jr. 1971. 'Are You a Keynesian?' *National Review*, Vol. 23 (9 February): pp. 162–3.

Burawoy, Michael. 1979. *Manufacturing Consent* (Chicago: University of Chicago Press).

Calomaris, Charles W. and R. Glenn Hubbard. 1990. 'Firm Heterogeneity, Internal Finance and "Credit Rationing".' *The Economic Journal*, Vol. 100, No. 399 (March): pp. 90–104,

Carey, John. 1990. 'Can U.S.Defense Labs Beat Missiles into Microchips?' *Business Week* (17 September): pp. 84–92.

Carlson, Bo. 1989. 'Flexibility and the Theory of the Firm.' *International Journal of Industrial Organization*, Vol. 7, No. 2 (June): pp. 179–204.

Carlson, John A. 1977. 'A Study of Price Forecasts.' *Annals of Economic Social Measurement*, Vol. 6, pp. 27–56.

Carter, Anne P. 1970. *Structural Change in the American Economy* (Cambridge, Massachusetts: Harvard University Press).

Carver, Thomas Nixon. 1925. *The Present Economic Revolution in the United States* (Boston: Little Brown).

Castells, Manuel. 1980. *The Economic Crisis and American Society* (Princeton: Princeton University Press).

Cerruzzi, Paul. 1986. 'An Unforseen Revolution: Computers and Expectations, 1935–1985.' In Joseph J. Corn (ed.) *Imagining Tomorrow* (Cambridge: MIT Press).

Chall, Daniel E. 1981. 'The Economic Costs of Subway Deterioration.' *Federal Reserve Bank of New York Quarterly Review*, Vol. 6, No. 1 (Spring): pp. 8–14.

Chandler, Alfred D. Jr. 1969. 'The Structure of American Industry in the Twentieth Century: A Historical Review.' *Business History Review*, Vol. 63 (Autumn): pp. 255–98.

——. 1990. *Scale and Scope: The Dynamics of Industrial Capitalism* (New York: Alfred A. Knopf).

Chipello, Christopher J. and Marcus W. Brauchli. 1990. 'Japan Has Greatly Boosted Its Resistance to Oil Shocks.' *Wall Street Journal* (9 August): p. A7.

Choate, Pat and Susan Walter. 1981. *America in Ruins: The Decaying Infrastructure* (Durham: Duke University Press).

Chposky, James and Leonisis, Ted. 1988. *Blue Magic: The People, Power and Politics Behind the IBM Personal Computer* (New York and Oxford: Facts on File Publications).

Clark, Gregory. 1987. 'Why Isn't The Whole World Developed? Lessons from the Cotton Mills.' *Journal of Economic History*, Vol. 47, No. 1 (March): pp. 141–73.

Cohen, Stephen S. and John Zysman. 1987. *Manufacturing Matters: The Myth of the Post-industrial Economy* (New York: Basic Books).

Collins, Robert. 1981. *Business Response to Keynes, 1929–1964* (New York: Columbia University Press).

Committee for Economic Development. 1987. *Children in Need: Investment Strategies for the Educationally Disadvantaged* (New York: Committee for Economic Development).

Cowherd, Raymond G. 1977 *Political Economists and the English Poor Laws: A Historical Study of the Influence of Classical Economics on the Formation of Social Welfare Policy* (Athens: Ohio University Press).

Craypo, Charles. 1990. 'The Decline of Union Bargaining Power.' in Bruce Nissan, ed. *U.S. Labor Relations, 1945–1989* (New York: Garland): pp. 3–40.

Cross, Rod. 1987. 'Hysteresis and Instability in the Natural Rate of Unemployment.' *Scandinavian Journal of Economics*, Vol. 89, No. 1: pp. 71–89.

Cusumano, Michael A. 1991. *Japan's Software Factories: A Challenge to U.S. Management* (Oxford: Oxford University Press).

Cutler, David M. and Lawrence H. Summers. 1988. 'The Costs of Conflict Resolution and Financial Distress: Evidence from the Texaco-Penzoil Litigation.' *Rand Journal of Economics* Vol. 19, No. 2 (Summer): pp. 157–72.

Cwiklik, Robert. 1990. 'Serious Money.' *The Nation*, Vol. 250, No. 15 (16 April): p. 524.

Cypher, James M. 1991. 'Military Spending After the Cold War.' *Journal of Economic Issues*, Vol. 25, No. 2 (June): pp. 607–16.

Daly, A., D. M. W. N. Hitchens and K. Wagner. 1985. 'Productivity, Machinery and Skills in a Sample of British and German Manufacturing Plants.' National Institute Economic Review, No. 111 (February): pp. 48–61..

Danziger, Sheldon and Peter Gottschalk. 1986. 'Do Rising Tides Lift All Boats? The Impact of Secular and Cyclical Changes on Poverty.' *American*

Economic Review, Vol. 76, No. 2 (May): pp. 405–410.

Davidson, Paul. 1972. *Money and the Real World* (New York and Toronto: John Wiley).

Dawson, Michael and John Bellamy Foster. 1991. 'The Tendency for the Surplus to Rise, 1963–88.' *Monthly Review*, Vol. 43, No. 4 (September): pp. 37–50.

Deci, Edward L., Connell, James L. and Ryan, Richard M. 1985. 'Self-Determination in a Work Organization.' (mimeo).

DeMarco, Tom and Lister, Timothy. 1987. *Peopleware: Productive Projects and Teams* (New York: Dorset House).

Denison, Edward F. 1964. 'The Unimportance of the Embodiment Question.' *American Economic Review*, Vol. 54, No. 1 (March): pp. 90–4.

Denison, Edward F. 1985. *Trends in American Economic Growth, 1929–1982* (Washington, D.C.: Brookings Institution).

Dertouzos, Michael L., Richard K. Lester, Robert M. Solow and the MIT Commission on Industrial Productivity. 1989. *Made in America: Regaining the Productive Edge* (Cambridge, MA: The MIT Press).

Dione, E. J. 1981. 'Many Billions Necessary to Restore Public Works, Albany Aides Say.' *New York Times* (13 October): p. B1.

Doyle, P. M. 1985. 'Area Wage Surveys Shed Light on Decline of Unionization.' *Monthly Labor Review*, Vol. 105, No. 9 (September): 13–20.

Drago, Robert. 1986. 'Capitalism and Efficiency: A Review and Appraisal of the Recent Discussion.' *Review of Radical Political Economy*, Vol. 18, No. 4 (Winter) pp. 71–92.

DuBoff, Richard. 1989. 'What Military Spending Really Costs.' *Challenge*, Vol. 32, No. 5 (September/October): pp. 4–10.

DuBoff, Richard B. and Herman, Edward S. 1972. 'The New Economics: Handmaiden of Inspired Truth.' *Review of Radical Economics*, Vol. 4, No. 4 (August): pp. 54–84.

——. 1989. 'The Promotional-Dynamic of Merger Movement: A Historical Perspective.' *Journal of Economic Issues*, Vol. 23, No. 1 (March): pp. 107–33.

Dumenil, Gerard, Mark Glick and Jose Rangel. 1987. 'Theories of the Great Depression: Why Did Profitability Matter?' *Review of Radical Political Economy*, Vol. 19, No. 2 (Summer): pp. 16–42.

Duncan, G. C. and F. P. Stafford. 1980. 'Do Union Members Receive Compensating Wage Differentials?' *American Economic Review*, Vol. 70, No. 3 (June): pp. 355–71.

——. 1982. 'Do Union Members Receive Compensating Wage Differentials? Reply.' *American Economic Review* Vol. 72, No. 4 (September): pp. 868–72.

Editors of *Business Week*. 1990. 'We Need to Repair our Economic Compass.' *Business Week* (13 August): p. 128.

Editors of *Business Week*. 1990. 'It's Time to Shrink the Weapons Labs.' *Business Week* (17 September): p. 164.

Editors of *Monthly Review*. 1983. 'Unemployment: The Failure of Private Enterprise.' *Monthly Review*, Vol. 35, No. 2 (June): pp. 1–9.

Edelstein, Michael. 1990. 'What Price Cold War? Military Spending and Private Investment in the US, 1946–79.' *Cambridge Journal of Economics*, Vol. 14, No. 4 (December): pp. 421–37.

Edwards, Edgar O. 1955. 'The Effect of Capital Depreciation on the Capital Coefficient of a Firm.' *Economic Journal*, Vol. 45, No. 260 (December): pp. 654–66.

Eisner, Robert. 1991. Infrastructure and Regional Economic Performance: Comment.' *New England Economic Review* (September/October): pp. 47–58.

Eisner, Robert and Robert Chirinko. 1983. 'Tax Policy and Investment Models in Major U.S. Macroeconomic Models.' *Journal of Public Economics*, Vol. 20, No. 2 (March): pp. 139–66.

Emmanuel, Arghiri. 1972. *Unequal Exchange: A Study of the Imperialism of Trade* (New York: Monthly Review Press).

Epstein, David F. 1990. 'The Economic Cost of Soviet Security and Empire.' in Henry S. Rowen and Charles Wolf, Jr. 1990. *The Impoverished Superpower: Perestroika and the Soviet Military Burden* (San Francisco: Institute for Contemporary Studies): pp. 127–54.

Epstein, Gerald. 1990–1991. 'Mortgaging America: Debt, Lies, and Multinationals.' *World Policy Journal* (Winter): pp. 27–59.

Etzioni, Amitai. 1988. *The Moral Dimension: Toward A New Economics* (New York: The Free Press).

——. 1991. 'The Socioeconomic View of Redevelopment.' *Review of Political Economy*, Vol. 3, No. 4 (October): pp. 373–92.

Etzold, Thomas H. and John Lewis Gaddis. 1978. 'NSC 68: The Strategic Reassessment of 1950.' in Thomas H. Etzold and John Lewis Gaddis, eds. *Containment: Documents on American Policy and Strategy, 1945–1950* (New York: Columbia University Press, 1978): pp. 383–855.

Fairris, David. 1990. 'Appearance and Reality in Postwar Shopfloor Relations.' *Review of Radical Political Economy*, Vol. 22, No. 4 (Winter): pp. 17–43.

Fazzari, Steven, R. Glenn Hubbard and Bruce Peterson. 1988. 'Investment, Financing Decisions and Tax Policy.' *American Economic Review*, Vol. 78, No. 2 (May): pp. 200–5.

Fenoaltea, Stefano. 1984. 'Slavery and Supervision in Comparative Perspective: A Model.' *Journal of Economic History*, Vol. 44, No. 3 (September): pp. 635–68.

Fiorito, Jack and Cheryl L. Maranto. 1987. 'The Contemporary Decline of Union Strength.' *Contemporary Policy Issues*, Vol. 5, No. 4 (October): pp. 12–27.

Fisher, Franklin M. and John J. McGowan. 1983. 'On the Misuse of Accounting Rates of Return to Infer Monopoly Profits.' *American Economic Review*, Vol. 73, No. 1 (May): pp. 82–97.

Fitzgerald, A. Ernest. 1989. *The Pentagonists* (Boston: Houghton Mifflin).

FitzRoy, Felix R. and Kornelius Kraft. 1985. 'Unionization, Wages and Efficiency: Theories and Evidence from the U.S. and West Germany.' *Kyklos*, Vol. 38, No. 4, pp. 537–54.

Flamm, Kenneth. 1988a. *Creating the Computer: Government, Industry, and High Technology* (Washington, DC: The Brookings Institution).

——. 1988b. *Targeting the Computer: Government Support and International Competition* (Washington, DC: The Brookings Institution).

Florida, Richard and Martin Kenney. 1990a. *The Breakthrough Illusion: Corporate America's Failure to Move from Innovation to Mass Production* (New York: Basic Books).

——. 1990b. 'High-technology Restructuring in the USA and Japan.' *Environment and Planning* A, Vol. 22, pp. 233–52.

Frankel, Boris. 1987. *The Post-Industrial Utopians* (Madison: University of Wisconsin Press).

Frankel, Max. 1972. 'The Budget: Defense vs Social Aims.' *The New York Times* (25 January): pp. 1 and 18.

Freeman, Richard B. and James Medoff. 1984. *What Do Unions Do?* (New York: Basic Books).

Friedman, Milton. 1968. 'The Role of Monetary Policy.' *American Economic Review*, Vol. 58, No. 1 (March): pp. 1–17.

——. 1980. 'The Changing Character of Financial Markets.' In Martin Feldstein (ed.) *The American Economy in Transition* (Chicago: University of Chicago Press): pp. 78–86.

——. 1988. 'Why the Twin Deficits Are a Blessing?' *Wall Street Journal* (14 December): p. A14.

Fuchs, Victor R. 1989. 'Women's Quest for Economic Equality.' *Journal of Economic Perspectives*, Vol. 3, No. 1 (Winter): pp. 25–41.

Garbarino, Joseph. 1962. *Wage Policy and Long Term Contracts* (Washington, DC: The Brookings Institution).

Gartman, David. 1986. *Auto Slavery: The Labor Process in the American Automobile Industry, 1897–1950* (New Brunswick: Rutgers University Press).

Gates, Paul W. 1960. *The Farmer's Age: Agriculture, 1815–1860* (New York: Harper and Row).

Gau, Robert S. 1984. 'Union Settlements and Aggregate Wage Behavior in the 1980s.' *Federal Reserve Bulletin* (December): pp. 843–56; reprinted in Ben Bernanke, ed. *Readings and Cases in Macroeconomics* (New York: McGraw-Hill, 1987): pp. 280–300.

Gaylord, W. W. 1940. 'Don't Expect All New Equipment to Pay Out in Three Years.' *Factory Management and Maintenance*, Vol. 98, No. 2 (February): p. 52.

Genovese, Eugene D. 1976. *Roll, Jordan, Roll: The World the Slaves Made* (New York: Vintage).

Gibbons, Joel C. 1984. 'Energy Prices and Capital Obsolescence: Evidence from the Oil Embargo Period.' *The Energy Journal*, Vol. 5, No. 1 (January): pp. 29–44.

Gilder, George. 1989. *Microcosm: The Quantum Revolution in Economics and Technology* (New York: Simon and Schuster).

Gillespie, Stephen. 1990. 'Are Economic Statistics Overproduced?' *Public Choice* Vol. 67, No. 3 (December): pp. 227–42.

Gintis, Herbert and Samuel Bowles. 1976. *Schooling in Capitalist America: Educational Reforms and the Contradictions of Economic Life* (New York: Basic Books).

Glasgall, William. 1988. 'The World's Top 50 Banks: It's Official – Japan Is Way Out Front.' *Business Week* (27 June): 76–8.

Gleckman, Howard. 1991. 'Washington's Misleading Maps of the Economy.' *Business Week* (3 June): pp. 112–3.

Glyn, Andrew, Alan Hughes, Alain Lipietz, and Ajit Singh. 1990. 'The Rise and Fall of the Golden Age.' Stephen A. Marglin and Juliet B. Schor, eds. *The Golden Age of Capitalism: Reinterpreting the Postwar Experience* (Oxford: Clarendon Press): pp. 38–125.

Gold, David. 1990. *The Impact of Defense Spending on Investment, Productivity and Economic Growth* (Washington, D.C.: Defense Budget Project).

Goldsmith, Raymond W. 1958. *Financial Intermediaries in the American Economy since 1900* (Princeton: Princeton University Press).

Gorbachev, Mikhail. 1987. *Perestroika: New Thinking for Our Country and the World* (New York: Harper and Row).

Gordon, R. A. 1969. 'The Stability of the U.S. Economy.' In Bronfenbrenner (ed.): pp. 3–35.

Gordon, Robert J. 1980. 'Postwar Macroeconomics: The Evolution of Events and Ideas.' In Martin Feldstein, ed. *The American Economy in Transition: A Sixtieth Anniversary Conference* (Chicago: University of Chicago Press): pp. 101–62.

Gordon, Robert J. and Veitch, John M. 1984. 'Fixed Investment in the American Business Cycle, 1919–83.' National Bureau of Economic Research Working Paper No. 1426 (August).

Gort, Michael. 1962. *Diversification and Integration in American Industry* (Princeton: Princeton University Press).

Gray, Patricia Bellew. 1986. 'Parties, Polls and Pejoratives: Lawyers Meet.' *The Wall Street Journal* (13 August): p. 25.

Green, Alison and David Mayes. 1991. 'Technical Inefficiency in Manufacturing Industries.' *The Economic Journal*, Vol. 101, No. 406 (May): pp. 523–38.

Griffin, Larry J., Michael Wallace, and Joel A. Devine. 1982. 'The Political Economy of Military Spending: Evidence from the United States, *Cambridge Journal of Economics*, Vol. 6, No. 1 (March): pp. 1–14.

Griliches, Zvi. 1988. 'Productivity Puzzles and R&D: Another Nonexplanation.' *Journal of Economic Perspectives*, Vol. 2, No. 4 (Fall): pp. 9–21.

Gruebler, Arnulf. 1990. *The Rise and Fall of Infrastructures: Dynamics of Evolution and Technical Change in Transport* (Heidelberg: Physica Verlag).

Habakkuk, H. J. 1962. *American and British Technology in the Nineteenth*

Century: The Search for Labour-Saving Inventions (Cambridge: Cambridge University Press).

Halberstam, David. 1986. *The Reckoning* (New York: William Morrow).

Hanushek, Eric A. 1986. 'The Economics of Schooling: Production and Efficiency in Public Schools.' *Journal of Economic Literature*, Vol. 14, No. 3 (September): pp. 1141–77.

Hargaves-Heap, S. P. 1980. 'Choosing the wrong natural rate, accelerating inflation or decelerating unemployment and growth.' *Economic Journal*, Vol. 90, No. 359 (September): pp. 611–20

Harris, Howell J. 1982. *The Right to Manage: Industrial Relations Policies of American Business in the 1940s* (Madison: University of Wisconsin Press).

Harris, Seymour E. 1964. *The Economics of the Kennedy Years and a Look Ahead* (New York: Harper and Row).

Harrison, Bennett. 1972. 'Education and Unemployment in the Urban Ghetto.' *American Economic Review*, Vol. 62, No. 5, pp. 796–812.

Harrison, Harrison and Barry Bluestone. 1988. *The Great U-Turn: Corporate Restructuring and the Polarizing of America* (New York: Basic Books).

——. 1990. 'Wage Polarisation in the US and the 'Flexibility' Debate.' *Cambridge Journal of Economics*, Vol. 14, No. 3 (September): pp. 351–73.

Heede, R. Richard and Amory B. Lovens. 1985. 'Hiding the True Costs of Energy Sources.' *Wall Street Journal* (17 September): p. 28.

Heller, Walter W. 1966. *New Dimensions of Political Economy* (New York: W.W. Norton).

Henwood, Douglas. 1990. 'A Compendium of Woes.' *Left Business Observer*, No. 40 (14 September): pp. 4–5.

——. 1991. 'The Uses of Crisis.' *Left Business Observer* (3 June): pp. 1–3.

Herz, Diane E. 1990. 'Worker Displacement in a Period of Rapid Job Expansion: 1983–87.' *Monthly Labor Review*, Vol. 113, No. 5 (May): pp. 21–33.

——. 1991. 'Worker Displacement Still Common the Late 1980's.' *Monthly Labor Review*, Vol. 114, No. 5 (May): pp. 3–9.

Hickok, Susan. 1991. 'The Shifting Composition of U.S. Manufactured Goods Trade.' *Federal Reserve Bank of New York Quarterly Review*, Vol. 16, No. 1 (Spring): pp. 27–37.

Hicks, John R. 1932. *Theory of Wages* (New York: St. Martin's Press, 1963).

Hill. T. P. 1977. 'On goods and services.' *Review of Income and Wealth*, Series 23, No. 4 (December): pp. 315–38.

Hillard, Michael and Richard McIntrye. 1991. 'A Kinder Gentler Capitalism? Resurgent Corporate Liberalism in the Age of Bush.' *Rethinking Marxism*, Vol. 4, No. 1 (Spring): pp. 104–14.

Hirschleifer, Jack. 1987. *Economic Behaviour in Adversity* (Chicago: University of Chicago Press).

Hooks, Gregory. 1991. *Forging the Military-Industrial Complex: World War II's Battle of the Potomac* (Urbana: University of Illinois Press).

Hulbert, Mark. 1982. *Interlock: The Untold Story of American Banks, Oil Interests, the Shah's Money, Debts and the Astounding Connection Between Them* (New York: Richardson and Snyder).

Hulten, Charles R. 1992. 'Growth Accounting When Technical Change is Embodied in Capital.' *American Economic Review*, Vol. 82, No. 4 (September): pp. 964–80.

Hungerford, Thomas and Gary Solon. 1987. 'Sheepskin Effects in the Returns to Education.' *Review of Economics and Statistics*, Vol. 49, No. 1 (February): pp. 175–7.

Hunter, Helen Manning. 1982. 'The Role of Business Liquidity During the Great Depression and Afterwards: Differences Between Large and Small Firms.' *Journal of Economic History*, Vol. 42, No. 4 (December): pp. 883–902.

Institute of Science and Technology, Industrial Development Division, University of Michigan. 1984. 'Revitalization of Industrial Buildings: An Investigation of Economic Impact Resulting from Closing of Aged Industrial Plants.' U.S. Research and Development Report, NTIS PB 84–162478.

Jackman, Richard and Richard Layard. 1991. 'Does Long-term Unemployment Reduce a Person's Chance of a Job? A Time Series Test.' *Economica*, Vol. 58, No. 229 (February): pp. 93–106.

Jenks, Jeremiah. 1890. 'The Economic Outlook.' *Dial*, 10; cited in Livingstone 1986.

Jensen, Michael. 1988. 'Takeovers: Their Causes and Consequences.' *Journal of Economic Perspectives*, Vol. 2, No. 1 (Winter): pp. 21–48.

Jerome, Harry. 1934. *Mechanization in Industry* (New York: National Bureau of Economic Research).

Jordan, J. S. 1989. 'The Economics of Accounting Information Systems.' *American Economic Review*, Vol. 79, No. 2 (May): pp. 140–5.

Juster, F. Thomas, Chairman of the American Economic Association Committee on the Quality of Statistics. 1988. 'The State of U.S. Economic Statistics: Current and Prospective Quality, Policy Needs, and Resources.' prepared for the 50th Anniversary Congress on Income and Wealth, Washington, D.C. (12–14 May).

Kanabayashi, Masayoshi. 1990. 'Rebuilding Japan: Prompted by the U.S., Tokyo Slates Trillions in Domestic Spending.' *Wall Street Journal* (3 January): pp. A1 and A8.

Kaplinsky, Raphael. 1988. 'Restructuring the capitalist labour process: some lessons from the car industry.' *Cambridge Journal of Economics*, Vol. 12, No. 4 (December): pp. 451–70.

Kapstein, Ethan B. 1990. 'From Guns to Butter in the USSR.' Vol. *Challenge*, Vol. 32, No. 5 (September/October): pp. 11–5.

Keezer, Dexter M. 1958. *New Forces in American Business* (McGraw-Hill: New York).

Kenney, Martin and Richard Florida. 1988. 'Beyond Mass Production: Production and the Labor Process in Japan.' *Politics and Society*, Vol. 16,

No. 1 (March): pp. 121–58.

Keynes, John Maynard. 1931a. 'The Consequences to the Banks of the Collapse of Money Values.' *Essays in Persuasion.* Vol. ix. *The Collected Writings of John Maynard Keynes,* Elizabeth Johnston, ed. (London: Macmillan, 1972): pp. 150–8.

——. 1931b. 'An Economic Analysis of Unemployment.' in Philip Quincy Wright, (ed.) *Unemployment as a World-Problem: Lectures at the Harris Foundation, 1931* (Freeport, New York: Books for Libraries Press), pp. 3–43, reprinted in Elizabeth Johnston, (ed.), *The Collected Works of John Maynard Keynes,* Vol. XIII, *The General Theory and After,* Part I, *Preparation* (London: Macmillan, 1973): pp. 343–67.

——. 1936. *The General Theory of Employment, Interest and Money* (London: Macmillan).

King, F. H. 1911. *Farmers of Forty Centuries or Permanent Agriculture in China, Korea and Japan* (Emmaus, Pa.: Rodale Press, 1972).

Kislev, Yoav and Peterson, Willis. 1982. 'Prices, Technology, and Farm Size.' *Journal of Political Economy,* Vol. 90, No. 3 (June): pp. 578–95.

Klein, Lawrence R. 1983. *The Economics of Supply and Demand* (Baltimore, Maryland: The Johns Hopkins University Press).

Komiya, R. 1975. 'Planning in Japan.' in M. Bernstein, ed. *Economic Planning: East and West* (New York: Ballinger).

Kopcke, Richard W. 1980. 'Potential Growth, Productivity, and Capital Accumulation.' *New England Economic Review* (May/June), pp. 22–41.

Kravis, Irving B. and Richard E. Lipsey. 1988. 'The Effect of Multinational Firms' Foreign Operations on their Domestic Employment.' National Bureau of Economic Research Working Paper No. 2760.

——. 1989. 'Technological Characteristics of Industries and the Competitiveness of the U.S. and Its Multinational Firms.' National Bureau of Economic Research Working Paper No. 2933.

Krugman, Paul. 1990. *The Age of Diminished Expectations* (Cambridge, Ma.: MIT Press.

Labaton, Stephen. 1988. '200 Million in Wall St. Fees Seen From Federated Deal.' *New York Times* (5 April).

Lamfalussy, A. 1961. *Investment and Growth in Mature Economies: The Case of Belgium* (London: Macmillan).

LaPlante, Alice and Ed Scannell. 1989. 'View from the Top.' *Infoworld,* Vol. 11, No. 40 (2 October): pp. 53–60.

Lawrence, Robert Z. 1983, 'Is Trade Deindustrializing America? A Medium Term Perspective.' *Brookings Papers on Economic Activiety,* No. 1, pp. 129–71.

Layard, Richard. 1988. 'Comments on Michael Burda. 'Wait Unemployment' in Europe.' *Economic Policy,* No. 7 (October): pp. 416–9.

Lazonick, William. 1989. 'Controlling the Market for Corporate Control: The Historical Significance of Managerial Capitalism.' Barnard Working Paper No. 90–04.

——. 1990. *Competitive Advantage on the Shop Floor* (Cambridge: Harvard

University Press).

Leibenstein, Harvey. 1983. 'Property Rights and X-efficiency: Comment.' *American Economic Review*, Vol. 73, No. 4 (September): pp. 831–42.

Lekachman, Robert. 1966. *The Age of Keynes* (New York: Random House).

Leontief, W. 1981. 'Testimony.' in United States House of Representatives. 1981. 97th Congress, 1st Sess. Committee on Energy and Commerce. Subcommittee on Oversight and Investigations. *Capital Formation and Industrial Policy, Part 1. Hearings, 27 and 29 April, 1, 22 and 24 June* (Washington, D.C.: U.S. Government Printing Office).

Levin, Henry M. 1989. 'Economics of Investment in Educationally Disadvantaged Students.' *American Economic Review*, Vol. 79, No. 2 (May): pp. 52–6.

Levitan, Sar A. and Isaac Shapiro. 1987. 'What's Missing in Welfare Reform?' *Challenge*, 30: 3 (July–August): pp. 41–8.

Levy, Frank. 1988. *Dollars and Dreams: The Changing American Income Distribution* (NY: Norton).

Lewis, Michael. 1989. *Liar's Poker: Rising Through the Wreckage on Wall Street* (New York: W.W. Norton).

Light, Jay O. and Andre F. Perold. 1987. 'The Institutionalization of Wealth: Changing Patterns of Investment Decision Making.' in Samuel P. Hayes, III, ed. *Wall Street and Regulation* (Harvard University Press).

Linbeck, Assar. 1981. 'Industrial Policy as an Issue in the Economic Environment.' *The World Economy*, Vol. 9, Nos. 11 and 12 (November/December): pp. 391–405.

Lippert, John. 1978. 'Shopfloor Politics at Fleetwood.' *Radical America*, Vol. 12, No. 4 (July/August): pp. 25–44.

Livingston, James. 1986. *Origins of the Federal Reserve System: Money, Class, and Corporate Capitalism, 1890–1913* (Ithaca, New York: Cornell University Press).

Locay, Luis. 1990. 'Economic Development and the Division of Production between Households and Markets.' *Journal of Political Economy*, Vol. 98, No. 5 (Part 1) (October): pp. 965–82.

Lucas, Robert E., Jr. 1970. 'Capacity, Overtime, and Empirical Production Fuctions.' *American Economic Review*, Vol. 60, No. 2 (May): pp. 23–27; reprinted in his *Studies in Business Cycle Theory* (Cambridge, MA: MIT Press, 1983): pp. 146–55.

Lucia, Joseph L. 1983. 'Allan Sproul and the Treasury-Federal Reserve Accord of 1951.' *History of Political Economy*, Vol. 15, No. 1 (Spring): pp. 106–21.

Lundberg, Erik. 1985. 'The Rise and Fall of the Swedish Model.' *Journal of Economic Literature*, Vol. 23, No. 1 (March): pp. 1–36.

Lynd, Staughton. 1989. 'Industry goes for the steal.' *In These Times*, Vol. 13, No. 11 (1–7 February): p. 20

McElhattan, Rose. 1985. 'Inflation, Supply Shocks and the Stable Rate of Capacity Utilization.' *Federal Reserve Bank of San Francisco Review* (Winter): pp. 45–63.

McHugh, Richard and Lane, Julia. 1987. 'The Role of Embodied Techno-logical Change in the Decline of Labor Productivity.' *Southern Economic Journal*, Vol. 53, No. 4 (April): pp. 915–24.

Maddison, Angus. 1964. *Economic Growth in the West: Comparative Experience in Europe and North America* (New York: Twentieth Century Fund).

Madison, Bernard L. and Therese A. Hart for the Committee on the Mathematical Sciences in the Year 2000. 1990. *A Challenge of Numbers: People in the Mathematical Sciences* (Washington, D.C.: National Academy Press).

Magaziner, Ira and Robert Reich. 1981. *Managing America's Business: The Decline and Rise of the American Economy* (Harcourt, Brace, and Jovanovich).

Magdoff, Harry and Paul Sweezy. 1983. 'International Finance and National Power.' *Monthly Review*, Vol. 35, No. 5 (October): pp. 1–13.

——. 1985. 'The Strange Recovery of 1983–1984.' *Monthly Review*, Vol. 37, No. 5 (October): pp. 1–11.

——. 1990. 'Investment for What?' *Monthly Review*, Vol. 42, No. 2 (June): pp. 1–10.

Magnusson, Paul, Eric Schine, Barbara Buell and Bruce Hager. 1990. 'American Smart Bombs, Foreign Brains.' *Business Week* (4 March 1991): p. 18.

Malabre, Alfred L., jr. 1988. 'Shaky Statistics Pose Peril for Forecasters.' *Wall Street Journal* (9 May): p. 1.

——. 1990a. 'Economic Roadblock: Infrastructure Neglect.' *Wall Street Journal* (30 July): p. A1.

Malabre, Alfred L., Jr. 1990b. 'The Economy's Faulty Barometer's.' *Wall Street Journal* (26 December): p. 6.

Malcomson, James M. 1975. 'Replacement and the Rental Value of Capital Equipment Subject to Obsolescence,' *Journal of Economic Theory*, Vol. 10, No. 1 (February): pp. 24–41.

Malecki, Edward J. 1991. *Technology and Economic Development: The Dynamics of Local, Regional, and National Change* (New York: Longman Scientific and Technical).

Mandel, Michael J. and Aaron Bernstein. 1990. 'Dispelling the Myths that are Holding Us Back.' *Business Week* (17 December): pp. 66–70.

Marglin, Stephen A. 1990. 'Lessons of the Golden Age: An Overview.' in Stephen A. Marglin and Juliet B. Schor, eds. *The Golden Age of Capitalism: Reinterpreting the Postwar Experience* (Oxford: Clarendon Press): pp. 1–38.

Markides, Constantinos and Norman Berg. 1988. 'Manufacturing Offshore Is Bad Business.' *Harvard Business Review*, Vol. 66 (September–October): pp. 113–20.

Marshall, Alfred. 1920. *Principles of Economics: An Introductory Volume*, 8th ed. (London: Macmillan & Co.).

Marshall, Andrew. 1987. 'Commentary.' in United States Congress. Joint

Economic Committee. *Gorbachev's Economic Plans*, 2 vols. (Washington, D.C.: U.S. Government Printing Office): pp. 481–4.

May, Ann Mari and Randi R. Grant. 1991. 'Class Conflict, Corporate Power, and Macroeconomic Policy: The Impact of Inflation in the Postwar Period.' *Journal of Economic Issues*, Vol. 25, No. 2 (June): pp. 373–81.

Mayer, Martin. 1974. *The Bankers* (New York: Ballantin Books).

——. 1990. *The Greatest-Ever Bank Robbery: The Collapse of the Savings and Loan Industry* (New York: Charles Scribner).

Melman, Seymour. 1983. *Profits Without Production* (New York: Alfred A. Knopf).

——. 1988. 'Economic Consequences of the Arms Race: The Second-Rate Economy.' *American Economic Review*, Vol. 78, No. 2 (May): pp. 55–9.

Melman, Seymour and Lloyd J. Dumas. 1990. 'Planning for Economic Conversion.' *The Nation*, Vol. 250, No. 15 (16 April): pp. 509 and 522–8.

Meltzer, Allan H. 1988. 'Economic policies and actions in the Reagan administration.' *Journal of Post Keynesian Economics*, Vol. 10, No. 4 (Summer): pp. 528–40.

Metzenbaum, Senator Howard M. 1991. 'Testimony.' Hearings of the Senate Committee on Labor and Human Resources, Subcommittee on Labor *Retirees at Risk: The Executive Life Bankruptcy*. (21 June).

Michl, Thomas R. 1988a. 'The Two-Stage Decline in U.S. Profitability.' *Review of Radical Political Economics*, Vol. 20: No. 4 (Winter): pp. 1–22.

——. 1988b. 'The Wage-Profit Frontier and Declining Profitability in U.S. Manufacturing.' *Review of Radical Political Economics*, Vol. 20, Nos. 2 & 3 (Summer and Fall): pp. 80–86.

——. 1991. 'Wage-Profit Curves in US Manufacturing.' *Cambridge Journal of Economics*, Vol. 15, No. 3 (September): pp. 271–86.

Miller, Edward. 1990. 'Can a Perpetual Inventory Capital Stock Be Used for Production Function Parameter Estimation.' *Review of Income and Wealth*, Vol. 36, No. 4 (March): pp. 67–82.

Miller, John. 1989. 'Social Wage or Social Profit? Net Social Wage and the Welfare State.' *Review of Radical Political Economy*, Vol. 21, No. 3 (Fall): pp. 82–90.

Mills, David E. and Laurence Schumann. 1985. 'Industry Structure with Fluctuating Demand.' *American Economic Review*, Vol. 75, No. 4 (September): pp. 758–67.

Minsky, Hyman P. 1982. 'Debt Deflation Processes in Today's Institutional Environment.' *Banca Nazionale del Lavoro Quarterly Review*, Vol. 143 (December): pp. 375–93.

——. 1986. *Stabilizing an Unstable Economy* (New Haven: Yale University Press).

Mishel, Lawrence. 1988. *Manufacturing Numbers: How Inaccurate Statistics Conceal U.S. Industrial Decline* (Washington, D.C.: Economic Policy Institute).

Mishel, Lawrence and David M. Frankel. 1991. *The State of Working America, 1990–1991* (Armonk, New York: M.E. Sharpe).

Morse, David. 1985. 'The Campaign to Save Dorothy Six.' *The Nation* (7 September): pp. 174–5.

Moseley, Fred. 1988. 'The Increase of Unproductive Labor in the Postwar U.S. Economy.' *Review of Radical Political Economics*, Vol. 20, Nos. 2 & 3 (Summer and Fall): pp. 100–6.

——. 1991. *The Falling Rate of Profit in the Postwar United States Economy* (New York: St. Martin's Press).

Mowery, David C. and Nathan Rosenberg. 1989. *Technology and the Pursuit of Economic Growth* (Cambridge: Cambridge University Press).

Moykyr, Joel. 1990. *The Lever of Riches: Technological Creativity and Economic Progress* (New York: Oxford University Press).

Mueller, Hans. 1984. Protection and Competition in the U.S. Steel Market: A Study of Managerial Decision Making in Transition. Monograph Series, No. 30 Middle Tennessee State College, Murfeesboro, Tn. (May).

Munnell, Alicia H. 1990. 'Why Has Productivity Growth Declined? Productivity and Public Investment.' *New England Economic Review of the Federal Reserve Bank of Boston* (January/February): pp. 4–22.

Murnane, Richard J. 1988. 'Education and the Productivity of the Workforce: Looking Ahead.' In Robert Litan *et al.* eds. *American Living Standards: Threats and Challenges* (Washington, D.C.: The Brookings Institution): pp. 215–45.

Murnane, Richard J. and Randall J. Olsen. 1990. 'The Effects of Salaries and Opportunity Costs on Length of Stay in Teaching: Evidence from North Carolina.' *Journal of Human Resources*, Vol. 25, No. 1 (Winter): pp. 106–24.

Murphy, Kevin M., Andrei Shleifer and Robert Vishny. 1991. 'The Allocations of Talent: Implications for Growth.' *Quarterly Journal of Economics*, Vol. 106, No. 2 (May): pp. 503–30.

Murray, Charles. 1986. *Losing Ground: American Social Policy, 1950–1980* (New York: Basic Books).

Myrdal, Gunnar. 1962. *An American Dilemma: The Negro Problem and Modern Democracy*, 20th Anniversary Edition (New York: Harper and Row).

Naj, Amal Kumar. 1988. 'Chemical Firms Resist Lures to Expand.' *Wall Street Journal* (12 January): p. 6.

Nakarmi, Laxmi. 1991. 'At Lucky-Goldstar, The Koos Loosen the Reins.' *Business Week* (18 February): pp. 72–3.

National Education Association. 1991. *Almanac of Higher Education* (Washington, D.C.: National Education Association).

National Machine Tool Builders Association. 1982–1983. *Economic Handbook of the Machine Tool Industry, 1983* (McLean, Virginia: National Machine Tool Builders Association).

Neal, Alfred C. 1981. *Business Power and Public Policy* (New York: Praeger).

Neild, R. R. 1964. 'Replacement Policy.' *National Institute Economic Review*, No. 30 (November): pp. 30–43.

Nelson, Richard R. 1989. 'What is Private and What is Public About Technology?' *Science, Technology, and Human Values*, Vol. 14, No. 3 (Summer): pp. 229–41.
——. 1990. 'U.S. technological leadership: Where did it come from and where did it go?' *Research Policy*, Vol. 19, No. 2 (April): pp. 117–32.
Niggle, Christopher J. 1988. 'The Increasing Importance of Financial Capital in the U.S. Economy.' *Journal of Economic Issues* Vol. 22, No. 2 (June): pp. 581–8.
Noble, David. 1984. *Forces of Production: A Social History of Industrial Automation* (New York: Alfred A. Knopf).
O'Brien, Anthony Patrick. 1989. 'A Behavioral Explanation for Nominal Wage Rigidity During the Great Depression.' *Quarterly Journal of Economics*, Vol. 104, No. 4 (November): pp. 719–36.
O'Leary, James J. 1945. 'Consumption as a Factor in Postwar Employment.' *American Economic Review*, Vol. 35, No. 2 (May): pp. 37–55.
Offer, Avner. 1989. *The First World War: An Agrarian Interpretation* (Oxford: Clarendon Press).
Okun, Arthur M. 1970. *The Political Economy of Prosperity* (New York: W.W. Norton).
Oshima, H. T. 1984. 'The Growth of U.S. Factor Productivity: The Significance of New Technologies in the Early Decades of the Twentieth Century.' *Journal of Economic History*, Vol. 44, No. 1 (March): pp. 161–70.
Pennar, Karen. 1991. 'Slash-and-Burn Cost-Cutting Could Singe the Recovery.' *Business Week* (6 May): p. 73.
Pentzinger, Thomas, Jr. 1988. 'Williams Cos. Transforms "Lazy Assets" Into No. 4. Telecommunications Service.' *Wall Street Journal* (5 May) p. 30.
Perelman, Michael. 1983. *Classical Political Economy, Primitive Accumulation, and the Social Division of Labor* (Totowa, New Jersey: Rowman and Allanheld).
——. 1987. *Marx's Crises Theory: Scarcity, Labor and Finance* (New York: Praeger).
——. 1989. *Keynes, Investment Theory and the Economic Slowdown: The Role of Replacement Investment and q-Ratios* (London: Macmillan).
——. 1991. *Information, Social Relations, and the Economics of High Technology* (London: Macmillan).
Phillips, Albert. 1958. 'The Deep Roots of Inflation.' *International Socialist Review*, 2 Parts, 19, 3 and 4 (Summer and Spring): pp. 93–98 and pp. 147–52.
Pindyck, Robert S. and Julio Rotemberg. 1983. 'Dynamic Factor Demands and the Effects of Energy Price Shocks.' *American Economic Review*, Vol. 73, No. 5 (December): pp. 1066–79.
Piven, Frances Fox and Richard A. Cloward. 1971. *Regulating the Poor: The Functions of Public Welfare* (New York: Pantheon).
Pollard, Sidney. 1982. *The Wasting of the British Economy* (New York: St Martin's Press).

President of the United States. 1990. *Economic Report of the President* (Washington, D.C.: U.S. Government Printing Office).

Putka, Gary. 1991. 'Making the Grade: Teacher Quality Rises with Improved Pay, Concern for Schools.' *Wall Street Journal* (5 December): p. 1A.

Rae, John. 1834. *Statement of Some New Principles of Political Economy* (Boston); Volume II in R. Warren James (ed.), *John Rae, Political Economist: An Account of his Life and an Compilation of his Main Writings* (Toronto: Toronto University Press, 1965).

Rattner, Steven. 1979. 'Volcker Asserts U.S. Must Trim Living Standard.' *New York Times* (18 October): p. A1.

Reagan, Ronald. 1984. Speech at Georgetown University's Center for Strategic and International Studies 'American Foreign Policy Challenges in the 1980s.' *Weekly Compilation of Presidential Documents*, No. 2086, pp. 1–6.

Register, Charles A. and Paul W. Grimes. 1991. 'Collective Bargaining, Teachers, and Student Achievement.' *Journal of Labor Research*, Vol. 12, No. 2 (Spring): pp. 91–111.

Reich, Robert B. 1990. 'Who Is Us?' *Harvard Business Review*, Vol. 90, No. 1 (January-February): pp. 53–64.

Reppy, Judith. 1985. 'Military R&D and the Civilian Economy.' *Bulletin of the Atomic Scientists*, Vol. 41, No. 9 (October): pp. 10–14.

Richards, E. M. 1933. 'To Buy or Not to Buy Equipment.' *Factory Management and Maintenance*, Vol. 91 (December): pp. 499–500.

Riddell, Tom. 1987. 'Military Build Up, Economic Decline? The Economy's Trillion-Dollar Habit.' *Dollars and Sense*, No. 129 (September): pp. 6–9.

——. 1988. 'U.S. Military Power, the Terms of Trade, and the Profit Rate.' *American Economic Review* Vol. 78, No. 2 (May): pp. 60–5.

Romer, Christina. D. 1989. 'The Prewar Business Cycle Reconsidered: New Estimates of Gross National Product, 1869–1908.' *Journal of Political Economy*, Vol. 97, No. 1 (February): pp. 1–37.

Romer, Christina D. and David H. Romer. 1989. 'Does Monetary Policy Matter? A New Test in the Spirit of Friedman and Schwartz.' Olivier Jean Blanchard and Stanley Fischer, eds. *NBER Macroeconomics Annual* (Cambridge: MIT Press): pp. 121–70.

Romer, Paul M. 1987. 'Crazy Explanations for the Productivity Slowdown.' in Stanley Fischer, ed. *NBER Macroeconomics Annual, 1987* (Cambridge, MA: The MIT Press): pp. 163–202.

Rose, Frederick. 1984. 'Occidental's Purchase of Cities Service Does Little to Increase U.S. Oil Reserves.' *Wall Street Journal* (5 December): p. 24.

Rothschild, Emma. 1974. *Paradise Lost: The Decline of the Auto-Industrial Age* (New York: Vintage Books).

Rubin, Laura S. 1991. 'Productivity and the Public Capital Stock: Another Look.' Board of Governors of the Federal Reserve System, Economic Activity Section, Division of Research and Statistics, Working Paper No. 118 (May).

Ruhm, Christopher J. 1991. 'Are Workers Permanently Scarred by Job

Displacement?' *American Economic Review*, Vol. 81, No. 1 (March): pp. 319–24.

Rustow, Hanns-Joachim. 1967. 'The Development of Shares of Wages and Profits in an Industrial Society.' *German Economic Review* No. 5, No. 2, pp. 92–115.

——. 1978. 'The Economic Crisis of the Weimar Republic and How it was Overcome – A Comparison with the Present Recession.' *Cambridge Journal of Economics*, Vol. 4, No. 2 (December): pp. 409–21.

Sahling, Leonard and M. A. Akhtar. 1984–85. 'What is Behind the Capital Spending Boom?' *Federal Reserve Bank of New York Quarterly Review*, Vol. 9, No. 4 (Winter): pp. 19–30.

Salamon, Gerald L. 1985. 'Accounting Rates of Return.' *American Economic Review*, Vol. 75, No. 3 (June): pp. 495–504.

Salpukas, Agis. 1971. 'Workers' Use of Drugs Widespread in Nation.' New York Times (21 June): pp. 1 and 16.

Sampson, Anthony. 1975. *The Seven Sisters: The Great Oil Companies and the World They Made* (New York: Viking).

Sansolo, Michael. 1987. 'Take this job . . . please.' *Progressive Grocer* (January): p. 75.

Santoni, G. J. 1986. 'The Employment Act of 1946: Some History Notes.' *Economic Review of the Federal Bank of St. Louis*, Vol. 68, No. 9 (November): pp. 5–16.

Sato, Ryuzo and Ramachandran, Rama. 1980. 'Measuring the Impact of Technical Progress on the Demand for Intermediate Goods: A Survey.' *Journal of Economic Literature*, Vol. 18, No. 3 (September): pp. 1003–24.

Schlesinger, Arthur M., jr. 1986. *The Cycles of American History* (Boston: Houghton Mifflin).

Schlesinger, Jacob M. 1990. 'Japan Makes Strides in Software Design: "Factory" Approach Contrasts with U.S. Production.' *Wall Street Journal* (8 February): p. B5.

Schmenner, Roger W. 1980. 'Choosing New Industrial Capacity: On Site Expansion, Branching, and Relocation.' *Quarterly Journal of Economics*, Vol. 44, No. 4 (August): pp. 103–19.

Schmid, Gregory. 1981. 'Productivity and Reindustrialization: A Dissenting View.' *Challenge*, Vol. 23, No. 6 (January/February): pp. 24–9.

Schoenhof, Jacob. 1893. *The Economy of High Wages: An Inquiry into the Cause of High Wages and their Effects on Methods and Cost of Production* (New York: G. P. Putnam's Sons).

Schor, Juliet B. 1991. *The Overworked American: The Unexpected Decline of Leisure* (New York: Basic Books).

Schorsch, Louis. 1984. 'The Abdication of Big Steel.' *Challenge*, Vol. 27, No. 1 (March/April): pp. 34–40.

Schultz, Theodore. 1961. 'Investment in Human Capital.' *American Economic Review*, Vol. 51, No. 1 (March): pp. 1–17.

Schumpeter, J. A. 1950. *Capitalism, Socialism and Democracy*, 3d. edn. (New York: Harper & Row).

——. 1939. *Business Cycles: A Theoretical, Historical and Statistical Analysis of the Capitalist Process*, 2 vols. (New York: McGraw Hill).

Scitovsky, Tibor. 1990. 'The Benefits of Asymmetric Markets.' Journal of Economic Perspectives, Vol. 4, No. 1 (Winter): pp. 135–48.

Scotchner, Suzanne. 1991. 'Standing on the Shoulders of Giants: Cumulative Research and the Patent Law.' *Journal of Economic Perspectives*, Vol. 5, No. 1 (Winter): pp. 29–41.

Semiconductor Industry Association. 1989. *Meeting the Global Challenge: Advanced Electronics Technology and the American Semiconductor Industry* (Cupertino: Semiconductor Industry Association).

Serrin. William. 1974. *The Company and the Union* (New York: Vintage).

Shaiken, Harley. 1985 *Work Transformed: Automation and Labor in the Computer Age* (New York: Holt, Rinehart & Winston).

Shaikh, Anwar and Ertugrul Ahmet Tonak. 1987. 'The Welfare State and the Myth of the Social Wage.' in Robert Cherry *et al.* eds. *The Imperiled Economy.* book 1. *Macroeconomics from a Left Perspective* (New York: Union for Radical Political Economics): pp. 183–94.

Shelton, Judy. 1989. *The Coming Soviet Crash* (New York: The Free Press).

Sherman, Howard J. 1983. 'Cyclical Behavior of Government Fiscal Policy'. *Journal of Economic Issues*, Vol. 17, No. 2 (June): pp. 379–88.

——. 1991. *The Business Cycle: Growth and Crisis Under Capitalism* (Princeton: Princeton University Press).

Shleifer, Andrei and Robert W. Vishny. 1988. 'The Efficiency of Investment in the Presence of Aggregate Demand Spillovers.' *Journal of Political Economy*, Vol., 96, No. 6 (December): pp. 1221–31.

Shoven, John B., Scott B. Smart, and Joel Waldfogel. 1992. 'Real Interest Rates and the Savings and Loan Crisis: The Moral Hazard Premium.' *Journal of Economic Perspectives*, Vol. 6, No. 1 (Winter): pp. 155–67.

Shrag, Peter. 1991. 'The Myth of Quick School Reform.' *The Sacramento Bee* (22 May): p. B6.

Silk, Leonard. 1985. 'The Pressures In Geneva.' *New York Times* (November 20): p. D2.

Sloan, Allan. 1985. 'Why Is No One Safe?' *Forbes* (11 March).

Smith, Adam. 1776. *An Inquiry into the Nature and Causes of the Wealth of Nations* (Oxford: Clarendon Press, 1976).

Smith, Hedrick. 1977. 'A Rare Call for Sacrifices.' *New York Times* (19 April): pp. 1 and 24.

Smith, James P. and Finis R. Welch. 1989. 'Black Economic Progress after Myrdal.' *Journal of Economic Literature*, Vol. 27, No. 2 (June): pp. 519–64.

Solow, Robert M. 1963. *Capital Theory and the Rate of Return* (Amsterdam: North Holland).

Spero, John Edelman. 1980. *The Failure of the Franklin National Bank* (New York: Columbia University Press).

Staehle, Hans. 1955. 'Technology, Utilization and Production.' *Bulletin de l'Institue Internationale de Statistique*, Vol. 34, Part 4, pp. 112–36.

Stein, Herbert. 1969. *The Fiscal Revolution in America* (Chicago: University of Chicago Press).

———. 1984. *Presidential Economics: The Making of Economic Policy from Roosevelt to Reagan and Beyond* (New York: Simon and Schuster).

Stewart, James B. 1991. *Den of Thieves* (New York: Simon and Schuster).

Stiglitz, Joseph E. 1987. 'The Causes and Consequences of the Dependence of Quality on Price.' *Journal of Economic Literature*, Vol. 25, No. 1 (March): pp. 1–48.

Stiglitz, Joseph E. and Andrew Weiss. 1981. 'Credit Rationing and markets with Imperfect Information.' *American Economic Review*, Vol. 71, No. 3 (June): pp. 393–411.

Stollman, Rita. 1981. 'Economic Diary.' *Business Week* (15 June): p. 22.

Stout, Hilary. 1989. 'Shaky Numbers: U.S. Statistics Mills Grind Out More Data that are then Revised.' *Wall Street Journal* (31 August): pp. A1 and A2.

Strassman, W. P. 1959. *Risk and Technological Investment* (Ithica: Cornell University Press).

Sullivan, Allanna. 1990. 'Stretched Thin: Exxon's Restructuring in the Past is Blamed for Recent Accidents.' *Wall Street Journal* (16 March): pp. A1 and A14.

Summers, Lawrence H. 1989. 'Some Simple Economics of Mandated Benefits.' *American Economic Review*, Vol. 79, No. 2 (May): pp. 177–83.

———. 1990. 'What is the Social Return to Capital Investment?' *Growth, productivity, employment: essays to celebrate Bob Solow's birthday*, Peter Diamond, ed. (Cambridge: MIT Press): pp. 113–41.

Summers, Lawrence H. and Victoria P. Summers. 1989. 'When Financial Markets Work too Well: A Cautious Case for a Securities Transactions Tax.' *Journal of Financial Services Research*, No. 3.

Tanzer, Michael. 1975. *The Energy Crisis: World Struggle for Power and Wealth* (New York: Monthly Review Press).

Terborgh, George. 1949. *Dynamic Equipment Policy* (New York: McGraw-Hill).

Thornton, William Thomas. 1869. *On Labour: Its Wrongful Claims and Rightful Dues* (London: Macmillan).

Thurow, Lester C. 1987. 'Economic Paradigms and Slow American Productivity Growth.' *Eastern Economic Journal*, Vol. 13, No. 4 (October-December): pp. 333–45.

Tilly, Chris. 1991. 'Continuing Growth of Part-Time Employment.' *Monthly Labor Review*, Vol. 114, No. 3 (March): pp. 10–18.

Tocqueville, Alexis de. 1848. *Democracy in America*, 2 vols. tr. Henry Reeve (New York: D. Appleton, 1899).

———. 1989. *Toward a High-Wage, High-Productivity Service Sector* (Washington, D.C.: Economic Policy Institute).

Toffler, Alvin. 1990. *Powershift: Knowledge, Wealth, and Violence in the 21st Century* (New York: Bantam Books).

Tonak, E. Ahmet. 1987. 'The U.S. Welfare State and the Working Class,

1952–1980.' *Review of Radical Political Economy*, Vol. 19, No. 1 (Spring): pp. 47–72.

United States Department of Agriculture. 1980. *Agricultural Statistics* (Washington, D.C.: U.S. Government Printing Office).

United States Department of Commerce, Bureau of Economic Analysis. 1987. *Fixed Reproducible Tangible Wealth in the United States, 1982–1985* (Washington, D.C.: U.S. Government Printing Office).

Unites States Department of Commerce, Bureau of the Census. 1990. *Statistical Abstract of the United States, 1990* (Washington, D.C.: U.S. Government Printing Office).

United States Department of Education. National Center for Education Statistics. 1991. *Digest of Education Statistics, 1991* (Washington, D.C.: U.S. Government Printing Office).

United States Department of Justice. 1990. *Sourcebook of Criminal Justice Statistics* (Washington, D.C.: U.S. Government Printing Office).

United States Department of Education, National Center for Education Statistics. 1991. *The Condition of Eduction, 1991.* Vol. 1. *Elementary and Secondary Education* (Washington, D.C.: U.S. Government Printing Office).

United States Department of Labor, Bureau of Labor Statistics. 1977. *Multiple Jobholders in May 1977*, Special Labor Force Report 211.

——. 1989. *Handbook of Labor Statistics*, Bulletin 2340 (Washington, D.C.: U.S. Government Printing Office).

——. 1990. *Employment and Earnings*, Vol. 37, No. 6 (June).

——. Bureau of Labor Statistics. 1989. *The Impact of Research and Development on Productivity Growth*, Bulletin No. 2331 (September) (U.S.G.P.O.: Washington, D.C.).

United States Department of Transportation. 1978. *A Prospectus for Change in the Freight Railroad Industry* (Washington D.C.: U.S. Government Printing Office).

United States House of Representatives, Committee on Education and Labor, Subcommittee on Elementary, Secondary and Vocational Education. 1989. *Child Nutrition Programs: Issues for the 101st Congress*, One Hundredth Congress, 2d Session (December).

United States House of Representatives. 1981. 97th Congress, 1st Session, Committee on Energy and Commerce, Subcommittee on Oversight and Investigations, *Capital Formation and Industrial Policy, Part I, Hearings, 27 and 29 April, 1, 22 and 24 June* (Washington, DC: US Government Printing Office.

United States National Security Council. 1950. 'NSC 68: United States Objectives and Programs for National Security.' in Thomas H. Etzold and John Lewis Gaddis, eds. *Containment: Documents on American Policy and Strategy, 1945–1950* (New York: Columbia University Press, 1978): pp. 385–442.

United States Senate. 1982. 97th Congress, 2nd Session. Committee on Labor and Human Resources, Subcommittee on Employment and Productivity.

Productivity in the American Economy, 1982., Hearings. 19 and 26 March, 2 and 16 April 1982 (Washington, DC: US Government Printing Office).

United States Senate, Committee on the Judiciary, Subcommittee of Separation of Powers. 1970. *The Philadelphia Plan*, 91st Cong., 1st Sess. (27 and 28 October 1969).

United States Department of Transportation. 1990. *Moving America: New Directions, New Opportunities* (Washington, D.C.: U.S. Government Printing Office).

United States President. 1990. *Economic Report of the President* (Washington: D.C.: U.S. Government Printing Office).

Varian, Hal R. 1988. 'Symposium on Takeovers.' *Journal of Economic Perspectives*, Vol. 2, No. 1 (Winter): pp. 3–5.

Vatter, Harold G. 1985. *The U.S. Economy in World War II* (New York: Columbia University Press).

Vicker, Ray. 1981. 'Hazardous Highways: Deterioration of the Nation's Roads Accelerates, Sparking a Race in States to Increase Fuel Taxes.' *Wall Street Journal* (15 October): p. 48.

Vidal, Gore. 1992. 'Time for a People's Convention.' *The Nation*, Vol. 254, No. 3 (27 January): pp. 73 and 88–94.

Viner, Jacob. 1933. *Balanced Deflation, Inflation or More Depression.* Day and Hour Series, No. 3 (Minneapolis: University of Minneapolis Press).

Vives, Xavier. 1990. 'Information and Competitive Advantage.' *International Journal of Industrial Organization*, Vol. 9, No. 1, pp. 17–35.

Volcker, Paul A., Chairman of the Board of Governors of the Federal Reserve System. 1981. 'Testimony before the Committee on Banking, Finance and Urban Affairs of the U.S. House of Representatives, 21 July 1981.' *Federal Reserve Bulletin.* Vol. 67, No. 8 (August): pp. 613–8.

——. 1982. 'Testimony before the Joint Economic Committee, 26 January 1982.' *Federal Reserve Bulletin.* Vol. 68, No. 2 (February): pp. 88–90.

Wagoner, Harless D. 1968. *The U.S. Machinetool Industry from 1900 to 1950* (Cambridge, Massachusetts: MIT Press).

Waldstein, Louise. 1990. *Service Sector Wages, Productivity and Jobs Creation in the U.S. and Other Countries* (Washington, D.C.: Economic Policy Institute).

Walton, Richard E. 1985. 'From Control to Commitment in the Workplace.' *Harvard Business Review*, Vol. 85, No. 2 (March-April): pp. 76–84.

Waterson, Albert. 1964. 'Good Enough for Developing Countries?' *Finance and Development*, Vol. 1 (September): pp. 89–96.

Watson, Bill. 1971. 'Counter-Planning on the Shop Floor.' *Radical America*, Vol. 5, No. 3 (May–June): pp. 77–85.

Webb, Roy H. 1991. 'The Stealth Budget: Unfunded Liabilities of the Federal Government.' *Economic Review of the Federal Reserve Bank of Richmond*, Vol. 77, No. 3 (May–June): pp. 23–33.

Weidenbaum, Murray L. and R. DiFina. 1978. *The Cost of Federal Regulation of Economic Activity* (Washington, D.C.: American Enterprise Institute).

Weingartner, H. Martin. 1969. 'Some New Views on the Payback Period and Capital Budgeting Decisions.' *Management Science*, Vol. 15, No. 12 (August): pp. B594–607.

Weisskopf, Tom. 1979. 'Marxian Crisis Theory and the Falling Rate of Profit.' *Cambridge Journal of Economic*, Vol. 3, No. 4 (December): pp. 341–78.

Weld, Issac. 1799. *Travels thought the States of North America and Provinces of Upper and Lower Canada During the Years 1793, 1796 and 1797* (London: J. Stockdale).

Welles, Chris. 1990. 'Exxon's Future: What Has Larry Rawl Wrought.' *Business Week* (2 April): pp. 72–6.

Wells, David A. 1885. 'The 'Foreign Competitive Pauper Labor' Argument for Protection.' in his *Practical Economics: A Collection of Essays Respecting Certain of the Recent Economic Experiences of the United States* (New York: G.C. Putnam; New York: Greenwood Publishers, 1968): pp. 133–52.

White, Merry I. 1991. 'Higher Education: A Comparative Examination.' *Thought and Action: The NEA Higher Education Journal*, Vol. 7, No. 2 (Fall): pp. 5–18.

Williams, Harry B. 1989. 'What Temporary Workers Earn: Findings from New BLS Survey.' *Monthly Labor Review*, Vol. 112, No. 3 (March): pp. 3–6.

Wion, Douglas W. 1990. 'Working Wives and Earnings Inequality Among Married Couples, 1967–1984.' *Review of Social Economy*, Vol. 48, No. 1 (Spring): pp. 18–40.

Wolfe, Alan. 1981. *America's Impasse: The Rise and Fall of the Politics of Growth* (New York: Pantheon).

Wolff, Edward N. 1987. *Growth, Accumulation, and Unproductive Activity: An Analysis of the Postwar U.S. Economy* (Cambridge: Cambridge University Press).

Wolfson, Martin H. 1988. *Financial Crises: Understanding the Postwar U.S. Experience* (Armonk, New York: M. E. Sharpe).

Woodham, Douglas M. 1984. 'Potential Output Growth and the Long-Term Inflation Outlook.' *Federal Reserve Bank of New York Quarterly Review*, Vol. 9, No. 2 (Summer): pp. 16–23.

Wright, Gavin. 1990. 'The Origins of American Industrial Success, 1870–1940.' *American Economic Review*, Vol. 80, No. 4 (September): pp. 651–68.

Wright, Patrick. 1979. *On a Clear Day You Can See General Motors: John Z. DeLorean's Look Inside the Automotive Giant* (New York: Avon).

Zaslow, Jeffrey. 1985. 'Building on the Past: The Challenge of Turning an Aged Plant into a Showpiece Factory of the Future.' *Wall Street Journal* (16 September): pp. 6c and 18c.

Zuboff, Shoshana. 1988. *In the Age of the Smart Machines: The Future of Work and Power* (New York: Basic Books).

Index

Aaron, Henry J., 85–6
Abelson, Alan, 162
Abken, Peter A., 55
Adams, Gordon, 56
Adams, Larry, 38
Adams, Walter, 121
Adler, Stephen J., 162
Aitken, Howard, 162
Akerlof, George, 200, 215, 220
Akthar, M., 189–90
Anders, George, 163, 165, 189
Arthur, Brian, 28
Aschauer, David, 76, 79, 81, 83,
    85–7, 98
AT&T 141

Bahl, Roy, 79
Bailey, Stephen Kemp, 13
Baily, Martin Neil, 13, 74, 136
Baran, Paul, 132
Barber, William, 205–6, 221
Barnett, Don, 129, 133, 140
Bassie, V. L., 11
Baumgarner, Mary, 79
Baytown, Texas, 159
Beck, E. M., 37
Bedwell, Donald E., 69
Berg, Norman, 177
Berkeley Round Table on the
    International Economy, 175
Bernanke, Ben, 207
Berndt, Ernst, 136
Bernstein, Aaron, 54, 76, 174, 175
Bernstein, Peter, 120
Bethlehem Steel, 155
Bhaduri, Amit, 193
Bils, Mark, 183
Bishop, John H., 74–5
Blinder, Alan, 41, 43
Bluestone, Barry, 44, 52, 54, 160
Boskin, Michael, 90
Bosworth, Barry, 189–90

Bowles, Sam, 18, 71, 137
Broderick, David, 160
Bronfenbrenner, Martin, 15
Bruck, Connie, 158
Buchsbaum, W. E., 165
Buckley, William F., 41
Burawoy, Michael, 196
Burlington Industries, 163–4
Butcher, Bernard, 134

Calomaris, Charles W., 138
Campeau, 162
Canada, 39, 83, 205
Cardigan Sweater Speech, 64
Carter, Anne P., 127
Carter, Jimmy, 64–5
Carver, Thomas Nixon, 206
Castells, Manuel, 24
Cerruzzi, Paul, 102
Chall, Daniel E., 82
Chandler, Alfred D. Jr., 209
Chipello, Christopher J., 24
Chirinko, Robert, 189
Choate, Pat, 80
Chposky, James, 219
Chrysler Corporation, 55
Cincinnati Milling Machine Co., 130
Citibank, 174
Citicorp, 155
Clark, Gregory, 205
Cohen, Laurie P., 162
Cohen, Stephen, 175
Collins, Robert, 12
Committee on the Quality of Statistics,
    92
Connell, James L., 215
Conoco, 165
Continental Airlines, 55
Coolidge, Calvin, 12, 58, 144
Cornell University, 87, 203
Cost of Living Council, 41
Council of State Planning Agencies, 80

Craypo, Charles, 38, 45, 51
Cusumano, Michael A., 177
Cutler, David M., 163
Cwiklik, Robert, 93
Cypher, James M., 101, 107

Danziger, Sheldon, 23
Defense Advanced Research Projects
    Agency, 102
Davidson, Paul, 137
Dawson, Michael, 166
Denison, Edward F., 70–1
Dertouzos, Michael L., 105, 124, 161
Detroit, Michigan, 31–2, 131, 178, 181
Devine, Joel A., 99
DiFina, R., 67
Doyle, P. M., 38
Drago, Robert, 215
Drexel Burnham Lambert, 162
DuBoff, Richard, 16, 95, 161–2
Dulles, John Foster, 62
Dumas, Lloyd J., 93
Dumenil, Gerard, 206
Duncan, G. C., 213
DuPont Corporation, 165

Edelman, Asher, 163
Edelstein, Michael, 99, 195
Edwards, Edgar O., 125
Eisenhower, Dwight David, 14, 19, 63
Eisner, Robert, 86, 189
Ellis, Wilson, 164
Emmanuel, Arghiri, 211
England, 9, 143
Epstein, David F., 97, 164, 181
Etzioni, Amitai, 67, 127, 159
Etzold, Thomas H., 62
Exxon, 159

Fairris, David, 31
Fazzari, Steven, 208
Fenoaltea, Stefano, 194
Fiorito, Jack, 39
Fisher, Franklin M., 168
Fitzgerald, A. Ernest, 104
FitzRoy, Felix R., 213
Flamm, Kenneth, 101–2
Florida, Richard, 106, 176–7, 179, 214
First Boston, 162

First New Jersey Bank, 165
Frankel, Boris, 173
Frankel, David M., 22, 66–7, 78
Frankel, Max, 94–5
Franklin National Bank, 153–5
Fraser, Douglas, 31
Friedman, Milton, 13, 40, 69
Fukuyama (Japan), 129

Garbarino, Joseph, 14
Gartman, David, 30
Gau, Robert S., 46
Gaylord, W. W., 123–4
General Electric, 160
Geier, Frederic V., 130–1
General Motors, 31
Genesco, 160
Genovese, Eugene D., 194–5
Getty Oil, 162–3
Gibbons, Joel C., 136
Gilder, George, 176
Gillespie, Stephen, 89–90
Gintis, Herbert, 71
Glasgall, William, 174
Glass-Steagall Act, 150
Gleckman, Howard, 90–1
Glick, Mark, 206
Glyn, Andrew, 198, 210
Gold, David, 96
Goldsmith, Raymond W., 156
Gollop, Frank, 128
Gorbachev, Mikhail, 97
Gottschalk, Peter, 23
Gordon, David 18, 137
Gordon, R. A., 15
Gordon, Robert J., 11–12, 99–100, 137
Gort, Michael, 209
Greenspan, Alan, 90
Grenada, 108
Griffin, Larry J., 99
Griliches, Zvi, 16
Gruebler, Arnulf, 86
Gulf-Socal merger, 106

Habakkuk, H. J., 203
Haitian Road to Development, 1, 3, 42,
    55, 56, 57, 184, 199, 210, 217
Halberstam, David, 31–2, 105
Hamburg (Germany), 218

Hanushek, Eric A., 72
Hargaves-Heap, S. P., 52–3
Harris, Howell J., 31
Harris, Seymour E., 63
Harrison, Bennett, 44, 54, 74, 160
Hart, Therese A., 75
Hartman, Howard, 76
Hawthorne Experiment, 215
Heller, Walter, 13–14
Henwood, Doug, 47–66
Hershey, Lewis, 95
Herz, Diane E., 51
Hickok, Susan, 183
Hicks, John R., 133
Hillard, Michael, 177
Hiroshima, 219
Hirschleifer, Jack, 218–19
Hirschmann, Albert, 214
Hooks, Gregory, 60–1, 108
Hoover, Herbert, 205–7
Houlthan, Lokey, Howard and Zukin, 164
Hubbard, Glen, 208
Hulbert, Mark, 24
Hulten, Charles, 85
Hungerford, Thomas, 71
Hyundai Corporation, 177

India, 211
Intel, 176
Intellectual Property, 90, 102, 173, 176
International Business Machines, 184, 219–20
International Business Machines (Japan), 184
International Harvester, 209
Iran, 24
Iraq, 106, 108

Jackman, Richard, 53
Jackson, Andrew, 143–4
Japan, 18, 24–5, 50, 56, 72, 77, 83, 87–8, 92, 105, 106, 129, 133, 134, 174–9, 181, 184–5, 198, 204–5, 214–16, 218–9, 221
Jenks, Jeremiah, 203
Jensen, Michael, 158–9
Jiler, William, 89
Jerome, Harry, 206

Johnson, Lyndon, 93
Jordan, J. S., 168
Juster, F. Thomas, 189

Kanabayashi, Masayoshi, 88
Kaplinsky, Raphael, 198
Kapstein, Ethan B., 61
Keezer, Dexter M., 131–2
Kennedy, John F., 14–15, 63, 93
Kenney, Martin, 106, 176–7, 179, 214
Keynes, John Maynard, 59, 98, 109–23, 133–4, 146, 149, 170
Kidder, Peabody and Co., 162
Kidder, Tracy, 195
Kislev, Yoav, 210
Kissinger, Henry, 24
Klein, Lawrence, 136
Koford, James, 176
Komiya, R., 92
Kopcke, Richard W., 210
Korea, 56, 212
Kraft Foods, 162
Kraft, Kornelius, 213
Kravis, Irving B., 184
Krugman, Paul, 43–4
Kuehler, Jack D., 174

Labaton, Stephen, 162
Lamfalussy, A., 216
LaPlante, Alice, 219
Latin America, 22, 38
Layard, Richard, 53
Lazonick, William, 30, 41, 156
Leibenstein, Harvey, 215–16
Lekachman, Robert, 13
Leonisis, Ted, 219
Leontief, W., 134
Levin, Henry M., 78
Levitan, Sar A., 23
Lewis Galoob Toys, Inc., 174
Lewis, Michael, 95
Linbeck, Assar, 26
Lipietz, Alain, 198
Lippert, John, 32
Lipsey, Richard E., 184
Lister, Timothy, 215
Livingston, James, 203
Livingston, Joseph, 11
Lordstown, 31

Lovens, Amory B., 98
Lucas, Robert E., 218
Lucia, Joseph L., 121
Lucky Goldstar, 212
Lynd, Staughton, 45

Maddison, Angus, 132
Madison, Bernard L., 75
Magaziner, Ira, 123, 129, 134
Magdoff, Harry, 10, 158, 179, 189
Magnusson, Paul, 106
Malabre, Alfred L., jr. 80–1, 89–91
Malcomson, James M., 123, 129
Malecki, Edward J., 178
Manchester, England, 205
Mandel, Michael J., 174
Manhattan, 82
Maranto, Cheryl L., 39
Marglin, Stephen A., 193, 202
Markides, Constantinos, 177
Marshall, Alfred, 26, 53, 37, 201–2
Marshall, Andrew, 97
Martinez-Vazquez, Jorge, 79
Mayer, Martin, 152–3
McCarthyism, 59
McCracken, Paul, 41
McDonald's Corporation, 162
McElhattan, Rose, 139–40
McGowan, John J., 168
McHugh, Richard, 127
MCI Corporation, 141
Medoff, James, 38–9, 212–14
Melman, Seymour, 93, 103–4, 127, 133
Meltzer, Alan, 69
Metzenbaum, Howard, 55
Mexican debt, 43
Michl, Tom, 18–21, 137
Milken, Michael, 162
Miller, John, 66
Miller, Edward, 133
Minsky, Hyman, 16, 154
Mishel, Lawrence, 22, 44, 66–7, 78, 183
Mldainov, John K., 81
Morgan, Stanley Co., 161, 163–4
Morland, Howard, 96
Morse, David, 160
Moseley, Fred, 160
Mosely, A., 198
Moykyr, Joel, 25

Mueller, Hans, 121, 129
Munnell, Alicia, 83, 85
Murnane, Richard J., 73
Murphy, Kevin, 162
Murphy, Paul, 93
Murray, Charles, 67
Myrdal, Gunnar, 37

Nakarmi, Laxmi, 212
Neal, Alfred C., 12
Neild, R., 189
Nelson, Richard R., 102, 110
Niggle, Chris, 166
Nissan Co., 105
Nitze, Paul, 62
Nixon, Richard M., 17, 24, 35, 40–2, 94, 114, 206
NNB Semiconductor, 176
Noble, David, 131
NSC-68, 62
Nynex Co., 75

O'Brien, Anthony Patrick, 207–8
Offer, Avner, 199
Okun, Arthur, 15
Olsen, Randall J., 73
O'Leary, James J., 11
Oshima, H. T., 206

Panama, 108
Pennar, Karen, 161
Pension plans, 54–5
Pentzinger, Thomas, Jr., 141
Penzoil Co., 163
Perelman, Michael, 12, 59, 113–14, 116–17, 119, 126, 133, 144, 188
Phillip Morris Co., 162
Pindyck, Robert S., 136
Piven, Frances Fox, 35
Pollard, Sidney, 128
Prisons, 54, 70, 76, 88
Progressive Grocer, 48
Prussia, 205
Putka, Gary, 73

Rae, John, 126
Ramachandran, Rama, 127
Reagan, Ronald, 19, 36, 39, 44, 65,

67, 69, 88, 90, 91, 95, 96, 138, 189, 191
Register, Charles A., 213
Reich, Robert, 123, 129, 134, 184, 185
Reppy, Judith, 102–3
Richards, E. M., 130–1, 208
Riddell, Tom, 96
Romer, Chrisitina, 99, 142
Romer, David, 142
Romer, Paul, 110
Rosenberg, Nathan, 103
Rotemberg, Julio, 136
Rothschild, Emma, 31, 96, 101
Rubin, Laura, 85
Ruhm, Christopher J., 52
Rüstow, Hanns-Joachim, 142, 216–17
Ryan, Richard M., 215

Sahling, Leonard, 189–90
Sampson, Anthony, 23
Samuelson, Paul A., 14–16
Sansolo, Michael, 48
Santoni, G. J., 13
Ed Scannell, 219
Schlesinger, Arthur M., jr., 58
Schlesinger, Jacob M., 177
Schmenner, Roger W., 128
Schmid, Gregory, 210
Schoenhof, Jacob, 203
Schor, Juliet B., 47
Schorsch, Louis, 120, 129, 133, 140
Schultz, George, 41
Schultz, Theodore, 70
Schumann, Laurence, 208
Schumpeter, J. A., 111, 220
Scitovsky, Tibor, 213–14
Scotchner, Suzanne, 102
Serrin, William, 31
Shah of Iran, 24
Shaiken, Harley, 197
Shaikh, Anwar, 66
Shelton, Judy, 97–8
Sherman, Howard, 99, 207
Shleifer, Andrei, 26, 162
Shoven, John, 154
Shrag, Peter, 77–8
Sigler, Andrew, 156
Silk, Leonard, 97
Sindona, Michele, 153

Sjoquist, David L., 79
Smith, Adam, 111, 151, 172
Smith, Hedrick, 64
Smith, James P., 35
Solow, Robert M., 109
Soviet Union, 62, 96–8
Spero, John Edelman, 153, 155
Sperry Rand, 160
Staehle, Hans, 10, 131, 207
Stafford, F. P., 213
Stein, Herbert, 12, 14, 40, 42
Stiglitz, Joseph E., 151–2
Stollman, Rita, 89
Strassman, W. P., 203
Sullivan, Allanna, 159
Summers, Lawrence H., 54, 109–10, 163, 167
Summers, V., 167
Sweden, 26
Sweezy, Paul, 10, 132, 158, 179, 183

Tabellini, G., 69
Taft-Hartley, 39
Tanzer, Michael, 24
Terborgh, George, 123–8
Texaco Co., 163
Texas Instruments, 177, 184
Thornton, William, 25
Thurow, Lester, 44, 48–51, 108
Tilly, Chris, 47–8
Tocqueville, Alexis de, 202–3
Toffler, A., 173
Tonak, E. Ahmet, 66
Toyota Co., 177, 198
Truman, Harry S., 94

UNESCO, 77
Uniroyal Co., 55
United States Steel, 160
Ure, Andrew, 202

Varian, Hal, 158
Vatter, Harold G., 60–1
Vidal, Gore, 62
Vietnam War, 17, 19, 23–4, 32, 36–8, 64, 100, 153, 184
Viner, Jacob, 207
Vishny, Robert W., 26, 162
Vives, Xavier, 92

Volcker, Paul, 42–4, 137–8

Wachtell, Lipton, 162
Wage and Price Control, 40
Wagoner, Harless D., 130
Waldstein, Louise, 44, 46, 49–50
Walton, Richard, 198
Watergate Scandal, 17, 41
Waterson, Albert, 141
Watson, Bill, 32–4
Webb, Roy H., 67

Weber, Arnold, 41
Weidenbaum, Murray L., 67
Weingartner, H. Martin, 133
Weiss, Andrew, 151–2
Weiskopf, 18–21, 137
Welch, Finis R., 35
Wells, David A., 204–5
Williams Cos., 141–2
Wolfe, Alan, 11, 13, 15, 137
Wolff, Edward N., 166
Wolfson, Martin H., 153